In Search of Greater Syria

In Search of Greater Syria

The History and Politics of the Syrian Social Nationalist Party

Christopher Solomon

I.B. TAURIS
LONDON • NEW YORK • OXFORD • NEW DELHI • SYDNEY

I.B. TAURIS
Bloomsbury Publishing Plc
50 Bedford Square, London, WC1B 3DP, UK
1385 Broadway, New York, NY 10018, USA
29 Earlsfort Terrace, Dublin 2, Ireland

BLOOMSBURY, I.B. TAURIS and the I.B. Tauris logo are trademarks of
Bloomsbury Publishing Plc

First published in Great Britain 2022
This paperback edition published 2023

Copyright © Christopher Solomon, 2022

Christopher Solomon has asserted his right under the Copyright, Designs and
Patents Act, 1988, to be identified as Author of this work.

For legal purposes the Acknowledgments on pp. xi–xii constitute an
extension of this copyright page.

Series design by Adriana Brioso
Cover image: SSNP members. (© Historic Collection / Alamy Stock Photo)

All rights reserved. No part of this publication may be reproduced or transmitted in any
form or by any means, electronic or mechanical, including photocopying,
recording, or any information storage or retrieval system, without prior
permission in writing from the publishers.

Bloomsbury Publishing Plc does not have any control over, or responsibility for, any
third-party websites referred to or in this book. All internet addresses given in this
book were correct at the time of going to press. The author and publisher regret any
inconvenience caused if addresses have changed or sites have ceased to exist, but
can accept no responsibility for any such changes.

A catalogue record for this book is available from the British Library.

A catalog record for this book is available from the Library of Congress.

ISBN: HB: 978-1-8386-0640-4
PB: 978-0-7556-4182-6
ePDF: 978-1-8386-0643-5
eBook: 978-1-8386-0642-8

Typeset by Newgen KnowledgeWorks Pvt. Ltd., Chennai, India

To find out more about our authors and books visit www.bloomsbury.com
and sign up for our newsletters.

We are a nation that loves life and one that loves death whenever it is a path to life.
—Antoun Saadeh, 1935

To Macrina and Elise

Contents

List of Figures	x
Acknowledgments	xi
Note from the Author	xiii
Key Factions and Figures	xv
1 Introduction: The Storm in the Shadows	1
2 The Party of the Martyr: The SSNP's Beginnings in Lebanon	11
3 Tahya Suriya! The SSNP's Ideology	33
4 We Have Avenged Him! The Party and Syria	47
5 In the Shadow of Nasser: The SSNP and the Arab Cold War	67
6 Broken Country, Fractured Party: The SSNP and the Lebanese Civil War in the 1970s	93
7 Guerrilla War to Politics: The SSNP's Role in Lebanon's Politics	109
8 Battles and Ballots: The SSNP and the Syrian Civil War	129
9 Fires on the Mountain Tops: Women, Youth, and Social Media	145
10 Invisible Leaders: The Future of the SSNP	155
Epilogue	167
A List of SSNP Presidents	169
A Timeline of the SSNP's Factions, Historic Splits, and Events	171
Notes	175
Bibliography	207
Index	213

Figures

1	An approximate sketch of the SSNP's short-lived redesigned flag used by the Lebanon School during Saadeh's exile	42
2	Antoun Saadeh, the SSNP's revered founder	87
3	Antoun Saadeh with his followers in 1949	87
4	Party members wait for the arrival of Antoun Saadeh's plane in Beirut on his return from exile in March 1947	88
5	Issam al-Mahayri, the first SSNP member to obtain a seat in Syria's parliament, 1954	88
6	Issam al-Mahayri in Mezzeh Prison in Damascus, walking along with fellow inmates who were members of the banned Armenian Dashnak party, 1957	89
7	"Antoun Saadeh – March 1, Birth of the National Consciousness." The party's founder's profile featured in this wartime poster from the 1970s, along with an outline of Greater Syria. Courtesy of www.signsofconflict.com and Abboudi Bou Jawde	89
8	Waseem Zineddine, known by his nom de guerre, Abu Wajib (the father of duty), mysteriously killed on May 23, 1975. Courtesy of www.signsofconflict.com and Abboudi Bou Jawde	90
9	SSNP martyrs who fell in the battle of northern Matn, December 1986. Courtesy of www.signsofconflict.com	91
10	SSNP comrade Sanaa Mehdaidli, the Bride of the South, widely believed to be the first female suicide bomber, who carried out her attack April 9, 1985	92
11	A graph illustrating the timeline of the SSNP's splits from 1932 to 2020	170

Acknowledgments

This book was inspired by the late Patrick Seale, whose classic work, *The Struggle for Syria*, is now unfortunately out of print. Seale's 1965 book documented Syria in the years following its independence up until its union with Egypt in 1958. The SSNP, referred to in the book by its French misnomer, the PPS, is one of the key factions described during these events. My aim with this book was not only to produce an update on the party's modern-day activities but also to harken back to a political history book from a time when nearly every other book had the word "struggle" in the title. I was also inspired by the Lebanese journalist Nour Samaha. Her *Foreign Policy* article, "Eagles of the Whirlwind," published on March 28, 2016, reported on how the SSNP's militia was fighting in the Syrian conflict and gave me the idea to bridge the party's early history to the present.

I wanted to extend my deepest gratitude to Joshua Landis for welcoming my guest articles on his Syria Comment website, some of which were partially repurposed for sections of this book. Dr. Landis was extremely generous and helpful in providing suggestions, contacts, and insights into Syrian affairs. My special thanks to Syrian historian Sami Moubayed for his consistent kindness in responding to my questions, providing pictures, and offering feedback on some sections of text.

I must offer my sincere thanks for Carl Yonker of Tel Aviv University. This book would not be possible without his endless insights, analysis, and sharing of documents and correspondence all hours of the day and night. Carl has also written a book on the SSNP's history, from the party's founding in 1932 through 1958, the Rise and Fall of Greater Syria.

My kind thanks to my friend Roland Bartetzko, a Kosovo Liberation Army veteran, who took the time to help me analyze images, weapons, and videos of the SSNP's training camps and militia propaganda activities. Other friends who helped by reviewing my work, suggesting edits, and providing valuable feedback on the manuscript chapters include Jon Neu, Jesse McDonald, Kevin Amirehsani, Nick Grinstead, and Winthrop Rodgers. I would also like to extend my thanks to Jacob Passel of The Middle East Institute, Erwin van Veen of the Clingendael Institute in the Netherlands, Antoun Issa, Lucas Winter, Matthias Baun Brubaker Christensen, Scott Preston, and Lili Fandrich. In addition,

I would like to express my gratitude to the team at Global Risk Insights for giving me the opportunity to begin writing about international affairs. I also wanted to remember Larry Katzenstein for his kindness and inspiration.

Ruwan Al-Rejoleh also deserves recognition for interviewing the son of the late former Syrian Defense Minister Mustafa Tlass, Firas Tlass, who relayed valuable information passed through his contacts with the party. Appreciation goes to Nour Al-Aameri and Duaa Malik for helping with translations and to the other Syrians and Lebanese who helped provide insights and information but wish to remain anonymous.

My thanks to Adel Beshara, who kindly answered all of my questions and provided valuable insights into the party. I am also thankful to the members and fellow travelers of the Syrian Social Nationalist Party, especially Elijah, the pseudonym for the party sympathizer who runs the SSNP News Twitter account. He provided many sources and helped with translations. Many party members were willing to answer my questions and send me tips and information. Throughout the course of writing this book, I was able to correspond with or interview members of all three of the party's factions: Markaz, Intifada, and Amana (the latter which was disbanded in 2019). I also want to thank the members of the Kataeb Party and Lebanese Civil War veterans who shared their experiences.

Thank you to the staff at I.B. Tauris–Bloomsbury—Sofie Rudland, Tomasz Hoskins, Joanna Godfrey, Yasmin Garcha, and Lizzy Collier—who were endlessly patient as I worked on this book for over four years. When I first received an I.B. Tauris book, *Hezbollah: The Changing Face of Terrorism* by Judith Palmer Harik, I had never believed that I would someday publish with them. Additionally, my sincere thanks go out to the Newgen KnowledgeWorks team in Chennai, Tamil Nadu, India.

I would like to thank my parents and family for all of their help, encouragement, and support to this project, in particular my brother Michael for reviewing some chapters. I am also forever grateful to my in-laws for watching over our daughter the first couple of years I began work on the manuscript.

Finally, most importantly, my gratitude to my wife for her infinite patience, keen eye for detail, feedback, editing, and advice. I began working on this manuscript only a few months after the birth of our daughter. Macrina, I am eternally thankful and glad that you joined me during this journey to see this project through.

Note from the Author

The Syrian Social Nationalist Party (SSNP), one of the Levant's oldest political movements, has long remained elusive and mysterious in one of the most widely studied and watched regions in the world. With the Syrian Civil War continuing and its long-term political outcome uncertain, the SSNP has found resurgence in activity within the coalition of the Syrian forces backing President Bashar al-Assad. With this revival comes a renewed interest in the party, along with its long, complicated history. Founded by Antoun Saadeh in 1932, the SSNP has been the subject of intense controversy and scrutiny. It is unclear how Syria will look in the aftermath of the civil war, or whether the country will relapse into multiple rounds of conflict; however, whatever happens, the SSNP will be a part of the larger picture.

Although I do not prescribe to the party's ideology or condone its violent actions, the prospect of a distant familial connection made researching the party all the more fascinating to me. It is remarkable how the early life of the party's founder Antoun Saadeh's mirrored that of so many Syrian immigrants who came to the Western Hemisphere around the start of the twentieth century. Coming from a Syrian Orthodox background, my family emigrated from a small village located in between Tartus and Homs, to the United States around 1907 and eventually settled in Western Pennsylvania. Another segment of the family emigrated from Syria to São Paulo, Brazil. Furthermore, it is likely that some of my distant relatives who remained in Syria became members of the SSNP, given their sectarian background and location. These migrations occurred at a time when Syria was still part of the Ottoman Empire. The future borders of Syria had yet to be determined. Even today, the issue surrounding the European colonial borders in the Middle East continues to be a very real, re-occurring political grievance, as we have seen recently with the rise of the so-called Islamic State terrorist group that smashed the sand barriers separating Iraq and Syria with bulldozers in 2014.

This book leaves much about the party uncovered. There are many more stories and details that, given the secretive and convoluted nature of the SSNP, remain untold. As the Syrian Civil War continues to evolve or wind down, the political developments on the ground will almost certainly involve the future of the SSNP and their relationship with the Syrian regime as well as their position in Lebanon, which is experiencing a period of extended political convulsion and financial collapse. Although it must be emphasized that the SSNP remains a small political movement within the Levant, it is still an interesting case study for gaging the region's trajectory. If the Syrian regime becomes inherently weakened or is removed entirely, the SSNP will be an essential factor to watch in the political reshuffle that would follow the collapse of the Syrian branch of the Arab Socialist Baath Party from power. On the other end, if President Assad is able to consolidate power, the SSNP is well positioned to be rewarded for its wartime service. However, if the party overplays its hand, it could risk punishment and experience a renewed persecution. By researching and documenting the SSNP, it is my aim that this book will be, in part, a way to better understand the Syrian government and the ruling Baath Party. The tragedy of the Syrian conflict is the responsibility of not only the Assad family's regime but also the Western nations that have miscalculated on the government's reaction, popular support structure, and political durability.

Since the political developments in the Syrian conflict remain unsettled, it is my plan to revisit this work sometime in the future to update and explore further the inner workings of the party and their future position in Lebanon and Syria, as well as the region. In addition, the SSNP has been mentioned in many different books and articles but always as a side story, and the information on the party, at least in English, is scattered. This work will tell the party's story in one place. It also discusses the pro-regime political factions in Syria, as well as the number of seats the SSNP gains in elections. Critics will rightly scoff, noting that there is no real parliamentary life in Syria and that the so-called tolerated opposition does not matter. However, while fully acknowledging that reality, the purpose of this book is to document and explore the ongoings of a valuable regime player. There is a growing interest in the SSNP and its role not only in the Middle East but also within the wider international debate on Western-oriented liberalism, democracy, identity-based nationalism, resurgent authoritariansm, and right-/left-wing populism. More works from others on the party are coming. It is my hope that this book will spark interest and perhaps act as a resource for Middle East scholars and researchers to pursue more information and documentation of a little-studied and fascinating political movement in the Levant.

Key Factions and Figures

SSNP Factions

SSNP-Intifada

Intifada, meaning "Uprising," is the small legacy faction of George Abd Messih, Antoun Saadeh's controversial successor who broke off from the main branch in 1957. This faction envisions itself as a reformist wing and is currently part of the "tolerated opposition" in Syria, along with a presence in Lebanon. Intifada is largely an intellectual and more doctrinal branch. It does not carry the same authoritarian stigma held by the main faction and seeks to return to the roots of Antoun Saadeh's vision. Intifada is headed by Dr. Ali Haidar and was entrusted with the Syrian regime's State Ministry of Reconciliation during the civil war. Efforts to negotiate a reunification with the other factions are still ongoing.

SSNP-Markaz

Markaz, or "Center," is by far the party's largest faction and is headquartered in Beirut. It has a strong reputation for militancy and is responsible for organizing and fielding the party's armed wing, the Eagles of the Whirlwind militia, in the Syrian conflict. This faction retains a close relationship with Syrian President Bashar al-Assad's government. Markaz recently resolved a licensing issue (regarding political parties receiving direction from foreign entities) in order to operate in Syria legally. The faction is currently in a leadership crisis with Assaad Hardan wielding strong influence. An internal reformist trend called the July 8th Movement is actively challenging Hardan for control over the party's future.

SSNP-Amana

Amana, meaning "Trusteeship," existed only in Syria and was a small faction that broke off from Markaz in 2012, a split that was made official in 2016.

This branch officially called itself the SSNP in the Syrian Arab Republic and was reportedly losing members to the other factions. Issam al-Mahayri, the party's elder statesman, led this branch along with Joseph Sweid. The Amana was in actuality the personal project of President Bashar al-Assad's cousin, Rami Makhlouf, who financed it. In November 2018, the faction's Supreme Council elected Ilyas Mtanious Shaheen to head the Amana faction. However, Amana was ultimately disbanded by the Syrian government in October 2019, and the majority of its members likely merged with Markaz.

July 8th Movement

The July 8th Movement is an internal reformist trend that emerged within Markaz in 2016. The former party presidents Faris Saad and Hanna al-Nashef are prominently involved. Rabi Zeineddine, Yousef Zidan, and Tammuz Qanayzeh are among its other notable figures. In the city of Tripoli in 2018, it officially declared itself as the Social Nationalist Renaissance Movement and stated its aim was to reform and unify the party and end all external influence.

Historical Members

Antoun Saadeh: Founded the Syrian Social Nationalist Party at the American University in Beirut in November 1932. The central part of Saadeh's ideology was the creation of a geographic entity he called Greater (or Natural) Syria. He devised this platform in response to the anticolonial sentiments prevalent in Lebanon at the time. Saadeh's confrontations with the French and Lebanese governments eventually led to his short-lived uprising that resulted in his capture and execution on July 8, 1949. Saadeh still remains highly venerated both within and outside of the party today as its founder, chief martyr, intellectual, and inspirational leader.

Juliette El-Mir Saadeh: A Lebanese-Argentinian immigrant and the wife of Antoun Saadeh. She became the first trustee of the party after her husband's execution. Party leader George Abd Messih moved into her home, and she was swept up in the mass arrests that followed the 1955 assassination of Baath Party supporter Adnan al-Malki. She spent over ten years of imprisonment in the Qala'a Dimashq (Citadel of Damascus) before being released in 1967 on health grounds. She died in 1976 in Beirut.

George Abd Messih: One of Antoun Saadeh's earliest followers, he became the head of the party after Saadeh's untimely death. Messih gained a negative reputation for his authoritarian leadership style but was hailed by some party members for guiding the SSNP through a difficult era after Saadeh's execution. Messih is perhaps best remembered for his role in the assassination of the charismatic and popular pro-Baathist Syrian army officer Adnan al-Malki. In 1957, he split off from the party to form his own smaller faction, which became known as the Intifada. He died on September 14, 1999.

Issam al-Mahayri: Both a historic and a modern-day member of the SSNP, Mahayri joined the party in 1944. He was the first member of the party to be elected to the Syrian parliament in 1950 and was close to the Syrian military ruler Adib al-Shishakli. Mahayri was put on trial and subsequently jailed in the wake of the Malki assassination and was later released in 1963. He was involved in several of the high-profile splits that occurred within the party during the Lebanese Civil War. In 2012, he headed a new split as Amana broke off from Markaz.

Ghassan Jadid: The brother of Salah Jadid, Ghassan is remembered in party lore for his anticolonial activities against the French, fighting in the 1948 Arab–Israeli War, and for his role in Syria's coups in 1949 as well as the Western-backed coup attempts in Syria in the 1950s.

Salah Shishakli: The brother of the military dictator Adib al-Shishakli, Salah was a Syrian army officer who took part in the 1948 Arab–Israeli War and was known for his role in the coups before and after Adib's four years of rule.

Said Taqiyaddin: Was the party's famous poet, writer, and "consultant." He was active in academic circles and was a political idealist. Taqiyaddin was considered a rising star in the party during the 1950s and took part in failed coup plots. He was subsequently targeted by the Syrian intelligence and left Lebanon where he lived the rest of his life in exile until his death in 1960.

Inaam Raad: Edited and wrote for the party's *al-Binaa* newspaper. As the party's leader in the 1970s, Raad had a strong leftist orientation and was largely responsible for the political reforms and changes that occurred within the party during the Lebanese Civil War, most notably the so-called Melkart Conference, the 1969 party congress held in Beirut. Raad had a close relationship with the Palestinian Liberation Organization and co-headed the Lebanese National

Movement alongside the powerful Druze figure and Progressive Socialist Party leader Kamal Jumblatt.

Assad al-Ashqar: A staunch anticommunist and considered to be more of a conservative figure in the party, Ashqar confronted George Abd Messih over the Malki assassination, which resulted in the SSNP's first official split in 1957. He was jailed in the aftermath of the failed 1961 New Year's Eve coup.

Abdullah Saadeh: Headed the party in the early 1960s, Saadeh (of no relation to the party's founder) was largely known for his antagonistic view toward the Lebanese ruling class and had a desire to carve out a larger space for the SSNP in the country's political sphere. Saadeh was primarily held responsible for the failed 1961 New Year's Eve coup attempt and was imprisoned along with other party members in the ensuing government crackdown.

Modern-Day Members

Assaad Hardan: Widely regarded as a Machiavellian figure by the party's critics and a product of the Lebanese Civil War, Assaad Hardan is known for his close relationship with the Syrian government. He made the transition from militancy to politics and became active in the Lebanese parliament after the end of the civil war. He is an elder statesman of the SSNP's Markaz faction in Lebanon and wields significant influence.

Ali Qanso: An SSNP Lebanese politician from the pro-Syrian March 8 Alliance, who served several ministerial positions, including the Ministry for Parliamentary Affairs and Ministry of Labor within the Lebanese government following the end of the civil war. Qanso was twice the president of the Markaz faction in Lebanon, first in the mid-2000s and again in 2016–17. He died in July 2018.

Ali Haidar: Currently heads the Intifada faction and steered the Syrian State Ministry for Reconciliation. Haidar is close to President Assad and was first elected to Syrian parliament in 2012, along with three other Intifada members. In November 2018, Haidar, as part of a cabinet reshuffle, took over a new entity designated as the National Reconciliation Authority.

Joseph Sweid: A Syrian politician who is affiliated with the Amana faction and acted as the Syrian State Minister of Expatriates. He headed the Amana faction until he turned over the presidency to Ilyas Mtanious Shaheen in November 2018.

1

Introduction: The Storm in the Shadows

The Syrian Social Nationalist Party (SSNP) is one of the most enigmatic and active political forces in the Middle East. It is one of the Levant's oldest secular party with its initial founding in 1932. The party is small, but loud and full of paradoxes. Anticolonial and revolutionary, the party has been a strong proponent of self-determination and sovereignty. Yet, early on, the SSNP was branded by the Baathist and other enemies as a foreign agent, in particular as an ally of the former British Empire and its Fertile Crescent Project in the aftermath of the Second World War. Today, the party has secured a base in Lebanon and Syria, and its network straddles the border of the two countries and, like many other political movements in the Levant, it fields its own militia, which has participated in both brief skirmishes to decades-spanning conflicts. From the early street clashes following Lebanon's independence, to its harrowing existence throughout the country's fifteen-year civil war, to the 2008 political crisis in Lebanon, to the current conflict in Syria, the SSNP has been there either as a key participant or as a player hidden in the shadows.

For observers in the West, the SSNP is usually regarded as an ally of Syria and is considered to be completely subservient to the Baathist government of President Bashar al-Assad. Westerns and Lebanese opponents of the party strongly associate the SSNP with the Syrian occupation that followed the end of the 1975–90 Lebanese Civil War as a supplemental resource of intelligence-gathering and intimidation for the Syrian regime on its opponents within Lebanon. Mainly regarded with fear, distain, and even disgust, Westerners have long described the party as a fascist terrorist organization with hypnotized members who serve the present-day cult of Antoun Saadeh, their martyred leader. Indeed, the SSNP has been the perpetrator of various acts of political violence since its founding. Their party comrades have been tied to the assassination of several Syrian and Lebanese historical political figures, and even holds the dubious distinction of being one of the first groups to cultivate and hone the tactics of suicide bombing.

In addition, observers tend to dismiss the party's history and its ideology of pan-Syrianism as too irrelevant or farfetched to be worth further study or analysis. The SSNP, therefore, is often overlooked and forgotten by the daily output of news, analysis, studies, policy recommendations, and commentary that is so often the norm for the Middle East.

The party has long been the subject of comparisons to the Nazis or fascist Italy. During the 1930s and 1940s, revolutionary movements in the former colonies occasionally looked to Nazi Germany as a response to colonialism, an answer for economic development, a powerful and centralized leadership, or as a progressive political force that could not only secure independence but also forge a new social order rooted in equality, justice and, ultimately, greatness to their country. The party's early history is indeed rooted in the early 1930s, a time when Adolf Hitler had obtained power and begun industrializing and rearmament in Germany. Lebanon, still under the French Mandate, was seething with nationalist inspiration along with a vast array of ideologies that were ripe for the picking. It was ultimately a transplant figure from the other side of the world who was able to devise and reformulate an old ideology that had been debated in the Levant since the late nineteenth century. Pan-Syrianism had existed in earlier forms and was surprisingly robust and resilient despite its two dominant competitors, pan-Arabism and Lebanese nationalism. Antoun Saadeh had repatriated to the place of his birth from Brazil and, within a decade, breathed new life into a line of thinking that has since fallen in and out of favor with the region's fast-changing political currents.

The Region's Ultimate Survivor

It is astonishing that Antoun Saadeh's ideology has largely survived multiple intraparty splinterings throughout the Levant's political turmoil, civil wars, foreign occupation and military interventions, and several high-level attempts to suppress and extinguish it before and after the early death of its founder in July 1949. How was a party with a ridged hierarchy that heeded to the commands of a single individual able to carry on? By not completely removing itself from an often-complex political platform and public discourse, the SSNP has so far failed to conjure itself into a popular mass movement. The irredentist geopolitical aspirations of the SSNP to create a single cultural and political entity from the Zargos Mountains of eastern Iran to the Western shores of Cyprus lump it into the category that it is not only a sinister party with a secretive, conspiratorial character but also often the object of ridicule in many conversations.

The party's members often acknowledge this; its partisans state that Antoun Saadeh's ultimate geopolitical achievement is the goal of a distant future when the region is ready to shake itself out of a long and painful slumber and realize its place as a multiethnic, diverse, progressive, and powerful entity called Greater (or Natural) Syria. The SSNP's ideology reaches far back into time before the advent of European imperialism and the modern political boundaries and finds itself in the glory and wisdom of the ancient empires of the Levant and Mesopotamia. In addition, the SSNP has been fairly or unfairly labeled as a Christian-tinged movement, a potential secular haven in the region for a sort of revamped Byzantium. It is this vein that the SSNP taps into, which for them the recent history of the Levant has been nothing short of a catastrophe. The establishment of the state of Israel, the division of Lebanon and Syria, the loss of Hatay (Antakyya) to Turkey, the capture of Syria's Golan Heights in the 1967 Six-Day War, Saddam Hussein's 1990 invasion of Kuwait, and now—with the outbreak of the Syrian Civil War in 2011—the very survival of Syria itself.

The SSNP has seen much violence and persecution since its establishment in the early 1930s. Saadeh's confrontations and maneuverings finally ran out of steam when he launched a rebellion against the Lebanese government in July 1949, which led to him being captured and summarily executed. His party, however, survived. It endured the ebb and flow of the Lebanese Civil War from 1975 to 1990. This fifteen-year period of civil strife, political and religious extremism, and terrible violence came as the party re-emerged from hiding after nearly two decades of harsh persecution. It survived and made itself useful during Syria's occupation of Lebanon by relying on its militia, unique ideology, and adopting a politically pragmatic approach that brought the SSNP from the right side of the political spectrum to its current place in the camp of the left. Embracing its anti-imperialist character, the party found a renewed solidarity with the Palestinians and won favor from the Syrian regime, which intervened steadily and heavily throughout Lebanon's long-running conflict, and subsequently, the SSNP has not left the side of its ally in Damascus since.

Antoun Saadeh had long since departed, but it appeared that his dream was finally a blip on the Levant's horizon. With the SSNP firmly established in a Syrian-dominated postwar Lebanon, it now reached across the border to clasp the hand of its once arch-competitor in Baathist Syria. It is this relationship that tested and tried itself through Syria's occupation of Lebanon and war of attrition against Israel throughout the 1980s to 2000. The stars appeared to be aligning for the party with Syrian troops based in Lebanon, a patron the SSNP could support and defend in the name of taking the long-awaited step toward establishing a unified Lebanon and Syria, the first rung of Greater Syria. In addition, pan-Arabism was beginning to lose its luster. The war in Lebanon had begun on the basis of protecting vulnerable Sunni Muslims against the whims and fears of Lebanon's powerful Christian factions. But ultimately, this view of the Lebanese conflict through this narrow prism did not last. Lebanon's civil war was far more complex and showed that the violence crisscrossed and defied an easy explanation of sectarian fault-lines. Sunnis fought Sunnis, Christians fought Christians, and Shia fought Shia as nearly every camp was allied and opposed the other at some point in the conflict.

Pan-Arabism predominately resonates with Arab Sunnis throughout the Middle East. The hard realities of the civil war were brought to bear that inter-Arab rivalries manifest themselves in vicious ways. The failure of the Arab countries to remain united against Israel (Egypt and Jordan each secured their separate peace), the Gulf War against Iraq, and the reconstruction of war-torn Lebanon saw a turn away from the region's once-leading ideological champion. Closer, local identities began to return. Ideas such as Phoenicianism promoted the belief that the Lebanese people were a distinct ethnic group, but pan-Syrianism was quickly finding a new home. As Syria's main benefactor, Hezbollah, emerged and heralded itself as the victor in consecutive showdowns with Israel, the Syrian government could finally regard itself as a key player in the Levant. In 2000, following the passing of President Hafez al-Assad, Syria witnessed a transition of power to his son, Bashar. Damascus, in the immediate post-9/11 era, was well positioned in the Levant's geopolitical arena. Damascus along with Tehran, confidently held the reins to Hezbollah in Lebanon; yielded a strong influence over Lebanon's political elite, with Hamas in the Palestinian territories; fostered a close friendship with Turkey; acted as an essential mediator and facilitator for the West to ease every violent conflict into a productive dialogue. Syria dangled the promise of being the key to all of the region's woes. Pan-Arabism began to fade, and pan-Syrianism now had a chance to step in, and the SSNP, with its proud history, discipline, and doctrine, stood ready.

But the winds of change took a new turn, and pan-Syrianism once again found itself in danger. Following the February 2005 assassination of Lebanese Prime Minister Rafik Hariri, the withdrawal of some 14,000 Syrian soldiers from Lebanon, the subsequent Cedar Revolution, the Arab Spring, and finally the rise of the Islamic State group brought about new challenges for the SSNP and the future of Greater Syria. The Syrian state itself is now the central player in a brutal struggle for survival. The Syrian Civil War has brought a vast array of military, economic, and social troubles that the regime in Damascus will be dealing with for years to come. Once the master of a tangled web of multiple geopolitical fault-lines, the Syrian government will now devote a tremendous amount of energy inwards, nearly completely dependent on foreign assistance from Russia, Iran, and China. A festering Islamist insurgency lingers; entire territories have yet to be recovered; a whole economy will have to be re-created from nearly scratch; choking sanctions lifted; criminal networks dismantled; and a vast black market, the return of refugees, the implementation of a national reconciliation, and the confrontation of a Kurdish force in Syria's northeast backed by a super power that could potentially see Damascus turn to the SSNP more than ever.

The Wrath of the Baath

For the SSNP and the Baath, there is a lasting stigma of victim and aggressor. To the Baath, the SSNP was once a conspiratorial, hostile force backed by the West until it corrected its behavior. For the SSNP, the Baath unjustly punished it from within its natural environment. No other party in the Levant has the same relationship that has been subjected to extreme political competition, outright hostility, tentative cooperation, and reconciliation, as the alliance between the SSNP and the Baath Party. *Al-Baath* (meaning resurrection or resurgence) is far more familiar in the West than the SSNP. The Baath is well known for its ideology of pan-Arabism, strident nationalism, and eventual authoritarianism. Founded as a students' movement by the Syrian teacher Michel Aflaq in 1940, it later merged with a party of the same name headed by Zaki al-Arsuzi. The Baath Party eventually joined with the Arab Socialist Party of Akram al-Hawrani and adopted the full name of the Arab Socialist Baath Party. Aflaq envisioned the party as a vehicle for political reform, modernism, and a mechanism that could unify the Arab World, which he felt had been artificially divided by European colonialism. The party's early history indeed had this character in mind, which won it the public support needed to build it into a mass movement. It was a movement that was secular, nationalist, socialist, and militaristic all at once. In addition, the party was modern and regarded as avant garde in its outlook, with forward-thinking views toward women and antisectarian in identity. It was on this platform that the Baath would bring glory, honor, and enlightenment back to the Arab World in the wake of European colonialism. In 1943, Aflaq stood at a podium in the University of Damascus and outlined his vision of the Arab renaissance in his famous speech titled "In Memory of the Arab Prophet."

> Today we stand witness to a conflict between our glorious past and shameful present. The Arab personality was in our past unified in one body: there was no divide between its soul and its intellect, no divide between its rhetoric and its practice, its private and its public codes of conduct. It was a fulfilled and rich life, where its intellect, spirit, and practice were working together, in harmony with its strong instincts ... It is time we removed this contradiction and returned to the Arab personality in its unity, and make whole Arab life once again.[1]

The high water mark of the Baath Party may very well have been in conjunction with the establishment of the United Arab Republic (UAR) in February 1958. This project was to be a solution for all the woes that plagued the region: the desires for independence, wealth, power, and social justice. At the center of this scheme was Gamal Abdul Nasser, the "champion of Arabism" who placed Egypt in the heart of the prevailing ideological trends developing at the time.[2] The union between Egypt and Syria, which only lasted a few years, hoped to signify the first step toward the creation of a united Arab World. The late intellectual Fayez Sayegh, a former-SSNP-member-turned-staunch-Arab-nationalist, characterized the political and ideological vision of Arab unification in June 1958:

> Two proud names, as ancient as history itself, evoking venerable memories ... have now been relegated to the past. By the choice of the peoples themselves, these names have been abandoned as designations of national identification, and have given way to a new name—the United Arab Republic.[3]

The Baath Party during this period underwent the first of several drastic changes that would permanently alter its character. The Baath has been described as a vanguard party with the aim to both protect Arab societies against Western imperialism and to unify and modernize the Arab World. However, the UAR scheme came to a sudden end when a coup in 1961 plucked Syria out of the union and the country experienced what was described as "near anarchy" between 1961 and 1963, as street battles between the communists, Nasserists, Baathists, and army factions unfolded.[4] By the mid-1960s, the party in Syria effectively became completely integrated into the governing system it was "virtually indistinguishable," and its membership increased dramatically to evolve from an elite vanguard to a mass organization.[5] The Baath Party had gradually become more and more authoritarian. Syria's emergency law was enacted after the Baathists launched the coup d'état in March 1963 against the anti-UAR secessionist government. This allowed the ruling party to arrest individuals and imprison them at will.

Various forms of the emergency law and a range of presidential decrees that favor and protect the state security services continue to exist in Syria today. These are described as shielding the country's citizens from terror and conspiracy but nevertheless have heightened the stigma of authoritarianism associated with the Baath Party.[6] The party headed into further internal turmoil with the 1966 interparty coup that toppled President Amin al-Hafiz and installed the leftist regime led by Salah Jadid. Old guard figures such as Michel Aflaq and Shibli al-Aysami fled to Iraq into the arms of the faction of the Baath Party based in Baghdad. Aysami became a prominent figure in the National Alliance for the Liberation of Syria, backed by Saddam until his retirement in 1992 and later disappeared in 2011, allegedly by the Syrian regime.[7] Aflaq went on to become an intellectual figurehead in Saddam's Baath Party and was designated the "founding leader"; however, he never wielded any sort of tangible political influence in Saddam's regime and died in Paris in June 1989.[8]

For a time, the Baathists sought to place themselves within the ranks of the Non-Aligned Movement amidst the Cold War.[9] However, in the long run, Baathist Syria drifted into Soviet orbit as part of President Hafez al-Assad's confrontation with Israel. The 1973 October War was lost but briefly managed to regain some of the Arab nationalism's lost luster, which proved to be short-lived. In 1976, protests in Syria broke out when Assad sent the Syrian army to support the Christian militias against the PLO–leftist coalition in the first phase of the Lebanese Civil War.[10] By the end of the 1970s and start of the 1980s, the Syrian government began to experience its first major internal challenges. The attack on the Alawite military cadets in Aleppo in 1979 by the Muslim Brotherhood led to the infamous Hamah uprising and massacre.

The Syrians faced another crisis among their Arab comrades when Yasser Arafat's PLO entered into the 1993 Oslo Accords with Israel. The agreement again left Damascus in the cold and rendered Assad diplomatically isolated as he had experienced earlier with Sadat's peace agreement with Israel in the 1970s.[11] The Damascus Spring of 2000 brought about another era of change. After the death of Hafez al-Assad and the easing up on the banned opposition parties, the SSNP also began to feel its way forward in a newly expanded political sphere. Following Hafez al-Assad's long period of rule, Syria became the first Arab republic to stage a hereditary succession. One Egyptian professor, Sa'ad Eddin Ibrahim, even developed an Arabic term for it, *Jumalikaya*, a merging of the words *Jumahuriya*, republic, with *Mamluka*, monarchy.[12]

Bashar al-Assad purged the old guard and expelled Abdul Halim Khaddam in December 2005. Prior to the outbreak of the 2011 protests, the government had lost ground to the wave of religious revival taking place in the countryside. The ruling party's ideology of pan-Arab nationalism that had attracted and sustained membership for so long had largely given way to the vastly more popular Sunni conservatism of the Muslim Brotherhood (al-Ikhwan al-Muslimun) and Salafist Islam.[13] The trend of Islamist movements had endured since the turn of the nineteenth century, even under the auspice of dictatorship. The first of these movements in Syria were primarily associations (jam'iyyat) oriented toward religion and providing social services and later evolved into full-fledged political parties.

Amidst all of these challenges to the Baath Party, lurking in the background was the ever-present specter of Syrian nationalism, which was informally adopted by Hafez al-Assad during the Lebanese Civil War. Some argued that Bashar al-Assad sought to move away from the notions of pan-Syrianism by ending Syria's claims to the Turkish Province of Hatay in 2004 and sending an ambassador to Lebanon in 2008, thereby distancing his government from the Pax-Syriana era of his father.[14] However, the Baath Party today now has the difficult tasks of wrestling with the outcome of the Syrian Civil War, the international demands for political reform, and a leadership transition. The government appears to have calculated that some outreach to the Sunni community will be vital to reconstitute its power across all of the country's sectarian components. This includes signals that Damascus intends to empower the Ministry of Awqaf (religious endowments), and Assad clearly aims to keep Syria within the Axis of Resistance security framework by adhering to a total alignment with Iran in the name of the Palestinian cause against the state of Israel. Refurbishing Syria's hold on Lebanon and revamping the Baath Party's political mechanisms on all of Syrian society will also be important for the government to re-establish its postwar control.

Reliance on Russia and Iran threatens to weaken Syria's long-term sovereignty, and the government will work to keep both powers off-balance in order to protect its own foreign policy goals. The question of return of the Syrian refugees will also be difficult. Allowing a massive influx of Syrians angry, disillusioned, and waiting for a repeat of the 2011 revolution will force the ruling Baath Party to rely on a mix of political theater, token reform, and state repression in order to secure its future. A new generation of Syrians, testing the waters of political pluralism and economic development, has denounced the Baath Party's "fake socialism."[15] Still, the Baath Party remains the largest and most organized political force in Syria. Before the outbreak of war in 2011, the party had some 1.2 million members in Syria.[16] It is actively rebuilding and recruiting a new generation of younger members. The Baath Party will likely rapidly reinsert itself into the areas recaptured by the government from the many rebel factions and will actively pursue an aggressive return to the territories held by the Kurdish-led Democratic Union Party (PYD) and the US-supported Syrian Democratic Forces (SDF) coalition. Assad's government and the SSNP have complimented one another throughout the Syrian crisis. What is uncertain as to how this relationship will continue as the country restructures and reasserts itself. The Baath Party is highly unlikely to allow any real sort of political competition to develop in the postwar environment. How the Baath and the SSNP will approach these issues in the coming decades will be essential to understanding the revival of the Syrian government's power and Syria's overall internal political stability in the postwar era.

2

The Party of the Martyr: The SSNP's Beginnings in Lebanon

The prisoners listened as the condemned man shuffled past their cells through the courtyard in Lebanon's al-Raml prison. They could not see the figure, but one prisoner, Gibran Jreige, later claimed to have recognized Antoun Saadeh from the sound of his footsteps.[1] The SSNP had experienced government crackdowns before the summer of 1949. The first in 1935 and later efforts to curtail the party that followed during Saadeh's exile. Even behind bars, the leader's very presence inspired hope in his followers, despite the most oppressive circumstances. However, the SSNP's leader would not live to see the 1950s. It is the story of the SSNP's founder and leader that best exemplifies the movement, its outlook, and its troubled history. As with much of the party's characteristics and activities throughout the region's modern history, the personal story of Antoun Saadeh is subject to controversy and debate. The legacy of the man's life struggle and his ideology continues to frame the foundations of the party.

Saadeh is venerated and adored by party members as well as a significant portion of nonpartisan Lebanese and Syrians, as well as other parties.[2] For them, Antoun Saadeh's story represents a rare figure that stood up to foreign interference and a corrupt, authoritarian Lebanese government. It was Saadeh's determination to remain utterly uncompromising in his politics, along with his secular beliefs, that still resonates with nonparty members ranging from the idealistic and highly educated to the social and political outcasts of Lebanon. His impact on Lebanese and Syrian politics during the 1930s and 1940s came at a time when the independence struggle was under way and the future scope of both nations' political identity was still fragile. For Saadeh's critics, he was a dangerous radical who sought to destroy the heart of Lebanon's national identity and existence by readily employing the use of violence and intimidation. Many of the SSNP's opponents to this day still regard him as an ideological fascist, who had established ties with Nazi Germany and whose organization was responsible for indirectly creating or influencing a number of authoritarian parties in the Middle East.³

What is remarkable, however, is the short timeframe of Saadeh's political agitation and subsequent role as the party's leader. Although born in Lebanon, he lived in Brazil for much of his youth before returning to his homeland. In just under twenty years, the benign-looking self-styled intellectual had repatriated to Lebanon from the diaspora in South America and challenged the geopolitical dictates of France, a world power; created a lasting armed militia; and established an ideology that penetrated deeply into the Syrian army's officer corps, leading to several of the first coups in the region. Aside from leading the party he founded, Saadeh never reached the status of national leader in Lebanon, either by force or election. It was his role as an agitator and disrupter that ultimately carved out his legacy. Perhaps in some ways, untainted by the decision making of public office, this helped facilitate his veneration by the party's later generations. Syrian historian Sami Moubayed emphasized the lasting impact of Saadeh's party on France's colonial history in Lebanon and how the SSNP leader continues to bask in his own rebellious character, long after his untimely death: "The Lebanese-born philosopher after all was the only politician of his day and era who was truly focused on doing away with the borders of Sykes-Picot, imposed on the Middle East by the infamous agreement of 1916."⁴

From the start of his activities in 1932 to his death in 1949, Saadeh left a tremendous impact on the politics and history of Lebanon and Syria. For people familiar with the party and its founder, the story of Saadeh's early career in journalism and teaching, his establishment of the party in secret, his imprisonment and confrontations with the French and Lebanese state, and the failed uprising in 1949 have been told many times and from multiple perspectives. For others studying the party for the first time, Saadeh's journey toward leadership and martyrdom is essential for understanding the SSNP as it exists today. However, it is critical to note that the Saadeh period and the birth of his party were not the sole undertaking of one individual. All too often, the history of the SSNP during this period predominantly focuses only on Saadeh and his actions. The era was also the formative years for many other figures who would later go on to shape Syrian–Lebanese politics with some leading the party in their own ways, such as George Abd Messih, Issam al-Mahayri, Inaam Raad, and Said Taqiyaddin. For that reason, other party figures will be introduced throughout the book and discussed as well. In addition, much of the party's history was documented during this time by the early followers such as the intellectual and party propagandist Labib Zuwiyya Yamak, who went on to publish a critical take on the SSNP, Hisham Sharabi, the pan-Arab nationalist who later settled in Washington, DC, and Fayez Sayegh, who became a Lebanese diplomat and champion of the Palestinian cause.

Saadeh's Early Life and the Founding of the SSNP

Antoun Saadeh came from a Greek Orthodox family from the village of Dhour el-Shuwayr in Ottoman Lebanon. He was born on March 1, 1904, to Dr. Khalil Saadeh, a physician who had been socially and politically active during the years of Ottoman rule, and Naifa Nassir Khneisser. The elder Saadeh left Lebanon for a new life, first in Egypt and later in Sao Paolo, Brazil. Antoun's father was an intellectual with a Western outlook. While in Egypt, Dr. Saadeh wrote an Arabic–English dictionary and a novel about Caesar and Cleopatra.[5] Antoun Saadeh joined his father and spent time studying in Egypt, but returned to Lebanon during the First World War, where he studied at a school in the town of Brummana in the Matn hills, which overlooked Beirut. After the end of the First World War, he spent a year in the United States, working with his uncle at a train station in Springer, New Mexico, before finally immigrating to Brazil where he began a career in journalism by editing his father's journal *al-Majallah*.[6] His father had previously headed the *al-Jarida* newspaper, which Saadeh first edited when he arrived in Brazil. When *al-Jarida* ceased publication in 1923, they then republished *al-Majallah* from 1923 to 1925 in the city of São Paulo, which had been earlier published in Buenos Aires until 1919.

During his time in Brazil, he pieced together his irredentist interpretation of Syrian nationalism. It is believed that Saadeh's father's writings and activities had a strong influence and shaped his political and social beliefs during his formative years in São Paulo. Antoun's early nationalism was well within the broader currents of Syrian nationalist thought that was trending during this time. Historians point to Saadeh's father's nationalist activities as evidence of his son's worldview.[7] Others said Antoun was influenced by his own readings and pointed to the works of Henri Lammens, a Jesuit priest with Beirut's University of Saint Joseph, who in 1921 wrote a two-part account on Syrian identity, which existed prior to the onset of Arab culture and political influence.[8] Another example often cited is Philip Hitti's *Syria and the Syrians in History*, published in 1926, which discussed an enduring connection between Syria's ancient history and that of a modern Syrian nation.[9]

In 1930, 25-year-old Saadeh returned to the Middle East where he joined the *al-Ayyam* newspaper in Damascus. The paper's owner, Nasuh Babil, was known for his hardline anti-French views, which likely appealed to Saadeh.[10] However, the restrictive and regressive environment in the French Mandate of Syria compelled him to relocate to Beirut, an environment with a certain level of freedom. At first, Saadeh struggled to support himself financially. It was these circumstances that led him to the American University in Beirut (AUB), where he gave German lessons and socialized in the staff areas. He was often teased for his bearded appearance and argumentative nature and spent much of his time talking with students and swimming.[11] He occasionally published articles and used his time on the campus to network within the university and to test his ideas. Despite these efforts, he initially had trouble gaining any sort of close following.[12]

For Saadeh, the campus offered some protection against the prevailing authoritarian climate under French rule in Lebanon, which he believed kept the country intellectually stymied. He wrote later:

> The situation in the country was one of desperation and fear. Espionage was widespread in all places and treachery concealed in every corner. Foreign armies occupied the strategic positions, and the intelligence bureau sent its agents into all milieus of the populace. People's thoughts were uneasy for they found themselves in a chaotic condition, which prevented mutual understanding. Everyone's spirits were in darkness and the future looked gloomy. The ordinary citizen had been reduced to sub-human level: he was unacquainted with the past, unable to comprehend the present, or perceive the future, and unwilling to share with others his true opinion, if he dared to think at all.[13]

Saadeh eventually developed a good relationship with the AUB staff and spoke at cultural functions staged by Al-Urwa al-Wuthqa, an influential AUB student association established in 1918 that espoused Arab nationalist thought, and others, such as the Palestine Club. In addition, there were active secular parties, such as the Syrian-Lebanese Communist Party, which had been founded earlier in 1924. The Communist Party was established during a period of an intellectual awakening that followed the intense economic hardships Lebanon faced as a part of the Ottoman Empire during the First World War. With the success of the Bolsheviks in Russia, middle-class and upper-class thinkers had sought to form a labor-oriented socialist party in Lebanon. Headed by the Syrian Kurd, Khalid Bakdash, the Communist Party had previously been suppressed by the French for taking part in the Great Syrian Revolt of 1925 and had since found refuge in Lebanon. Described as "a brilliant, bold individual, an unexcelled and fiery public speaker,"[14] fluent in French, Arabic, and Kurdish, Bakdash was a powerful personality, of a similar mold that of Saadeh, and he went on to become one of Saadeh's primary political opponents and critics.

It was against this backdrop of political competition and oppression that Saadeh began his first steps toward forming his own party in 1931. Saadeh took great care in selecting the first nine members, who were both Lebanese and Jordanian. Nevertheless, he grew to have doubts about his recruits and, through his discussions with them, soon came to believe that most of the students had been overly exposed to competing ideologies. In addition, he was not certain his party would remain secret from the authorities. In early November 1932, Saadeh abruptly gathered his small group and announced the party was disbanded. He explained that he was unsatisfied with two members he felt were not completely loyal, thus a risk to the nascent party's survival. About a week later, on November 16, he secretly reformed the party with the other students, naming it the Syrian National Party (SNP)—al-Hizb al-Suri al-Qawmi. The first members of this group were George Abd Messih, Fouad Girgis Haddad, Jamil Abdou Sawaya, Zahauddin Hammoud, and Wadi Talhouq.

The party remained secret over the next three years under the guise of the Societe Syrienne de Commerce (al-Sharika al-Tijariya al-Suriya).[15] Girgis Samaan Haddad, Fouad's father, owned a restaurant opposite of AUB, which became an informal meeting place for teachers and students. Fouad's sister, Afifah, acted as a look-out when the meetings were held, and she soon became tasked with recording the proceedings. By the summer of 1934, word of the SNP's existence had spread to other cities in Lebanon, and its membership increased to roughly a thousand. Orthodox Christians, Alawites, Druze, and other sectarian minorities of upper- and middle-class backgrounds were primarily drawn to the party. As the SNP continued to grow, party members around the country were largely isolated and organized by cells, each knowing little about the true size and scope of the rest of the organization. The leading members began to formulate its structure, and its constitution was drafted in November 1934.

Throughout 1934 and into 1935, the party experienced limited but consistent growth in its membership. It was not long before the SNP was discovered by the Lebanese and French authorities, which both worked together to infiltrate the party. Once exposed, the party's ideological purity and revolutionary goals would be tested in its first initial rounds of confrontation with the ruling establishment. Party members began their long journey of becoming acquainted with state persecution and repression, a dynamic that would shape the SNP's behavior, both internally and externally. Saadeh's party was uncovered in November 1935 after the French colonial security services, the Surete Generale, looked into the inner workings of the Societe Syrienne de Commerce and found out it was a front for Saadeh's subversive political activities. He was arrested, along with his chief lieutenant, Ni'mah Thabit. Saadeh's comrade, Ni'mah Thabit, was a Lebanese Christian who came from a prominent family. He had joined the party after its founding and quickly climbed the party's nascent power structure to become chairman of the Higher Council.[16] The court sentenced Saadeh to six years imprisonment. While in jail, he wrote the first of several published works, which was called *Genesis of Nations*.

The French began assessing the movement to find out what they were up against. Informants had already infiltrated Saadeh's party. One spy reported meeting Saadeh in person at the club room in the Hotel Imperial on Rue Foch on October 2, 1935. They discussed the location of French military weapon depots, the number of members in Saadeh's party (which the party leader said was around 3,000–4,000), party's finances, and how to procure weapons from overseas.[17] The colonial authorities, in their reports to Paris, mistranslated the party's name as the Parti Populaire Syrien (PPS). They mistakenly thought the Arabic word, *qawmi*, to have meant popular, not nationalist. The nomenclature PPS subsequently appeared in many of the early news publications and scholarly works that discuss the party's history in the decades that followed and is still occasionally used today.

The colonial authorities subsequently embarked on a series of incursions throughout Lebanon in order to snuff out the clandestine movement. Raids on the SNP comrades' homes yielded maps and documents from the SNP's own intelligence network, which showed the location of French military garrisons and ammunition depots.[18] It also revealed an organization of 5,000–6,000 members that spanned across both Lebanon and Syria. Each SNP branch had a political section called *munafidhiyyat* (administrative regions) and subsections referred to as *mudiriyya* (a village or city directorate).[19] Given the need for secrecy, the head of each political district only knew the identity of their direct superior and so on. The SNP was especially dominant among the Levant's sectarian minority communities: the Greek Orthodox (Marj Ayun and Matn), the Druze (Chouf mountains), and the Alawites (Tartus, Syria). The French viewed Saadeh's party as a movement that was dedicated to overthrowing the colonial mandate and, from then on, sought to confront, cajole, and repress the SNP with force.

Now shorn of its disguise, Saadeh's movement quickly became the target of a variety of competing political forces in Lebanon due to the very nature of its ideology, which was opposed to the two ideologies most prominent in the country at the time. The first envisioned a Christian, Western-oriented Lebanon with a distinct Lebanese national identity. This brand of Lebanese nationalism was aligned with the existing social order in Lebanon that empowered the religious establishments and safeguarded Lebanon's traditional ruling families, the Zaim. The other, pan-Arabism, was rooted in a Sunni Muslim-based, anti-Western, liberation framework and espoused an independent Lebanon as an essential geographic component of the wider Arab World. As discussed in Chapter 3, Saadeh rejected both of these platforms in favor of an older, ancient Syrian identity that saw Lebanon and Syria as one united entity in a long-forgotten geographic region he called Natural Syria. Patrick Seale relayed the view of the Baath Party founder Michel Aflaq in his renowned 1965 study of the post-independence period, *The Struggle of Syria*:

> The whole movement was an odd mixture of modernism, of scientism, with something extremely old, even archaeological; a resurrection of the local past and grudges a thousand years old. Among the many movements of the Arab rebirth, this was one which aborted and lost itself in unhealthy romanticism, due perhaps to the fact that Saadeh's mind was directed mainly towards the past.[20]

Seale also acknowledged that many of the party's early comrades did not fully grasp or understand the SNP's pan-Syrian doctrine and noted that it was the party's discipline, alleged fascist outlook, and emphasis on social change that brought in most of its average members.[21]

Saadeh was released from his first jail stint in May 1936. A short time later, on June 15, 1936, Saadeh delivered the so-called Blue Declaration in Beirut, which slammed the French and British Mandates and decried the Lebanese elite for engaging in diplomacy for the imperial powers without consulting his party and its proposed solutions.[22] Reaction to the discovery of Saadeh's party continued to reverberate across the Lebanese political spectrum. He was quickly arrested again when SNP members assaulted two Lebanese journalists who had criticized the party. Now exposed, the SNP benefited from a dramatic boost in membership in 1936. By and large, the party's chief political opponent for recruitment was the Lebanese Communist Party (LCP), which painted the SNP as an aggressive right-wing party. The LCP, earlier known as the Lebanese People's Party (in an effort to tone down the anticolonial communist label and to avoid unwanted French harassment), like the SNP, was also a party of elites. Many of its early members were journalists, academics, intellectuals, who sought both social and economic change in Lebanon and Syria. The LCP also benefited from a short-lived burst of toleration from the French due to the French–Soviet alliance during the Second World War. With the 1936 election of the leftist coalition and the Popular Front government of Leon Blum in Paris, the communists in the Levant found a wider opening to operate and grow in Syria.[23]

Meanwhile, Saadeh defended the party's structure, strict organizational hierarchy, and view toward democracy saying: "[The system can] mold our new national life and protect this unusual renaissance, which shall change the history of the East, from the reactionary elements that can never be trusted."[24] The SNP's four-point motto consisted of Freedom, Organization, Discipline, and Power. Labib Zuwiyya Yamak, himself a former member of the party, wrote in his ideological analysis of the party in 1966 that Saadeh was opposed to political pluralism because

> the reactionary elements, primarily sectarian and feudal, thrive within a traditional democratic system because such a system lacks the power to mold and change ... to admit the suitability of the democratic system to the Syrian nation was to him tantamount to giving the reactionary elements a free hand to scuttle the nationalist renaissance which the party engendered. The choice of the dictatorial system became, therefore, a matter of necessity (and of belief) as the only means by which the danger of corruption could be averted, the reactionary elements crushed, and the community transformed into a unified homogeneous entity.[25]

However, Saadeh's ultimate challenge came from the forces of the right through Pierre Gemayel and the hizb al-Kata'ib al-Lubaniya or the Lebanese Phalanges Party or Kataeb Party, which Gemayel had established in November 1936 in order to counter Saadeh's pan-Syrian movement with his own brand of Lebanese nationalism.[26] Pierre Gemayel formed his new party to not only preserve Lebanese sovereignty by countering the SNP but also, like its pan-Syrian nemesis, to act as an anticommunist force in Lebanon.[27] Gemayel attended the 1936 Olympics in Berlin, and the power and order of Nazi Germany left a deep impression on him.[28]

With the earlier outbreak of the Spanish Civil War in 1936, Kataeb had adopted a right-wing ideology akin to Francisco Franco's Spanish nationalist forces of Falangism (hence the Kataeb Party's name), a platform with an intense emphasis on Catholic identity, anticommunism, and an antiliberal belief in the power of the state over the nation's destiny. The party's motto was "God, Nation, and Family." Lebanese President Emile Edde tried to curb the influence and spread of these nationalist movements and issued an order to ban them in 1937. Gemayel denounced the move and said his party's goal was to protect Lebanon from "anarchy" and called for hundreds of Kataeb members to hit the streets where they gathered in Beirut's central square and battled the French colonial forces amid stone-throwing and gunfire. In the subsequent crackdown, Kataeb was largely forced into hiding where they waited for the departure of the French.[29]

The SNP continued to clash with both of these political rivals and the government authorities into the late 1930s. The SNP held a military-style parade in February 1937 in Bikfaya, where the SNP's militia skirmished with the Lebanese security forces. However, Saadeh occasionally sought to maintain the cordial relations with the colonial French authorities, visiting the Pine Residence palace for ceremonies commemorating the Bastille Day. French High Commissioner Damien de Martel met Saadeh in the receiving line and asked him, "*Za'im* means leader, *n'est ce pas*, so where do you want to lead us?" Saadeh replied, "To what is best for both of our countries."[30] In November 1937, Saadeh journeyed throughout Lebanon and Syria to review his party's militia wing. He was arrested a third and final time before heading off into his self-imposed exile. He was released after two months when his party threw its political support behind the pan-Arab Lebanese politician Khayreddin al-Ahdab for the parliamentary elections. Without this deal, Saadeh would have remained in prison longer. After Saadeh departed Lebanon in 1938, the French authorities, amid an expanding crackdown on all political dissents, sentenced him to ten years imprisonment in absentia. The SNP issued a communique to bid farewell to their chief:

> Let us be ready for the day when our leader will call us to the field of freedom and honor. Let our hearts accompany the national hero on his travels and uphold him at every moment with our thoughts and feelings.[31]

Self-Exile to Europe and the Americas

With the Second World War commencing in Europe, Saadeh's repeated confrontations with the French colonial authorities led him to leave Lebanon and attempt to build the party's membership overseas. Saadeh's decision to go into self-exile would, like everything else he did, become a point of contention in the party's history. His activities, the purpose of his movements abroad, and his relations with the Axis Powers would provide additional fuel for the region's partisans, scholars, and commentators to argue that the SNP was in fact linked with the Nazis.

These accusations were repeated extensively, but no conclusive evidence of a relationship with Nazi Germany or Fascist Italy was ever validated. Saadeh fled Lebanon, stopping first in Jordan, meeting with King Abdullah I, and traveled through Palestine.[32] Then he went on to Europe. According to Beshara, he stopped briefly in Rome and Berlin and met with local officials.[33] Back in Lebanon, the French Mandatory authorities judged it as a telltale sign that the SNP was a fascist organization and rounded up its leadership. The French government alleged that Saadeh spoke on Radio Berlin, a charge that Patrick Seale said remained unproven.[34] Party sympathizers usually defend against the accusations of fascism by pointing to what Saadeh stated in a speech in 1935:

> I want to use this opportunity to say that the system of the Syrian Social Nationalist Party is neither a Hitlerite nor a Fascist one, but a pure social nationalist one. It is not based on imitation, but is instead the result of an authentic invention— which is a virtue of our people.[35]

However, in his 2010 book on Riad al-Solh, Seale wrote that Saadeh stopped in Berlin, where "Nazi authorities are believed to have given him a warm welcome." The party explained the stop as an "informational visit." Saadeh continued his travels through Europe, giving radio speeches in Budapest and Bern before heading to Italy and boarded a transatlantic ocean liner for the Western Hemisphere.[36] The exact nature of Saadeh's stopover in Europe and the full extent of his relationship with the Nazi regime in Berlin remain largely unknown.

Upon his arrival in Brazil, Saadeh was briefly detained because of his time in Berlin. However, he was not indicted and was released. From Brazil, he set sail for Argentina, where he ran into more trouble. He soon learned that the French had sentenced him to ten years imprisonment. When he tried to renew his visa at the French consulate in Buenos Aires,[37] his passport was confiscated. Saadeh was unable to return to Lebanon or to continue his trip beyond Argentina. It was during this crucial time that Saadeh sought to establish the first foothold of the SNP outside of the Levant within the Latin American Sírio-Libanês community. The *mahjar*, meaning "land of emigration," was for the most part a familiar and comfortable environment for Saadeh during his years in exile since he had already spent nearly a decade of his life in Argentina before his first return to Lebanon. It was here in the *mahjar* he married Juliette El-Mir and built financial and political networks for the SNP, but, like his time in the Levant, he soon found enemies in the Western Hemisphere. Through debates in Argentina's

Arabic newspapers, Saadeh received opposition from both communists and conservative thinkers that were present and active among the Sírio-Libanês in Latin America.

The outbreak of the Second World War further compounded his troubles. Saadeh was cut off from his party, and his chances of covertly traveling back to the Levant were greatly diminished. In addition, Saadeh heavily depended on financial donations from supporters. As a result, Saadeh entered the realm of the *mahjar*'s business leaders and community's elite, receiving help from key figures such as Camel Auad and Yusef Musa Azizeh, joining the latter's social club, Honor Y Patria.[38] Azizeh's publication, *Diario Siriolibanes*, became a perch for Saadeh to spread word of the party and its ideas within the local Arabic-speaking community, also printing articles in Spanish. The articles toned down the full scope of the SNP's political persecution at home and sought to portray Saadeh's time in Latin America as an educational and goodwill visit. The club Honor Y Patria even hosted a large banquet for Saadeh's birthday on March 1, 1940, at the Jousten Hotel in Buenos Aires. The birthday celebration was described as having an atmosphere of "general excitement and cordiality" with local journalists, prominent families, intellectuals, and poets in attendance. A local poet named Zaki Qonsol read a poem he drafted in Saadeh's honor. After the other speakers had finished, Saadeh gave a speech and shared "his hopes with respect to a progressive future for Syria" to the joy of the banquet hall.[39] However, the years overseas following the banquet did not fare well for Saadeh. He started a new paper called *Zawbaa* (or *El Ciclon* in Spanish) named after his party's storm logo. A selection of summaries from his editorials is as follows:

The Syrian Social-Nationalist Ideology, June 15, 1942[40]

The Syrian Social Nationalist Creed and the Democrat's Search for a Creed

Saadeh starts off with going through a number of recent statements made by Western politicians and academics trying to gain the public's support by appealing to the working class' hopes of equality and higher standards of living, and also attempting to create a creed for the people to fight under the same banner against the enemies of the Allies.

He examined the Western governments' efforts and says that the Democratic countries now realized they are fighting without an ideology against enemies with strong creeds. Saadeh proceeded to compare the workers' situation in the Western Democracies with the situation of their peers in the USSR, Nazi Germany, and Fascist Italy. He cites the high unemployment rates and poor living conditions for the workers in the Western countries and the much lower unemployment rates in the latter. However, Saadeh notes that the Communist USSR's ideology remains just as materialistic as the capitalist West and left very little space for the human spirit.

He criticized the Western-worshipping segments of the Middle East's intellectual class. Saadeh described the revolutionary aspects of the Social Nationalist creed and states that Karl Marx and Friedrich Engels' socialism shed light on the economic issues of human society, but failed to solve "the complex human social issues."

The Leader's Speech on the 1st of March, June 15th, 1943[41]

Location: Córdoba, Argentina. Time: 12 AM, March 1st, 1943.

Saadeh praised Argentina and thanked it for allowing the party the freedom to operate in its territory. Then Saadeh explained that he and his comrades in Lebanon were facing persecution, describing the court martial that sentenced him to prison in absentia, along with many of his comrades. He raised his glass in their honor. Saadeh then went on to speak of the tradition of celebrating his birthday with his comrades in the party, which started in 1935 and still continued. He said that it shows that the spiritual bond between him and his comrades was only getting stronger. Saadeh compared the French oppression and persecution of political thought in Syria to the Ottoman oppression. The speech also discussed Arabism and Phoenicianism and the religious sectarian agenda hidden behind their veils.

He said the Lebanese nationalists who claimed Phoenicia has always been separate from Syria should read the Bible to see where it said that Christ had visited the Syrian city of Tyre. Saadeh stressed that the party's position on Arabism was no less critical than their position on Phoenicianism but noted that the SNP's interest was in the dignity of the Arab World's nations and this was an indisputable matter. He said, "Whenever it comes to the dignity of the whole Arab World, then we are its front, its sword and shield, and the defenders of the language of Dhad (a term for the Arabic language)[42] and the bearers of its banner."

Greater Syria, July 1st, 1943[43]

Saadeh highlights what he believes were Egypt's imperialist ambitions in Natural Syria, and notes certain statements made by the Egyptian prime minister and members of parliament indicated their intentions to annex Palestine. He goes on to connect this threat to a long history of bloody Syrian-Egyptian conflicts and wars in Southwestern Syria. Saadeh notes a change in Abdullah of Transjordan's positions from Arabism to Syrian Nationalism and mentioned Abdullah's call for the unification of Greater Syria.

Saadeh stated that, with Iraq and Jordan's new orientation towards Syrian Nationalism, Egypt's goals had failed. Saadeh viewed Arabism as an Egyptian imperialist tool but commented that it was the SNP's efforts that had caused the royal Hashemites in Iraq and Jordan to switch positions. The article then goes back to old statements that Saadeh made regarding Levantine-Iraqi unity, as early as 1936. In a statement from 1938 Saadeh said he wishes to erase the desert between the Levant and Iraq and forest it. He added that social unity must come before a political unity and suggested changing the name from Greater Syria to Souraqia.

The *Zawbaa* editorials proved to be divisive within the Sírio-Libanês community as his views on Syrian nationalism became more pronounced. Although Saadeh still retained the respect of some elements of the community for his anti-imperialist positions, the advocates of Arab nationalism and political Islam rallied to take him down. Articles printed in *Ad-Difah* painted Saadeh as an outsider, an opportunist, a con artist, and a Nazi fifth columnist. In particular, Abd al-Malik, a community leader responsible for hosting the infamous banquet, helped cut off the flow of donations for Saadeh and slammed him in public for "deceptions Rasputin is incapable of." The poet Zaki Qonsol distanced himself from rumors that he had joined the SNP and denounced his personal ties to Saadeh.[44]

At the end of the Second World War, Saadeh sought a resolution to his exile and tried repeatedly to return to Lebanon but was denied. Diplomatic negotiations finally yielded success in early 1947. Lebanon's President Beshara el-Khoury granted his blessing for Saadeh's repatriation and, in return, expected the SNP's political support in the general elections scheduled in May of the same year.[45] The opportunities were across the board. Kamal Jumblatt and Camille Chamoun, along with other Lebanese politicians, all sought backing from the SNP during the 1947 elections, which were widely considered to be the most corrupt in the country's history.[46] However, the SNP that was waiting at home for Saadeh had changed significantly during his long absence.

The exile period had witnessed a dramatic transformation in the SNP in order to adjust to the political landscape. This political reconfiguration became known in the party's history as the "Lebanon School," and the movement's attitude of confrontation toward the ruling establishment and the party's pan-Syrian ideology was significantly reduced. Its name and salute were all curtailed and, in the words of Adel Beshara, the SNP became "indistinguishable" from any of the other political parties operating in Lebanon during this time. The SNP's fierce red zawbaa symbol was retired and replaced by a benign-looking circle divided into four quadrants, each representing the four words of the party's motto. This new logo was designed by the party's secretary of broadcast, Ibrahim Yamout, in 1945.[47] The party also cut the word "Syrian" from its name, becoming the National Party. This was done in order to placate the Lebanese political establishment, along with the growing independence movement, which greatly feared that a newly liberated Lebanon could be easily swallowed up by its larger neighbor, Syria. Without Saadeh at the helm, the Lebanon School period essentially saw the party scale back its irredentist vision in exchange for political accommodation.

But the external and internal changes instigated by the party members Saadeh left behind were not entirely made passively. The colonial government had banned the SNP on October 7, 1939, and a seven-month crackdown ensued, with hundreds of members rounded up into detention camps and its leaders imprisoned. The French charged that the SNP was in contact with the Axis Powers even though, ironically, the French Mandate in Lebanon during this time was under the authority of the Vichy government in Paris, an Axis ally. An eventual occupation by the Allies did not change their fortune. Ni'mah Thabit and an estimated seventy party members were jailed in the Rashaya citadel and the Mieh-Mieh Prison, which had been converted from an orphanage by the Free French and British Australian forces when they wrestled Lebanon back from the Vichy French troops in the summer of 1941.[48]

In June 1941, a delegation of Lebanese political figures lobbied the French General Henri Dentz to ease up on the party, an effort that eventually succeeded. Lebanon, finally freed from the French in 1943, began to sort out its political environment in the independence era. It was likely this measure of goodwill shown by the old guard of the Lebanese political establishment that facilitated the SNP's path into a temporary legitimacy, which was granted in April 1944. In addition, contact between the party and Saadeh was virtually nonexistent. From 1945 to 1946, the party focused on internal restructuring, rebuilding, and recruitment. It remained under the wary eye of the government but continued to grow, pulled in students and intellectuals from the urban areas, and waited patiently for the return of its founder.

Clashes and violent street battles continued throughout the 1940s as the SNP fended off political rivalries that sought to feed off its weakness during Saadeh's exile. The communists engaged the party and continued to accuse the SNP of fascism, a charge only heightened during the backdrop of the Second World War. The SNP, for its part, was all too willing to strike back. In November 1945, Edward Shartuni, the head of the communist publication *al-Tariq*, was fatally stabbed by an SNP member. The LCP alleged the Lebanese government had facilitated these attacks in order to play the two sides off each other.[49] The LCP would soon have its own troubles. The Soviet Union's recognition of the newly established state of Israel in 1948 plagued the Communist Party, with a number of communists leaving the LCP to join the staunchly anti-Zionist SNP.

The SNP also won converts from the primary constituents of pan-Arabism. The SNP had a small but established presence in Palestine since its founding. Many of the Palestinians refugees from the Arab-Israeli War of 1948 in Lebanon were kept in the confinement of refugee camps. However, some Palestinians, who had been living in Lebanon in the years prior to the arrival of the refugees, were able to gain access to Lebanon's intellectual circles and join the emerging political movements. Most notably was the case of Hisham Sharabi, who had been a student in Beirut before the Arab-Israeli War and described his youthful impatience with the secret pan-Arabist cell he was a part of in his memoir *Embers and Ashes*. The long meetings and boring discourse caused him to seek his political realization elsewhere.[50] Sharabi also touched on his conversion from Arab nationalism to pan-Syrianism in 1946. In his personal journal, he wrote:

> June 19, 1946. Today I joined the Syrian Nationalist Party. I joined it officially today, but I had joined it doctrinally when I studied the Party and understood it. This is a decisive step. It is decisive because of the responsibility which I took in joining this institution. As such, it makes me now—as never before—an active member like many other active members who work toward a goal and are united by an ideal. First of all, I have confidence in the doctrine that I adopted officially today. Second, I have confidence in the comrades and superiors I joined today. Finally, I have confidence in my leader, whom I don't know in person but in spirit and through the moral force embodied in the movement he created. I have taken an oath today to be loyal to the Party and to my comrades in it, to obey the commands of my superiors, and dedicate myself fully to the service of my doctrine and my leader. I have taken this oath in the presence of my two friends and the Party, and here I am now taking the oath in the presence of myself. This is my greatest oath.[51]

1947 Return to Lebanon and Confrontation

The Junkers Ju 52 descended over the Lebanese coast and slowed to a crawl on the runway of Beirut's airport on March 2, 1947. Euphoric crowds of men, women, and children waited to observe Saadeh emerge from the aircraft and amble his way across the landing field. It did not take him long to once again take up his mantle of pan-Syrian nationalism. He gave a rousing speech at the home of Ni'mah Thabit in al-Ghubayri. He stressed that Lebanon's future must be aligned with a wider Syrian nation and denounced the changes that had been made in his long absence by the "Lebanon School" and stated that Cyprus and Iraq would be added into the geography of his vision for Natural Syria. However, the jubilant atmosphere belied what was in store for the movement. The party's detente with the government would soon come to an end and, in a little over two years, Saadeh's dismal fate was sealed.

Kamal Jumblatt, the leader of Lebanon's Druze community and the founder of the Progressive Socialist Party (PSP), who later played a key role in the party's history after Saadeh's death, had worked with Minister of Interior Camil Chamoun to secure Saadeh's return. The two believed that this arrangement would help them win the SNP's backing in the May 1947 parliamentary elections. At one point, before the establishment of his own party, Jumblatt had even considered joining the SNP.[52] In addition, Saadeh entered into talks with Jumblatt on ways to merge the nascent PSP with the SNP, but they were unable to reach an agreement.[53] But it wasn't long after the celebrated homecoming that a series of confrontations unfolded that led to the final years of Saadeh's life and left the organization decapitated. The SNP's rivals were already aware of the plans for his homecoming and protested fiercely. The title of a communist party pamphlet from February 1947 blared, "There is No Place in Independent Lebanon for Spies and Traitors."[54] The LCP continued to blast Saadeh as the SNP's "Fuhrer" and an agent of imperialism. Despite these efforts, the communists still found the SNP to be an able competitor in the political arena. The LCP's troubles were largely due to its flip-flops on their views of the French during the Second World War, switching between viewing the French as an imperialist aggressor and then an ally of the Soviet Union. In addition, Bakhdash's tepid approach to the French over the Hatay issue in Syria, which saw the land transferred over to Turkish sovereignty, won the LCP little sympathy among the masses in the Levant. The SNP, with its distrust of communism as a foreign tool and consistent anticolonial outlook, remained steadfast.

The SNP had also shared a temporary common cause with the Lebanese establishment in the midst of the country's quest to secure independence from France. Lebanese President Khoury's prime minister, Riad al-Solh, was a prominent figure in the Lebanese independence movement, himself imprisoned during his November 1943 standoff with the French in the Rachaya citadel in Bekka, which loomed over the Taim Valley, where he mingled behind bars with members of Saadeh's party, including Ni'mah Thabit, Zakariya Lababidi, and Anis al-Fakhury.[55] However, Solh was closely tied to Saadeh not through comradeship but hostility. Saadeh and Solh's personal rivalry dated back to 1935 due to Saadeh's close relationship with then Prime Minister Khayreddin al-Ahdab, Solh's political competitor.[56] From this rivalry sprang two separate visions of the history of the Lebanese independence movement. One rooted in the mainstream of Solh and a pro-Western attitude, and the other in Saadeh that portrayed itself as deeply persecuted and above the corruption of the traditional Lebanese elite. Outside the walls of the citadel, as the French colonial forces battled Lebanese irregulars, many of the SNP's members or sympathizers took part in the independence skirmishes. To this day, the party lauds itself as the only movement that suffered a fatality in Lebanon's independence struggle. An SNP member named Said Fakhreddine, born in Ain Aanoub, Mount Lebanon, in 1903 and joined the party in 1941. On November 16, 1943, he was defending the Lebanese government headquarters in Bechamoun from French soldiers and threw a hand grenade at an armored vehicle, seconds before French bullets pierced his body. Fakhreddine was later posthumously awarded the Lebanon's National Struggle medal by President Khoury in 1946.[57]

Saadeh's first order of business was reversing the "normalization" of the party made by the so-called Lebanon School during the exile period. It essentially amounted to an internal purge, which many of the party's detractors use to exhibit Saadeh's assumed totalitarian tendencies. Some of the Saadeh's top lieutenants, Ni'mah Thabit, Ma'mum Ayas, and Assad al-Ashqar, were removed from their posts and denounced as having turned away from the national doctrine and making the SNP into a "provincial party."[58] Fayez Sayegh, the party's official ideologue and propagandist, was expelled later in December 1947. Sayegh had initially resisted the reformist trend during Saadeh's exile, but later agreed to the changes out of "necessity."[59] Sayegh, well respected for his oratory and debate skills and widely admired both inside and outside the party, stayed on after Saadeh's return but became bogged down in an internal philosophical debate with Saadeh over individuality and existentialism. One August night, he and Saadeh argued for hours outside in the party leader's home village of Dhour el-Shuwayr. He was finally ejected by the end of the year, taking with him a small cohort and forming a new group called "the Free Nationalists," which quickly fizzled out. Ghassan Tueini, a famous Lebanese journalist, was one party member who joined this short-lived group and left the party.[60] Despite these rifts, Saadeh was not beyond forgiveness. Assad al-Ashqar was rehabilitated in 1949 and later went on to become the party's president. The fact remained that the purge, by and large, did not cause any splits in the party. Yamak commented:

> The sharp ideological differences between [Saadeh] and Sayegh, for instance, should have caused a vigorous and continuous debate within the party. Yet, no debate took place … [his expulsion] was met with equanimity even by Sayegh's closest associates. The membership received the news of these expulsions not with consternation or jubilation but rather with resignation. They did so because they were brought up to believe that there was only one leader of the party, Saadeh, and only one true interpretation of the ideology, his own.[61]

By 1948, Saadeh renamed the party, adding the term *ijtima'i*, meaning "social." This term differed from the word *socialist* (*ishtiraki*) and emphasized a community-oriented outlook rather than a class or economic struggle. The party henceforth was known as the Syrian Social Nationalist Party (SSNP). From January 7 to April 4, 1948, Saadeh gave a series of lectures at the party's cultural club in central Beirut. Party secretary George Abd Messih documented the lectures, and they became Saadeh's final official doctrinal statements, which outlined the party's ideology. He also published a slew of articles blasting the Arab (and Lebanese) nationalists for the defeat of the campaign in the Arab-Israeli War. Yamak described the reaction of his opponents: "Many Arab nationalists who felt insulted by Saadeh's remarks rose to the defense of Arabism by accusing him and the SSNP of collaborating with the enemies of the Arabs. But it must be emphasized that Saadeh's point against the Arab nationalists was regarded in many well-informed Arab circles as legitimate criticism of the traditional point of view."[62] He further noted that the articles and speeches gave the SSNP a morale boost and actually converted a few prominent Arabists to the pan-Syrian cause, including Said Taqiyaddin, who was a famous writer and poet from a well-respected Druze family and later became a powerful figure in the party. In addition to correcting the party's ideology and stance toward the government, Saadeh revived his preferred version of the party's flag. Hisham Sharabi recalled the excitement felt by himself and his comrades when, on Saadeh's orders, they rushed to the printing office to prepare a new publication of *al-Jil al-Jadid* (*The

New Generation) and revived the old storm (zawbaa) logo to display on its pages, which appeared on its front page in May 1949.[63]

However, it should be noted that overall the SSNP remained a small, intellectual, and elite party, with a tightly controlled and guarded approach to recruiting and indoctrinating its members. In terms of popularity, the party largely failed to win over the vast majority of Sunni Muslims, Maronite Christians, and even the Greek Orthodox, who were concerned more with economic and political issues closer to home rather than creating a Natural Syria. Saadeh's brand of Syrian nationalism lacked the broad appeal that Arabism and Lebanese nationalism fostered among the wider population. Its strict adherence to the pan-Syrian doctrine limited its ability to tap into Lebanese society, and the SSNP in 1948–9 was unsuccessful in its attempt to become a mass party. Despite this, the SSNP sought to position itself at the forefront of the region's geopolitical struggles, particularly when it came to the issue of Palestine. In his infamous return speech, Saadeh said:

> You should always remember that Palestine, this southern wing of Syria, is very dangerously threatened. The will of the Social Nationalists is to save Palestine from Jewish ambitions and their consequences. You will probably hear people say to you that saving Palestine constitutes ill will against Lebanon and the Lebanese, and that it is a matter for which Lebanon has nothing to do. The saving of Palestine is, indeed, just as much a genuinely Lebanese concern as it is a genuinely Syrian and a genuinely Palestinian concern. The Jewish danger to Palestine is a danger to all Syria; it is a danger to all these entities. I repeat: these entities should not be prisons of the nation but rather strongholds in which the nation is fortified, and in which it prepares itself to pounce upon those who covet its rights. My charge to you, O' Social Nationalists, is to return to the battlefield of struggle.[64]

In addition, Saadeh blasted the Arab armies that fought in the 1948 Arab-Israeli War as "feudalistic" and was seen by his comrade Hisham Sharabi forming brigades of "Social Nationalist" troops preforming military drills in al-Ramla al-Bayda wearing a quasi-military uniform with binoculars.[65] Israel itself paid attention to the activities of Saadeh's party. Gamliel Cohen was a Jew of Syrian origin who infiltrated the SSNP in the spring of 1949 using the alias Yussef el-Hamed. Cohen was part of the *mista'aravim* (those who live among the Arabs) and used his cover as a Palestinian refugee from Jerusalem to meet with the party's finance official, Abdullah Mohsen, and volunteered as an SSNP cultural officer. He also participated in Saadeh's birthday celebrations. According to his memoir, Cohen's orders were to monitor the SSNP and see if it was receiving any support from the British government.[66]

In March 1949, a coup d'état in Syria brought a military regime headed by Husni Za'im to power in Damascus, ending Syria's brief experiment with democracy after independence. During this time, Cohen, still undercover, observed the unease that gripped the Lebanese government that the new military regime in Damascus had its sights on Lebanon. However, he did not believe the SSNP would attempt any militant action since it was facing financial hardships and by that time had ceased its training maneuvers. Cohen also noted the SSNP had hope that Za'im's new regime would support it.[67] In Beirut, the Lebanese government embarked on a path toward confrontation that forever relegated Saadeh to the role as disrupter and political outsider. Saadeh's subsequent moves marked him for death and deprived him of the chance to enter politics as a legitimate actor and eternalized his character as a revolutionary who refused to compromise to the very end.

The story of Saadeh's final months typically begins with the so-called Jummayziah incident.[68] The Kataeb Party raided the SSNP's printing press on June 9, 1949, and the Lebanese police allegedly stood by while armed Kataeb militants ambushed and routed the SSNP. The building was destroyed, but far worse for Saadeh was the Lebanese government's reaction to the violence. Khoury's government quickly announced its intention to dissolve Saadeh's party. Lebanese Army General Fuad Chehab directed his troops to fan out into Beirut and the countryside to locate and arrest party members. The new crackdown netted 2,500 SSNP followers who landed in prison and detention camps.[69] Members soon found themselves harassed, arrested, and tortured by the government. Backed into a corner, Saadeh and many SSNP members fled to Syria where they sought assistance from Za'im's military government.

The Popular Uprising

Za'im promised Saadeh arms and support in exchange for his party's loyalty. With the Damascus regime behind him, Saadeh quickly went into action, launching the so-called First Popular Social Uprising against Beirut on July 4, 1949. The plan intended to seize police stations and border outposts while hoping that the Lebanese people would rally to the cause. According to sympathizers, Saadeh's rebellion did not so much intend to force Lebanon into an immediate union with Syria, but rather pushed to alter Beirut's heavy-handed political environment so that the SSNP could operate in a more pluralistic atmosphere. However, Saadeh's armed revolt was an utter failure. His men were disorganized and frequently fell victim to government ambushes. Others found that they had the wrong type of ammunition for their weapons. One group led by party cadre Assaf Karam was ambushed in Mashgharah. Karam engaged in a shootout with the Lebanese authorities until he was killed. Another SSNP detachment, led by George Abd Messih, battled in Sarhamul and was quickly defeated. However, Abd Messih was able to escape in the wake of the fighting.[70] It soon became apparent that Saadeh had been betrayed by Za'im. He was arrested by the Syrians and turned over to the Lebanese government. In total secrecy, the Lebanese authorities expedited Saadeh's trial and found him guilty of treason. He was executed at dawn on Friday, July 8, just four days after his attempted coup.

The sudden and dramatic downfall of Antoun Saadeh has been told many times and in many ways. The narrative put forward by his supporters regarding his death has primarily focused on the unjust nature of the trial and the allegedly authoritarian decisions taken by the Khoury regime. Another view is that Saadeh was playing a dangerous game by fomenting an insurgency against a legitimate Lebanese state and, as Patrick Seale put it, "he had gambled and lost." For the party, the emotional sentiments that surround his treatment by the Lebanese authorities still remain the essential heart of the SSNP's soul and character. A lasting notion of injustice, outrage, and a desire for revenge ruminated throughout the party's membership. Even for nonpartisans, the dignity of an intellectual man who, in their view, had fought for social justice and independence from colonial rule and advocated against sectarianism and the social stagnation represented by the Lebanese government's authoritarianism resonates on some level a deep sense of respect and admiration.

The exact events of his execution have been researched and studied by party members and also depicted in films and described in presentations for the party's youth. A movie titled *Haddathani el Kahin Allathi A'arefah (The Priest Who Knew Him Told Me)* was produced in the 2000s by party members who were also film students at the Lebanese American University.[71] The production was approved by the party, but was regarded more as an internal education tool than a project slated for Lebanese cinema or TV. Most of the film's actors were SSNP members and it was based on the writings of the SSNP's famed literate and poet Said Taqiyaddin.

The black-and-white film shows a convoy of jeeps stop along an isolated tree-lined dirt road in the darkness of night. A group of Lebanese police escort a bound Antoun Saadeh who is forced to kneel before a wooden post. Blindfolded, he defiantly faces the firing squad as they raise their Russian SKS Simonov carbines and fire a volley into his chest. The scene is from the movie depicted from the point of view of the priest who received Saadeh's final confessions before he was executed.

Without Saadeh, the party's militant activities surrounding the uprising came to an abrupt halt. The government's purge of the party continued beyond Saadeh's execution. Anyone suspected of taking part in the revolt was arrested and put on trial, with sixty-eight party members given long prison sentences, and twelve sentenced to death. Of the twelve, only six were executed, and the unfortunate souls were selected by lot with a noted emphasis on maintaining a sectarian balance to the condemned. The party's two main bodies, the Higher Council and the Council of Commissioners, long powerless under Saadeh, suddenly gained new authority overnight. Saadeh had never specified their roles in the party's constitution, and this transformed the nature of the party's behavior after his execution. Yamak wrote that it took the party two years to deliberate the mechanisms of authority during a time of both simultaneous pressure and popularity.[72]

The sudden death of the organization's leader, and subsequent crackdown, would momentarily galvanize popular support for the SSNP, and the movement's energy then shifted across the border to Syria, where a series of military coups rocked the country's political foundations and the party stretched its influence and finally made the jump from a fringe revolutionary movement to a national parliament constituent. The abrupt exit of Saadeh left a vacuum that brought about tremendous challenges for the party. Without its leader firmly at the helm, the pan-Syrian movement became prone to factionalization, internal power struggles, and conflicting orders. How the party would have fared if Saadeh had lived is uncertain. As with most ideologically driven political movements, the Lebanon School trend that emerged during his exile was one example of a reformist, cooperative faction that sought to integrate itself fully into the Lebanese political environment. This trend even continued to be revived from time to time in various forms in the decades that followed Saadeh's execution. Over the subsequent decades, this reformist trend only worsened and would seek to maximize the party's interest by either heightening or minimizing the risks exposed to the party. These problems brought about many difficult years for the SSNP as it regrouped and began to politically and violently confront its ideological competitors in Syria: the pan-Arab Baath and the communists.

3

Tahya Suriya! The SSNP's Ideology

Despite the SSNP's sudden decapitation in July 1949, the ideological movement that Antoun Saadeh left behind proved to be remarkably durable. The notion of Greater Syria had existed prior to Saadeh. What gave the SSNP's Greater Syria longevity and stand-out was that, when Saadeh came to the scene, it was at a time of political transition from European colonialism to independence. He fine-tuned the idea of a Syrian nation-state into an ideology and created a political party. Saadeh's Syrian nationalism is often confused with a nationalism that focuses on the modern-day country of Syria that exists today. However, the SSNP's Syrian nationalism approaches Syria from a far wider and deeper context. The party's ideology was unique for several reasons, the first primarily being its irredentism that directly ran against the grain of pan-Arabism. Contrary to the goals of pan-Arabism, Natural Syria did not extend to the entire Arabian Peninsula and North Africa, but rather an ancient and romantic vision of what Saadeh viewed as an expanded definition of Syria's map from antiquity. Before he died, Saadeh's final concept of the Natural Syria homeland included all of the Levant—Syria, Lebanon, Jordan, and Palestine, along with extending to Iraq, Kuwait, and parts of Iran, Hatay, and Cilicia (the southern region of Turkey), stretching out into the northern parts of the Saudi Arabian desert, and the Sinai Peninsula. The island of Cyprus was also included within Natural Syria's boundaries. The SSNP's ideology was antisectarian, secular, and eschewed ethnicity and language in favor of history and territory.

The party was and remains a party of intellectuals, and a great deal of emphasis is placed on each member knowing the party's history and its doctrine. Comrades greet each other with the phrase *Tahya Suriya!* This means "Long live Syria!" Of course, this refers not to the Syria with the current borders but to the Saadeh's vision of Natural Syria. It is believed that these were his final words. Other phrases include *Truth, Beauty, and Goodness*, along with *Sons of Life*. Party cadres assume senior responsibilities at the regional and national levels.

They are expected to be versed in the ideology and preferably hold an academic degree. Higher-ranking cadres who obtain a 'Trustee' title are likely to earn more respect and obedience from the SSNP community than the non-ranking cadres.

The SSNP's ideology was rooted on four main points: Freedom, meaning complete independence and sovereignty of the Syrian nation; Organization; Discipline, and Power (or force), which were needed in response to the dearth of organization in the other nationalist movements that Saadeh believed had hindered Syria's success and progress. The party's platform also included fundamental principles, the first and most important of which was that Syria is for the Syrians, essentially meaning that only the land's indigenous people could determine their own destiny and rejected any notion of foreign interference.[1] Other key tenets included the need for a separate religion and state, breaking down sectarian barriers, abolishment of feudalism, forming a strong army, and completely uniting the homeland.

However, once Saadeh was out of the picture, the party's main faction was prone to making adjustments and showing political pragmatism in order to stay politically relevant as the regional situation evolved. For instance, in the beginning, it was extremely hostile toward communism. However, the SSNP by the late 1960s and into the 1970s was able to establish a kinship with the Lebanese Communist Party, the Soviet Union, and its arch-nemesis, the Baathists, by finding common ground on issues such as anti-imperialism. The SSNP, while still retaining its vision of a Natural Syria, was able to secure an understanding with the pan-Arab Baath Party under Hafez al-Assad that viewed relations with the Arab World as essential to the interests of Natural Syria.

Understanding the party's ideology is critical to analyzing the SSNP's relevance and stake in the Levant's current conflicts and politics today. The Syrian government has managed to survive the civil war and looks set to assume some place within the so-called counterrevolution that is unfolding in the Middle East. As we have seen with Egypt's military coup in July 2013 and Field Marshal Khalifa Haftar's 2019 military offensive in Libya, secular nationalism is experiencing a revival. How this counterrevolution will play out in Syria remains to be seen.

What is the SSNP fighting for in Syria? The SSNP's members are not technically fighting for the Baath party to indefinitely remain in power. At least officially, the party's members are not involved in the conflict to protect the interest of intervening foreign governments such as Russia or Iran. The party is also not participating on the conviction of any divine religious mandate. In fact, the party sees itself as one component in Syria's political landscape that positions the country against the bulwark of religious extremism and to preserve the nation-state. The party's distinctive ideology is the best place to begin to understand what sets the SSNP apart from its competitors and why the party is experiencing a revival in Syria.

Postcolonial Dream of Syria and Ancient Romantism

The Battle of Maysalun occurred on July 24, 1920, an event that is annually commemorated by the SSNP. A Syrian officer named Yousef al-Azma led Syrian rebels against the French colonial forces. Although the rebels lost the battle, it remains the earliest symbol of the indigenous resistance against a foreign power in modern Syria. Antoun Saadeh described the battle as "the greatest and most glorious battle this nation has witnessed in all of modern history, because it represents the spirit of a living nation and symbolizes its higher principals, it is the first regular battle by a Syrian army, led by a Syrian leader, for Syria's freedom in modern history."[2] Azma remains highly venerated by the party, and on the battle's anniversary, party members visit his grave site along with the Tomb of the Unknown Soldier in Damascus.[3] The party directly links the battle to the Levant's ancient civilizations. Saadeh called Azma "one of the greatest leaders and warriors in the history of Syria" and ranked him with ancient rulers such as Nebuchadnezzar II, Sargon of Akkad, and Ashurbanipal.[4] Furthermore, the party today emphasizes that Azma in fact desired a Syria that extended beyond the borders that outside powers had assigned it. In an interview with *Al Hayat* in November 2014, Azma's grandson Dr. Nazeer al-Azma, the head of the SSNP (Markaz faction) Political Bureau in Syria, said, "[Azma] did not fight for Sykes-Picot's Syria, he fought for a Greater Syria that includes Mosul, Cilicia, and Alexandretta!"[5] The SSNP's Intifada faction marked the hundredth anniversary of the battle with an article that quoted Saadeh explaining how Maysalun was the greatest proof that Syria could defend its land and had a hidden magical (ideological) power to inspire the nation.[6]

The first step toward understanding the party's platform of Natural Syria is to comprehend that the current borders of the Middle East were artificially imposed on the indigenous people who never agreed to these political divisions. Furthermore, the party believes that all of the region's woes, terrorism, and conflicts are the results of these borders. However, the SSNP does not proclaim itself to be an irredentist party since it does not envision Natural Syria as the rightful land belonging solely to the Syrian Arab Republic. For the SSNP, Natural

Syria is divided land, and its political entities are all equally representative of the nation. One party sympathizer even remarked:

> If we would go by size and population, Natural Syria is more of an Iraqi expansion than a Syrian expansion, just under the name of "Syria," which was carefully chosen because it is one of the few names that once included all of the Fertile Crescent, and some SSNP members also came up with the name Souraqia (The Arabic name for Syria, plus Iraq) to refer to Natural Syria.[7]

Initially, Natural Syria's geography only included the Levant countries. A Greek Catholic party member explained, "It's convincing even for me. I feel closer to a Palestinian or a Lebanese person than to an Emirati or an Egyptian or a Bedouin."[8]

Saadeh had added Iraq, Kuwait, and Cyprus to Natural Syria while in exile and without conferring with the other members of the party or the Higher Council.[9] Cyprus is an interesting case study for the SSNP since it embodies the land, history, and people that Saadeh had envisioned for his future state. For Saadeh, the desire for Cyprus to be used as a maritime defense of Syria's coast was one aspect of this inclusion. Another point was the belief that the Troodos Mountains in Cyprus were geographically linked to the Amanus (Nur) and Cassius (Jebel Aqra) Mountains in Hatay. The SSNP even hails the late archbishop and former president of Cyprus Makarios III as a hero and "Syrian nationalist" of sorts and still retain positive relations with the government of Cyprus today.[10]

The party's anthem was written by Antoun Saadeh during his second imprisonment and was allegedly to be sung to the tune of a Russian song titled "Stenka Razin." Another tune was later composed by Zaki Nassif. The party's anthem has long been plagued by accusations it was modeled after the one used by Nazi Germany. The lyrics are as follows:

> Peace be unto Syria,
> Which is our enlightenment,
> Peace be unto Syria,
> Which we will sacrifice for
> We are a nation that will never budge to the greedy dictators
> Our land has an undiminishing resource, of well-received men
> Everything in Syria is beautiful,
> Everybody is generous,
> Its climate is clear and healthy,
> Its people are lively and great
> O' mountains that shoot high and manifest like the castles,

O' souls that are unreachably high,
Over the times of death
The revival has shaken ages, and washed away our inactivity,
We certainly are a nation,
And a life that never disappears.[11]

A young fellow traveler explained that the SSNP presented a new form of nationalism, which he said could be called "Natural Nationalism." In this view, the SSNP believes that nature is the factor behind nations, essentially "horizontal interaction with the people and vertical interaction with the land creates a nation." He also called this "Romantic Nationalism."[12] In a documentary published by *Al Mayadeen* in January 2018, Lebanese SSNP members in Beirut talk about how Jerusalem and the rest of Palestine are just as important to him as Beirut. Another militia fighter with the SSNP in Syria remarked that the region's current boundaries were "fake borders, they don't exist, they bother us, and we do not recognize them." Another aspect of the party is to foment the national renaissance through cultural activities and social engagement. Antoun Saadeh was keen on the need to disburse his ideology through poetry, art, plays, songs, and film. From the very beginnings of the party, Saadeh established a cultural club in the 1930s. In addition, the SSNP's newspapers all contain a cultural section, and the party has a Directorate of Culture.

The SSNP's brand of nationalism primarily can be understood as uncompromising in its approach to Syria's positions in regard to its sovereignty, and this position has extended itself to the Syrian government's overall posture in international relations. In addition, the romantic aspects of Saadeh's doctrine of unity among Syria's various ethnic groups and his staunch opposition to colonialism is held in high regard by non-SSNP government figures. In September 2009, Syria's former ambassador to the United States, Imad Mustapha, speaking at an Arab American function in Detroit, honored Saadeh and said, "Even if you're not one of his partisans, you still respect the great things he did for our region."[13]

Secularism and Anti-Semitism

The party is strictly secular and, while not against the practice of organized religion outside of the party, it strongly discourages any notions of sectarian identity for the party as a whole. It does not track statistics on the sectarian composition of its overall membership. One former attendee of the party's youth camps in Australia remarked, "When you're inside the party, you're staunchly secular. It's militant secular. It's French-style laïcité secular. There is no mention of religion. There is no mention of anything, no symbols of religion … people wear headscarves and crosses if they want to. People still tend to be religious. It's not an atheist party."[14] However, since its founding, the SSNP has largely been associated with the Levant's Christian Orthodox community, an association it has sought to rebuff.[15]

One party historian explained, "The Greek Orthodox are more receptive to secular parties than the other groups, but they are not necessarily the backbone of the party. Maronites and Protestants have also found the SSNP appealing. As for the relationship with the local church organizational structures and religious figures, it is kept to a minimum in keeping with the Party's secular commitment."[16] Dr. Joshua Landis explained the origins behind the politics of this particular demographic and how it emerged out of a trend for how the region should frame its nationalism in the wake of the First World War. He wrote:

> The *Comite Central Syrien*, a largely Greek Orthodox inspired organization, grew up to challenge this conception of the [Middle East]. It presented Greater Syria as the alternative to a Hashemite-led Middle East and appealed to the French—particularly during the Paris Peace Conference after the War. People like Jacques Tabet, Chucri Ghanem and Semne, leading members of the movement—as well as the many chapters in the *mahjar*, Latin America, Europe, and North America, did not want toe-picking backward Arabian Arabs to take over. They also depicted Arabism as a scary fanatical movement coming from the desert that wanted to re-impose a caliphate on the Middle East and had no conception of modern nationalism. They tried to scare Christian Middle Easterners and Europeans alike about the ultimate results of empowering a largely Muslim, neo-Umayyad, Arabism in the region.
>
> When one scratched below the surface of the Greater Syria alternative, one found an imperial Byzantine sensibility and conception of history that had been built upon readings of the Bible and sought to reunite regions of the Middle East where large populations of Greek Orthodox lived. Greater Syrianism didn't just grow up as an anti-Arabist movement, it also emerged as an anti-Phoenicianist movement. It was an effort to present a nationalist conception of the region that suited the sensibilities and demographic of the Greek Orthodox in opposition to the largely Sunni and Maronite nationalist conceptions that were emerging.[17]

Fayez Sayegh also discussed the problem of overlapping political Islam with pan-Arabism. He wrote in 1958:

On the one hand, Islam is an essential ingredient of Arabism despite the logical distinctness and the actual historical separability of the two processes of Islamization and Arabization. On the other hand, the Arab national movement reflects the aspiration of Arabs of all faiths to establish a secular Arab society consolidated by the community of language, culture, history, and territory, and animated by a desire for national freedom, political unity, and human progress of which all Arabs will be beneficiaries and for the attainment of which all Arabs have struggled and will struggle, regardless of their faith.[18]

The Baath Party, in both Syria and Iraq, although officially secular, celebrated and cultivated an Islamic identity in order to tap into the street's anti-Western sentiments, in particular with regard to the Arab states' confrontation with Israel. However, this secular construct was also in part to preserve and protect the rule of the minority regimes in both Damascus (Alawi) and Baghdad (Sunni). By contrast, the SSNP largely has remained consistent in its approach to politics and religion. Members say they do not care or discriminate when it comes to ethnicity or religion. Over the decades, there has been speculation on the party's sectarian configuration. At one point during the later stages of the Lebanese Civil War, the party was even described as predominantly Sunni.[19] Despite this, it is difficult to gage the breakdown of sects presently in the party. The SSNP has been inclusive of the region's sects and ethnic groups since Saadeh's ideology emphasized that the modern-day Syrian was the end result of thousands of years of mixing between the various peoples, empires, and kingdoms that have dominated his geographic dream of Natural Syria. This inclusiveness is attractive to inhabitants of today's sectarian-riddled geopolitics in Lebanon and Syria. This platform of antisectarianism is a central point in the party's opposition to the rise of religious extremist militancy in the region. In a sense, this narrative offers a direct repudiation to the so-called Islamic State's exclusionary practices, in which members have to adopt the organization's strict interpretation of Sunni Islam, convert, or die.

Despite its antisectarianism, the SSNP was not completely inclusive. A young journalist named Ahmad Shuman, who joined the party during the Saadeh era, remarked, "However, Saadeh did not include the Jews in his new nationality. He stressed that the Jews were not equal to others that belonged to this nationality. Such a vagrant announcement would go as an anathema to the theory itself, since neglecting a group who possesses all the necessary elements to be within this nationality defaults the theory itself."[20] The reason behind this was, in Saadeh's view, the Jews held "alien and exclusive racial loyalties" that could not be reconciled as citizens of Natural Syria.[21] Never mind that the Jewish people had inhabited Syria, Iraq, and much of the region for ages. The SSNP has long been regarded as problematic in the West due to its strong anti-Zionism, which is widely acknowledged to be involved in anti-Semitic propaganda. It can be argued that a party can hold anti-Zionist positions without being anti-Semitic, but these boundaries often become blurred. The SSNP regularly used the term "Jew" in its political discourse to criticize the Israelis. Saadeh himself used the words Jew and Zionist interchangeably, and his quotes on this subject are still widely utilized to indicate support and solidarity with the Palestinian cause. Saadeh also never clarified what was the fate of the region's Jews who lived in Palestine, Lebanon, Syria, and Iraq.

As recently as September 2020, the head of the Higher Council, Amr al-Tal, spoke on al-Manar TV and warned about a "Jewish danger" and described Israel as a "cancer" to be removed. The party's outlets and ideological arms still perpetuate some of the most common anti-Semitic tropes and conspiracy theories.[22] The SSNP put out posters on social media commemorating its martyrs in the Syrian Civil War; they featured a statement reading that the fallen combatants died "fighting the internal Jews." However, in recent years, the martyrdom posters have shifted the language, removing the references to Jews in place of an alleged international conspiracy against Syria. Whether this is part of a calculated effort to distance the SSNP from its anti-Semitism or coincidental, the party's uncompromising and relentless approach to confronting the state of Israel led the majority scholars and observers to regard the SSNP as inherently anti-Semitic and racist. The party in turn believes that Israel is a colonial project that divides Natural Syria and holds the entire region in a state of division, conflict and strife.

It is possible that younger generations of the party could adopt a more prominent voice against anti-Semitism, but it remains unlikely. At its heart, the SSNP's anti-Semitism is perhaps best understood and rooted in the two competing and, ultimately, incompatible visions for the Levant, one that includes the existence of a designated Jewish homeland, and the other that favors the unified revival of the entity of Greater Syria from antiquity.

The Whirlwind

Adopted by the party in 1935, the party's signature red emblem is a powerful and ancient symbol emblazoned within a white circle. It was designed by Bahij Maqdisi and Raja Khouli. The red, white, and black colors project a serious, radical, and mysterious tone. The flag and logo of the party are its most recognizable symbols and, in some sense, the embodiment of the organization's controversy. To the SSNP's detractors, the flag's central design element, the whirlwind or *zawbaa*, is the poignant sign that the party is inspired by fascism. The fierce hurricane symbol appears often without the flag, stenciled on walls, ceremonial wreaths, necklaces, dinner plates, and in the form of a sun with rays on party propaganda posters. The zawbaa also frequently features an outline of Antoun Saadeh's profile, emphasizing his continuing legacy over the party. The color scheme has also been criticized for being an inverted version of the Nazi Party flag. The SSNP's flag has a black field, representing the darkness of colonialism, sectarianism, and feudalism that binds and restricts the Syrians. The white disc symbolizes the daylight's brightness that destroys the surrounding darkness of the regressive society.[23]

The flag's central whirlwind device is depicted at a forty-five-degree angle and has four arms. Each arm signifies the four fundamental pillars of the party's ideology: power, freedom, organization, and duty. Saadeh explained, "The symbol of the whirlwind was found engraved on more than one fossil in Syria. It symbolizes the interaction of matter and spirit. It symbolizes life, survival, immortality and within the four corners of freedom, duty, order, and power."[24] The zawbaa asserts its constructiveness over social servitude, social irresponsibility, social chaos, and social collapse. The whirlwind was also selected as the party's symbol since it was found on ancient artwork and pottery; one such example is a Sumerian bowl from around 6000 BC in the region representing the universe. One commentator explained:

> The universe is symbolized by a circle which is always moving. In the center is the mandala, a whirlwind that has a unique and close relationship with the circle. The center radiates towards the circle and the circle gives depth to the center. Why is this relevant? The SSNP believes this universe was centered in Syria when the land sprouted numerous advanced and powerful civilizations thousands of years ago.[25]

When approached with the proposed design for the flag, Saadeh was presented with a symbol that had four arms, but his associates suggested if they altered it to a three-pointed whirlwind, they could evade depicting a symbol with a likeness to the Nazi swastika. However, Saadeh, in his usual insistent manner, decided on the whirlwind with four points and denied that there was any resemblance. After Saadeh left Lebanon in his self-imposed exile, the party he left behind modified the flag to a far less revolutionary scheme.

Figure 1 An approximate sketch of the SSNP's short-lived redesigned flag used by the Lebanon School during Saadeh's exile.

The new version was white with horizontal stripes cutting through a circle containing four quadrants, presumably to honor the four pillars of the party. The redesigned flag can be seen in video footage of waving in the large crowds that greeted Saadeh in 1947 during his return to Lebanon.

Right or Left?

The SSNP has long been widely regarded as a right-wing party. The party's nationalism and early Cold War history of staunchly opposing communism was the primary basis for this, along with the lingering allegations of fascism. However, Saadeh himself was most prominently anti-establishment. Adel Beshara noted:

> It is customary to associate Sa'adeh with right-wing politics on account of his commitment to nationalism and extreme dislike of traditional electoral politics. That much is true. But Sa'adeh was also a strong advocate of leftist reforms, the kind that promotes intervention in favor of egalitarianism, and gives little or no authority to tradition. Most Lebanese regard him as neither left nor right but definitely anti-Establishment.[26]

However, even during the Saadeh years, the party still contained a communal outlook, with a strong emphasis on society, as opposed to the individual. One historian wrote, "Saadeh regarded the social dimension in human life as a value of the highest importance. He believed that the Syrian nation as a social community had managed to preserve its continuous distinctiveness throughout history."[27] Contrary to socialism or communism, Saadeh advocated for a Syrian nation that would be governed by "a social elite."[28] It was not until much later, during the SSNP's time in prison in the aftermath of the failed New Year's Eve coup attempt, that it began to change. In July 1965, party leader Abdullah Saadeh wrote in his prison letters to his wife Mary:

> The hope of humanity is in the left. The capital is the outcome of the public production, thus its ownership is public and not private. What is the value of a citizen who wastes his dignity for a living? What is the value of a citizen who kills the dignity of his brother to reward him with a living?[29]

During the Lebanese Civil War, the SSNP transitioned over to the left. It adopted a heightened anti-imperialist character and aligned itself with the left-wing nationalist Baath Party. In addition, the party looks to create a secular environment that empowers women and the desires to end sectarianism. However, it is spectral-syncretic politics that could perhaps describe the party's outlook today. The SSNP does not tend to identify with either the right or the left. Nationalism and self-determination are still key elements, along with a sense of community and shared responsibilities. One member with the party's Intifada faction explained why he joined:

> The most appealing aspect to me was the first Principle "Syria is for the Syrians, and the Syrians form one complete nation." This principle reflects the historical fact that Syria is an independent nation which has its own identity, history and interests, which are not necessarily identical to other Arab nations. Besides the above, the party pays a lot of attention to, and bares responsibility towards Syrian society. That is why it is "social." No other party gives any consideration to the social behavior to its members. Members of SSNP are supposed to be very committed to their community and its welfare, and should maintain the supreme values that serve the community and the whole country. SSNP is a secular party and believes in equal citizenship regardless of religion, ethnic background, or gender. The ultimate aim of SSNP is to provoke a resurrection in the Syrian society that serves the ultimate interest of the Syrians. After two years of reading SSNP literature and the writings of its founder, and after many sessions of discussion, I became to believe that the ideology of SSNP and its principles are the best way that leads to a democratic, free, and unified Syria. At that point, I made my decision to take the oath and join the SSNP.[30]

Corporatism is another element that is reflected in the party's discourse. The idea that the nation is essentially a living body and every citizen has their part in propelling the country forward. For example, in May 1949, Antoun Saadeh emphasized that the Syrian people themselves were the nation. "Syrian workers and farmers, artists and craftsmen, producers of science, knowledge, crops and goods; You are the veins of life and the arteries of strength in the living body of the Syrian nation. You are the nation." Economically, the SSNP does not view itself as socialist. One young member with the Markaz faction explained a common saying in party:

> "Capitalism is opportunism, a minority becomes rich and a majority becomes poor. Socialism benefits from other people's hard work and all people become equal in poorness." The SSNP believes in being fair to hard workers, "Justice [occurs when] the poor become rich, and the rich becomes richer," the SSNP believes in production, how much you produce is how much you deserve. In addition, the party believes in helping weak nations rise because "more capable nations equal more buyers" and "more strong nations equals a stronger front against imperialism and injustice."[31]

However, in his memoir *Embers and Ashes*, Hisham Sharabi remarked that the SSNP was never able to become a mass party because it "lacked class perspective." As a party that is at least nominally on the left today, the ideology aims to confront the status quo and traditional tribal and political elite. For many Lebanese in the countryside, they had a longstanding tradition rooted in Levantine rural culture of associating with a political chief, or *za'im* (which means leader), which conjures an image of a big man with a large beard or mustache. One member remarked on how, upon meeting Saadeh, his father was taken by surprise with the party *za'im*'s unimposing stature and clean-shaven appearance.[32] To many in the villages, seeing Saadeh in person for the first time did not initially elicit an impression that he was a powerful leader, but they were nevertheless won over by his speeches and nationalist-orientated idealism. Zeina Maasri, in her book *Off the Wall*, discussed the emphasis on personalities and leadership (*za'ama*) in Middle Eastern politics and noted how political parties often venerate their founders and lack sustainable programs, instead becoming "parties of leaders." She cited Arnold Hottinger's work that defined the notion of the leader: "the political leader who possesses the support of a locally circumscribed community and who retains this support by fostering or appearing to foster the interests of as many as possible from amongst his clientele." Maasri also noted that Farid el-Khazen, referring to Lebanon's Maronite community, described the representation of "strong men," which existed during times of crisis and eventual embodiment of a heroic mythology that exists within a community, "physical daring, defiance of authority, the self-inflated important of the community, and the unwavering willingness to resist and even to die for the cause." Saadeh's decision to go to the grave and not compromise his party or ideas was one such example of how his determined leadership and legacy of martyrdom still plays out prominently within the SSNP to this day.

On the other hand, Saadeh also confronted the traditional image of a *za'im*. He often criticized the very notion of the role of the *za'ama* in order to attract followers and build a populist base and reach the common people.[33] Maasri illustrated that a leader, especially after assassination, continues to be commemorated by a party as a role model to "lend its struggled credibility and continuity."[34] These leadership characteristics would later define Saadeh's place in the party long after his death. One example of the sectarian leadership was the struggle within the Lebanese Druze community. Yusri Hazran explained that the two prominent Druze factions, the Jumblatts and the Yazbakis, both saw members join the SSNP throughout the party's long history. He noted the Yazbakis in particular "lack both a coherent ideological vision and a modern political leadership," which led many to join Saadeh's party. However, he noted that a number of the Jumblatt loyalists also joined the SSNP. The party's recruitment of Druze was alarming enough for the community's religious leadership to threaten members with excommunication, especially in the wake of the Lebanese government's crackdown on the party following the 1949 uprising.[35] But perhaps most importantly, Saadeh's ideology was staunchly opposed to Lebanon's National Pact that had been devised to govern the country through a system of sectarian balancing. To Saadeh and his party, the National Pact was a painful reminder of how Lebanon was being held back based on a corrupt and an unofficial confessional divide across the major sects.

Regardless of whether or not the SSNP is designated as a leftist movement today, the party's ideology is inherently focused on its vision of a future state in the region. However, since the realization of this potential political entity remains far off, in the short run, the party's primary political and ideological goals will be on identity and social cohesion. This soft power aspect of the party's ideology will be one critical element of the Syrian government's attempts to rebuild and restructure a war-torn nation that has been horribly hit by a brutal conflict, separatism, a mass exodus of refugees, and sectarianism. This is also true for the widespread belief in a loss of legitimacy regarding Bashar al-Assad's presidency. Furthermore, in a nod to the Baath Party's pan-Arabism, Syria's name officially remains the Syrian Arab Republic. However, in the pro-regime population's view, what does it mean to be an Arab republic in the aftermath of such pain, devastation, and betrayal from fellow Arab countries? Fostering and developing a future identity will be essential for the government's postwar efforts. What does it mean to be a Syrian in the twenty-first century? Whether or not the Syrian Arab Republic simply reverts to a "Syrian Republic," the SSNP will deploy its ideology in order to play up the issue of a national identity in the war's aftermath. Finally, beyond the SSNP, identity remains a strong current in the rest of the Levant. What does it mean to be an Israeli, Palestinian, Jordanian, Lebanese, Kurd, or an Iraqi in the age of political upheaval, globalization, and social media? Is the region's future headed toward unity and cohesion or further fragmentation? The SSNP's vision of Greater Syria will be one aspect of these debates and controversies as the region's wars either simmer or settle down entirely.

4

We Have Avenged Him! The Party and Syria

Refuge in Syria

The events of July 1949 were tumultuous for the movement that Antoun Saadeh had created and left behind. His failed uprising, capture, sudden execution, and the party's subsequent purge in Lebanon would have surely destroyed other, less dynamic movements. But the SSNP persevered. Syria at this junction provided a window for the party to reorganize and tangle with the newly empowered elite of Damascus. The year 1949 was not quite finished with the violence and political upheaval that began in the Lebanese countryside with Saadeh's failed "First Popular Social Uprising." The storm that had begun along the Mediterranean coast would soon shift over the Lebanese mountains to the desert plains of Syria. From 1949 to 1955, Saadeh's party played a pivotal role in Syria's post-independence politics with drastic consequences. Many of his followers in Lebanon left the widening persecution for the safety of Syria where their Syrian party comrades were waiting for them.

The dream of creating a Greater Syria and shaking off French colonial rule already held a significant level of appeal within Syria. Many of the SSNP's earliest supporters were Syrian army officers, journalists, as well as members of the intellectual and political-social elite that stemmed from Saadeh's journalism and educational networks that straddled the two countries. Along with this, Syria was still smarting over the loss of the coastal region of Hatay to Turkey ten years earlier in 1939. Hatay, perhaps best known in the West for its two medieval cities of Alexandretta and Antioch, had been wrestled by the West out of the Ottoman Empire and changed hands after the end of the First World War. Hatay initially faired under a British military garrison, which was also occupying eastern Turkey and nearby Cyprus. The region was then passed on to the French. During the 1920s, Hatay, widely known as the Sanjak of Alexandretta, was administrated by the elite in the northern city of Aleppo for a short period of time, before the French administration sought to finalize its status with Turkey. As Turkey recovered from the First World War and transformed itself into a modern nation-state, Turkey's nationalist leader Mustafa Kemal Atatürk made the acquisition of Hatay a priority in his effort to secure territory.

In the 1930s and 1940s, the SSNP had established itself economically in Syria, especially in the Régie Company, a state-owned tobacco enterprise and relic of the Ottoman Empire. Patrick Seale described how the party members benefited from their domination of Régie in Syria's Latakia region, particularly in the village of Bustan al-Basha, and profited from a side scheme, which sold undeclared tobacco crop in the area's black market trade. The rise of anticolonial political parties in Syria often presented socioeconomic opportunities for young men who were largely isolated from the modern world and living in poverty.[1] One example was the Syrian playwright and poet Muhammad al-Maghout, who joined the party not so much out of ideology but for simple reasons. In an interview with Sami Moubayed, he explained, "There were only two parties in Salamiyya. One was the SSNP and the other was the Baath. Since I was very poor I joined the SSNP which was closer to our home and had a heater while the Baath Party office was far away and cold." But still it was Saadeh's untimely death that had a pronounced emotional impact even on Syrians with a minimal interest in politics. In addition, the deep personal admiration and devotion to Saadeh that existed in Syria from the party's early years was seen as far back as 1937 with the large demonstrations that occurred in Damascus after his second arrest. Al-Maghout went on to explain that, although he never took the time to learn the party's pan-Syrian ideology, he was upset when he learned of Antoun Saadeh's execution.[2]

However, for other Syrians, it was the SSNP's deep anticolonial sentiments that were the primary driver for joining. The party had earlier made contact and explored alliances with other nationalist movements, such as the Steel Shirts of Dr. Abdulrahman Shabandar, following his assassination in June 1940.[3] Having established itself in secret and successively extended its network into Syria, the SSNP predated the Baath, which would not be formally established as a party until 1947. Issam al-Mahayri was one of Saadeh's true believers who never accepted the region's artificial borders and went on to become a central figure in the party, rising through the ranks and living through many of the traumatic events in the SSNP's history. Having spent time in Cairo, he returned to Syria to study law at the University of Damascus.[4] As a young man, Mahayri saw the harsh oppression of the French colonial police who violently cracked down on protestors who took to the streets over the disputed status of Hatay. He recalled in an interview how he was struck by the SSNP's response to the arrest of a few party members for distributing leaflets protesting the government's inaction on the Alexandretta issue. The party ordered their comrades to gather outside the General Security Center where they all proclaim responsibility for the circulation of the leaflets.[5]

It was Europe's geopolitics that influenced the final shape of the modern Syrian nation-state's borders. As Paris watched the rise of the Nazis in Germany, offering up Hatay was a primary tactic for wooing Turkey. For the French, cutting away a piece of the Syrian coast from its dominion was a necessary diplomatic and strategic risk. And it came at a cost. Syrian President Hashim al Atassi's independence movement, the National Bloc, had cooperated with Paris and signed the Franco–Syrian Treaty of Independence of 1936. With the transfer of Hatay, Atassi resigned from office to illustrate the displeasure of Syria's ruling colonial political class. But Atassi's gesture did little to stem the growth of the new nationalist parties. The geographic decision regarding Hatay, forcefully imposed on Syria by the French, was seen as a violation of the treaty, which further diminished the general public's trust in the older independence movement dominated by elder statesmen. The younger parties with Arab nationalist ideological foundations were influenced by European politics and began to pick up steam through figures such as Zaki al Arsuzi. An Alawite from Latakia, Arsuzi had a love for French history and philosophy and lived and worked as a teacher in Antioch. He built a following based on Arab nationalism in response to the European's colonial injustice and established the early Baath (meaning resurrection, resurgence, or renaissance) movement, which eventually formed into a political party of the same name, headed by Michel Aflaq and Salah ad-Din Bitar.

In June 1939, the French colonial government facilitated the transfer of Hatay to Turkey. The dramatic events led to not only widespread violent demonstrations in Syria but large-scale population transfers, bringing thousands of Turks to Hatay and driving away thousands of Arab Christians, Armenians, Alawites, and Sunni Arabs.[6] The event helped form Mayahri's anti-imperialist views and led him to join the SSNP in 1944. Other major geopolitical events also fed into the growth of Saadeh's movement in Syria. The establishment of the state of Israel and the Arab states' loss in the 1948 war not only bolstered the party's membership there, but the war's outcome helped shape the lives and careers of the Syrian SSNP members.

One such player was the infamous Adib Shishakli, who was born in Hama of both Arab and Kurdish descent and served in the colonial French Troupes

Speciale. His participation in anticolonial actions against the French, such as the takeover and occupation of the Hama citadel in 1944, earned him a reputation as one of Syria's emerging national heroes. Shishakli later took on a leadership role with the Arab Liberation Army as the head of the Second Yarmuk Battalion in the 1948 Arab-Israeli War, and his exploits on the front lines and his family's affiliation with the SSNP branch in Hama earned him a following among Syria's officer corps. When his wife asked him what he would gain by leaving his family of seven children behind to fight in the Palestine campaign, Shishakli replied: "A good name! A good reputation! Pride in hearing people say; He left his family to die as a martyr for Palestine!"[7]

However, in May 1948, Shishakli's battalion found itself surrounded by Israeli forces in the city of Safad. Syrian President Shukri Quwatli, who intuitively saw the military campaign as futile, tried to minimize his country's direct involvement by sharing the responsibility with the other Arab countries and refused to send much needed supplies and ammunition to Shishakli's men. The Israeli mortar barrages and their ability to target the city's Arab neighborhoods at will left the Arab forces with few military options. By May 10, Shishakli's troops withdrew from Safad through corridors intentionally left open by the Israeli forces.[8] They returned to Syria defeated and demoralized. This wartime experience formed Shishakli's negative view of Syria's civilian leaders and left him with a bitter resentment.[9] Quwatli, while highly respected in Syria for leading the independence movement, was hence tainted in the public sphere with the brush of incompetence and corruption, a feeling that Shishakli shared and would not soon forget.

The SSNP and Syria's Coups

While an ardent nationalist, Shishakli was not known to be an ideologically driven figure. By the late 1940s, he was largely inactive with the SSNP, but still retained friendships and connections with many in the party's leadership and entertained many of Syria's nascent political activists at the officer's club in Damascus. His brother Salah was also a ranking member of the SSNP, a Syrian army captain who served in the Arab-Israeli War, the owner of the Syriana nightclub, and would later on remain an influential figure in the party after Shishakli's exile. In addition, Shishakli had a close relationship with Antoun Saadeh and his family. While Saadeh was in hiding from Lebanese authorities in July 1949, Shishakli was instrumental in advising and moving Saadeh's wife,

Juliette El-Mir, and his daughters to safety. The SSNP leader's widow wrote in her memoir that she frequently sought Shishakli's advice, such as whether or not to hide in the Orthodox Our Lady of Saidnaya Monastery.[10] But it wouldn't be Shishakli, or the SSNP for that matter, who first shattered the existing political order in post-independence Syria. The era of the independence movement's old guard nationalists was quickly coming to an end. The reigns of leadership held by the more esteemed parties such as National Bloc and the pro-Iraqi Aleppo-based People's Party would first be snatched away by a Western-backed army officer.

After the French relinquished their control of Syria, President Quwatli issued pardons to a number of army officers who had been jailed under colonial rule. As they re-entered the Syrian army, it was not long before the military would venture into the political scene. In April 1946, 52-year-old Husni Za'im emerged from prison to re-enter Syria's military life.[11] He had been jailed during the Second World War on orders of French General Charles de Gaulle for having fought on behalf of the French Vichy forces in Syria. Gruff and portly looking, Za'im served as the army's chief of staff during the Arab-Israeli War and, after the defeat, became bogged down in a war of words with Quwatli, who he blamed for the failed campaign. Za'im had forged a relationship with Syrian political elite that not only secured his spot in the army but also established contact with the US Central Intelligence Agency in November 1948 that recognized him as someone with the potential to secure Syria an anti-Soviet counterweight in the Middle East.[12] For the United States, Syria was primarily viewed through the prism of the Cold War and the global battle against communism.

When General Husni Za'im seized power from Quwatli in March 1949, the country experienced the first in a series of coups that plunged Syria into a volatile period of upheaval. This set the stage for Za'im's betrayal of Saadeh, which would galvanize the SSNP, as well as the later political intrigue that would pit the pan-Syrian party against its ideological competitor, the student-dominated pan-Arab Baath movement. Saadeh had reasons to believe Za'im would be receptive to his party. The Lebanese government at first refused to grant recognition to the new military regime in Damascus. Earlier signs had also shown that Za'im may have been susceptible to pan-Syrian ambitions. He once told an American diplomat, "Lebanon should be part of Syria. With one hundred additional armored trucks, I can take Lebanon."[13] However, despite the bravado, Za'im's secret channels with the Lebanese government soon showed otherwise. As discussed in Chapter 2, Za'im had engaged with Saadeh in what appeared to be a partnership aimed at setting up a friendly SSNP regime in Beirut, but in actuality was a betrayal that sent shockwaves through the Levant. Ultimately, Za'im's rule would be short-lived. Following Saadeh's death, discontent with Za'im's regime grew. This anti-Za'im trend in Syria stemmed from allegations that he was pursuing a peace treaty with Israel, as well as his hostility to the Hashemite monarchies in Jordan and Iraq, which led to a new conspiracy to oust the general from power.

Only one month after Saadeh stood before a firing squad in Lebanon, Syria's first military strongman who sent him there would meet the same fate. In August 1949, Za'im and his wife attended a charity dinner hosted by the Red Crescent.[14] Hours later, the SSNP, seething with a desire to avenge their fallen leader, seized the moment and sprang into action. Angry with Za'im over the betrayal of Saadeh, the coup leader, Sami Hinnawi, an officer with SSNP sympathies, took charge of setting the plan into motion. Shishakli, along with his army comrade, Lieutenant Fadlallah Abu Mansur, an SSNP member,[15] apprehended Za'im in person. Fadlallah punched Za'im and angrily accused him of betraying Saadeh. The country's second coup resulted in Za'im's execution in the courtyard at Mezzeh Prison on August 14. Facing the firing squad alongside him was his prime minister, Muhsin al-Barazi, a holdover from the Quwatli government who was held directly responsible by the SSNP for facilitating the secret extradition of Saadeh to the Lebanese government.

After Za'im was executed, Shishakli brought the fallen dictator's bloody shirt to Saadeh's widow, Juliette, and shouted, "We have avenged him!" One party elder remarked that this scene was a big shock to Juliette, being from Latin America.[16] Hinnawi began setting up his own regime and maneuvering Syria's diplomatic channels with the aim of merging Syria with Iraq. However, the Iraqi government was still under the control of the British-backed Hashemite monarchy and the country's Prime Minister Nuri al-Said was widely regarded as a Western stooge. The pan-Arab nationalist officers in Syria felt a union with Iraq would endanger the independence of their newly found republic, a view shared by Shishakli. Hinnawi ruled Syria from August to December and banned a number of left-wing parties, which only further fueled political resentment. It was this sense of endangerment that led them to decide Hinnawi had to go. The third coup stripped him from power, with Shishakli heading Syria's final military intervention of the year on December 19, 1949, and a short period of stability ensued.

Shishakli did not rule openly, but rather through the government of Fawzi Selu, an army friend he installed as the prime minister.[17] For some, the period of military rule under Shishakli had its benefits. The Shishakli regime cracked down on crime, enforced strict control of Syria's porous borders, and rebuild the army into a modern force. Shishakli also harnessed the power of the radio and was well known throughout the region for his oratory and zeal that reverberated through the airwaves. His radio speeches occurred even before those of Egyptian President Gamal Abdul Nasser. He was the first post-independence Arab leader to cultivate a cult of personality with his pictures appearing in shop windows and established a government ministry of information and propaganda.[18]

His spies and security agents were posted throughout the country to monitor any potential anti-Shishakli activity. All political parties were banned, especially the religious parties. Long before Egypt's deadly cat-and-mouse game with the Muslim Brotherhood (MB), Shishakli barred the Islamic Socialist Front (Syria's early incarnation of the MB) from participation in politics. Maarouf al-Dawalibi of the MB was close to the Aleppo's People Party and served as Syria's minister of economy and prime minister, until his removal following Shishakli's coup.[19] The SSNP, on the other hand, was largely left alone during Shishakli's rule. The party's leader, George Abd Messih, declined to take a more active role in the Shishakli regime. The writings of former party members indicate this was due to a general feeling that the SSNP was not ready to govern and also that Abd Messih did not want Shishakli to take over the party's leadership, which Abd Messih guarded for himself.[20] Prior to Shishakli's rise to power, Mahayri, took part in the drafting of Syria's constitution and later who used his platform in the Syrian parliament to give the party a voice in the public sphere.[21] Although no longer a party comrade, Shishakli kept a close friendship with Mahayri. Patrick Seale described how Mahayri gained a reputation as one of Shishakli's trusted companions during his rule and would often travel around the country with him. Shishakli was also likely close to another prominent SSNP figure, Elias Gergi Qanayzeh, who obtained legal recognition for the party in Syria in 1950.

The SSNP was also in the midst of its reprisals for the death of Antoun Saadeh. Most notable among them was the assassination of former Lebanese Prime Minister Riad al-Solh on July 17, 1951. Three SSNP gunmen had ambushed Solh on the way to Marka International Airport on the outskirts of Amman, Jordan, allegedly on Abd Messih's orders, to avenge the fallen Saadeh. The SSNP hit team included Michel Deek, Spiro Wadih, and Mohammed Adib al-Salah. They carried out the attack using two vehicles. Riad al-Solh en route to the airport, accompanied by two delegations' cars. Adib al-Salah, who was driving one of the two cars, slowed down. Then Deek's car, which was driven by Wadih, approached Solh's vehicle and pulled alongside it and aimed his gun at Solh. As he fired, Wadih shouted, "Take it from Saadeh's hand!" Solh's car flipped over and crashed. Deek then descended to make sure the operation has been completed and found that their victim had perished. The group then escaped and tried to smuggle themselves through the woods. However, Deek was injured by Riad Solh's bodyguards, which prompted him to shoot himself and commit suicide. Adib al-Salah also ended his life in suicide like his companion. Spiro Wadih survived and managed to escape with the help of a Bedouin who hid him. He then took refuge in a friend's safe house and hid until he had a passport that enabled him to flee to Brazil.

These dastardly actions were tied to the wave of sympathy that was still resonating in the Levant after Saadeh's death. This wave of support had the potential to appeal to the Syrian leader. However, Shishakli knew that the SSNP would have great difficulty venturing out of the sectarian minority communities and into the mainstream of Syria's Sunni majority where pan-Arabism was far more popular. Therefore, he abstained from fully embracing the party's central tenant of pan-Syrianism in favor of the vastly more popular pan-Arabism.

He founded his own party, the Arab Liberation Movement (ALM), to cultivate this Arabist trend. It was a pan-Arab, anticommunist, hierarchical organization and structured similarly to the SSNP. Patrick Seale described the movement's grandiose launch in Aleppo in October 1952 and noted how ALM "party militants could be seen marching in and out of their Damascus headquarters greeting each other with raised-arm salutes."[22] The ALM and SSNP, along with the Baath and Communist Party (the latter two that were both banned), were progressive in nature, allowing women and Syrians regardless of sect to join. In the October 1953 elections, Shishakli's regime funneled allegations into the media that the SSNP was in fact funded by Western powers.[23] The ALM and the SSNP were the only two parties allowed to run. The ALM took sixty out of eighty-two seats, and the SSNP grabbed only one, with independent candidates filling the other seats.[24] In the 1954 elections, the SSNP fielded fifteen candidates and won only two seats.[25]

Shishakli was able to court Egypt and Saudi Arabia and allowed France to maintain a level of nominal influence inside of the country. Shishakli knew how to utilize the region's players to keep Syria neutral during the Cold War and safeguard its independence. Shishakli made his own awareness of Syria's colonial-imposed borders and the country's precarious situation in the region known, "Syria is the current official name for that country which lies within the artificial frontiers drawn up by imperialism."[26] Like the SSNP, Shishakli was suspicious of Western interference in Syria, and his primary foreign policy concern was Syria's place in the contest of dominance between Iraq and its British-backed

Hashemite rulers, and the Egyptian–Saudi alliance. However, Iraq, under the direction of Nuri al-Said, was a key instrument in fomenting internal dissent and organizing the forces that ultimately united against him. Meanwhile, France continued to vie for influence in its former colonial dominion in order to check the British.

Shishakli's final years saw a wave of organized opposition, both in Syria's urban centers as well as outside the country that eventually led to his downfall. Although the city of Homs was the key urban center of anti-Shishakli activity, he had long perceived the Druze in the south as a threat to his regime. Shishakli was perhaps most notorious for his efforts to curtail the tribal-based power of the Druze.[27] The Druze never forgave him for the shelling and military assault on Jabal Druze (Druze Mountain), and many Druze officers in the Syrian army later formed the backbone of the coalition that conspired against him. Furthermore, Shishakli had begun to scale back the role of the military in Syria's political scene in an effort to legitimize his rule. Many well-connected officers who suddenly felt detached and disenfranchised turned to Shishakli's political enemies for help. With the assistance of Iraq, factions of the army were able to present a united front to subsequently oust him from Damascus. Faced with increasing pressure to resign, the military strongman turned to confidents in the SSNP for their views. One story relays that he sought out the advice of two Syrian Kurdish SSNP members based in Qamishli, named Zaki Nizameddine and Anees Mdiwaye.[28] They encouraged him to resign rather than have Syria face near-certain civil war. Shishakli went into exile and eventually found a quiet life in the Sírio-Libanês community in Brazil. However, he could not escape the long memory of Syria's politics and was later assassinated by a Druze assailant in the Brazilian village of Ceres in 1967.

The SSNP and the Confrontation with the Baath

Elections followed Shishakli's dictatorship and created the conditions that, four years later, led to the short-lived union with Egypt. Mahayri lost his seat to Salah al-Din Bitar, a Baathist politician, in the elections, and the Baath Party won twenty-two seats in total and significantly increased their control over Syria's power structure. The political upheaval was further compounded by the breakdown of the army, which had become factionalized without Shishakli. An array of officers organized and formed their own secret networks of political patrons; some allied with the Baath and others with the SSNP. However, an alliance of mutual interests between Aflaq's Baath Party and the Syrian Communists ushered in a new era of leftist-oriented Syrian politics that pushed the country toward a union with Nasser's Egypt. The figure who was essential for the expansion of the Baath Party and orchestrating the creation of the United Arab Republic was none other than Akram al-Hawrani, who had his own history with the SSNP, which will be discussed further in Chapter 5.

The Syrian Communist Party was formed in 1944 after a split occurred in the Syrian-Lebanese Community Party, a decision the party's politburo took in 1943. The party's leader, Khalid Baqdash, had traveled to Moscow in 1934 and studied in the Communist University of the Toilers of the East and returned to the Levant in 1936. The party managed to survive earlier political repression and hardships in Syria by cooperating with Quwatli and the influential establishment and staying within certain red lines.[29] Limited political activity would be tolerated as long as it did not overtly challenge Quwatli's government. However, despite the dismal state of the country's rural peasantry, Syria's communists struggled to gain a widespread following. This was due to the party's strong association with foreign powers, namely the Soviet Union, which had strongly backed the newly established state of Israel. As will be seen, it was the left-wing nationalists of the Baath who would attract Syria's rural poor and urban intellectuals. Meanwhile, the SSNP, still swirling about in Syria's increasingly leftist political sphere dominated by Arabism, soon found itself caught up in a violent confrontation with the Syrian Baathists, with drastic consequences. This dramatic clash primarily manifested itself in the fate of a young and popular pro-Baathist army officer.

Colonel Adnan al-Malki came from an influential Sunni family in Damascus, made his career in the Syrian army, and, like much of the country's officer corps, was a graduate of the Homs Military Academy. Despite never being an official member of Michel Aflaq's Baath Party, he was strongly affiliated with the movement and was well known as a firm supporter of Nasser and Arab nationalism. His brother Riad al-Malki was a staunch Baathist and later became an MP in the Syrian parliament. Even as a new recruit, he was at the center of Syria's political transformation and appeared destined for greatness. One photo taken in 1946 shows a young Malki proudly marching as an army cadet during Syria's first Independence Day. He also worked closely with Akram al-Hawrani and had encouraged him to unite his Arab Socialist Party with the Baath movement, which Shishakli had outlawed. At the Baath Party's 1947 congress, the merger was officially declared, with the party now renamed the Arab Socialist Baath Party, the name by which the party continues to be known to this day.

Malki's first major political intrigue came in 1953, when he famously confronted Shishakli on the Damascus airport runway after the president had returned from a visit to Egypt. The young officer handed over a list of demands that included allowing political pluralism, freedom of the press, and for Shishakli to abolish his ALM party and relinquish power. The strongman politely took the list from him and consequently rounded up the document's signatories to throw them in jail, Malki included. In fact, he had been a central player in the plot to overthrow Shishakli, organizing with former President Atassi and the influential Druze leader Sultan al-Atrash.

After the fall of Shishakli's regime, Malki enjoyed widespread popularity, which even overshadowed his army superior, Chief of Staff Shawkat Shuqayer. Politically astute, hardworking, and willing to risk his life for the Palestinian cause, his ideals, and justice he was widely admired and had a large following in the army. By all accounts, Malki appeared ordained to become a powerful political leader in Syria's post-Shishakli era. Malki was restored to his position in the army, becoming deputy chief of staff.

Malki continued his foray in politics and corralled his fellow army officers to support the political and military unification with Egypt. There was even speculation that Malki would launch a coup if Prime Minister Faris al-Khury did not abandon his attempts to move Syria toward the Western sphere of influence. He regularly represented the official position of the government and the army in the press. For example, in February 1955, Malki spoke to the Syrian newspaper *al-Jihad* for an interview, in which he downplayed the prospects of a Turkish military incursion along the Syrian border.[30] The Baath Party, during this time, had been in a fierce competition with the SSNP. George Abd Messih had just taken command of the party after the execution of Antoun Saadeh in 1949 and was struggling to implement his control over the party's factions. Malki soon became engaged in a public spat with Abd Messih, who accused him of using Arab nationalism to secure power for Syria's Sunnis.

Malki, in turn, tried to intimidate the SSNP leader by promising to hand him over to Lebanon, where he had been sentenced to death in absentia for the murder of former Lebanese Prime Minister Riad al-Solh. The fierce competition between the two parties played out within the army. Another opponent of Malki was a fellow army officer, Ghassan Jadid. Through his friendship with Shishakli, Jadid became the head of the Homs Military Academy and had been appointed defense chief of SSNP in 1954. The academy was the site of a full-fledged political recruitment operation by Syria's new ideological parties, and the SSNP was the first such movement to begin recruitment among the school's officers.[31] Jadid was an Alawite and used his position at the academy to recruit officers to the party, a move that riled Malki. Jadid also rivaled Malki in his charisma. He also served as a military attaché for Syria's UN delegation. The SSNP has many tales celebrating the exploits and legends of Ghassan Jadid, who joined the SSNP when he was eighteen years old. The party officials noted that the Germans referred to him as "Syria's Rommel" and described an adventure where, in 1945, he drove a truck filled with weapons and ammunition from Tripoli to Latakia, the location of a French military barracks.[32] A group of sympathetic Syrian soldiers based at the barracks helped him take it over and raise the Syrian independence flag.[33] According to SSNP lore, Ghassan was the first Syrian to raise the new independence flag in a French barracks in Syria and Lebanon. His rebellion against the French was ultimately crushed, and he was jailed until granted a pardon by Quwatli in April 1946.[34] Ghassan also fought in the 1948 Israeli-Arab War.

Jadid had two other brothers, Fuad, who was also in the SSNP, and Salah, who joined the party for a short period of time. However, he soon left for the ranks of the Baath Party but, through his brothers, he helped retain a level of contact between the two sides. Later on, he became a leading architect in the establishment of the United Arab Republic and was essential for aligning Syria with the Soviet Union. The political rivalry extended outside of the military all the way through Syria's educational institutions, polarizing a generation of youth. A young Hafez al-Assad recalled how during his school years, when students asked your "religion," the response was typically either *Baathi* or *Qawmi* (the latter meaning nationalist, taken from the SSNP's full name in Arabic, *al-Hizb al-Suri al-Qawmi al-Ijtima'i*).

The Malki Affair and Purge

The Malki Affair and its aftermath was one of Syria's earliest shifts toward authoritarianism along a sharp turn toward anti-Western sentiment. Malki's assassination rocked Syria and brought about a harsh crackdown on the SSNP that ultimately eradicated them from Syrian politics for fifty years. It was also a major political spectacle that marked a turning point away from the country's brief return to democracy back to a long era of authoritarianism under the Baath.

On April 22, 1955, Malki was attending a football match between the Syrian army's team and an Egyptian team at the Damascus Municipal Stadium. A figure suddenly approached and fired two shots, killing the colonel instantly. The assailant was Yunes Abd al Rahim, a military police officer and an Alawite member of the SSNP, who also killed himself on the spot. Two other SSNP members, Badi Makhlouf and Abdul Munim Dubussy, were in attendance at the match and arrested as accomplices. However, Rahim's fellow Alawites, possibility from fear of retribution, distanced themselves from his participation in the assassination. For the next twenty years, members of his Alawite sect would refuse to visit or do business with his family village of B'amrah in the Safita District of the Tartus countryside.[35]

The main theory is that Rahim was selected by George Abd Messih since the former had been denied entrance to the military academy due to his sect.[36] The most dominant story told, however, is that the assassination was ordered by Abd Messih due to his personal feud with Malki. Ghassan Jadid stated during his trial that this was the case since the assassination occurred without the knowledge of the party's leadership. Another view was that the plot was actually perpetrated by Egyptian intelligence in order to galvanize support for Arab nationalism and secure a free rein to eliminate the threat of the SSNP. Though Arab nationalism was already immensely popular in Syria, the country still had a slew of political parties across the ideological spectrum. Furthermore, anti-Western sentiment was not completely present at all levels of Syrian society, a trend that would change dramatically after the purge commenced.

Afif al-Bizri, a known leftist army officer, headed the show trials and later became the Syrian army's chief of staff. The trials that followed the assassination have often been compared to the trials carried out by Joseph Stalin during his 1930s purges in the Soviet Union. This period marked a turning point where the Baath now had the opportunity to finally isolate and eliminate their primary competitor. The Baath and Communists orchestrated a full-scale purge of the SSNP. First, the Arab nationalists and leftist factions urged the parliament to implement a state of martial law. Other parties resisted but eventually reached a compromise. A military tribunal would be carried out with full power to investigate and arrest anyone suspected of being connected to the assassination, which quickly had morphed into a larger antigovernment conspiracy.

The offices of the SSNP's party organ, *al-Bina*, were burned to the ground. The SSNP's members were accused of purposely destroying their own offices and documents to cover up evidence of their conspiracy against the Syrian government. The SSNP, shut out of the press, was reduced to facilitating their meetings and activities in secret. To offer a counternarrative, they handed out pamphlets and flyers in which they claimed they were the victims of a Zionist plot facilitated by the Communists and Baathists. Some of these materials took on an anti-Semitic tone with complaints of Jewish "exploitation and fraud."[37] However, these efforts ultimately proved futile amidst the highly organized onslaught orchestrated by the Baath.

A faded photo, titled "Accused of the crime of the assassination of Adnan al-Malki," showed Issam al-Mahayri and Saadeh's widow, Juliette El-Mir Saadeh, seated in rows of courtroom benches with other SSNP members grimly awaiting their fate. Thousands of the party's members were rounded up and paraded through the military tribunals for a certain guilty verdict and lengthy jail sentence. Issam al-Mahayri, the SSNP's leader in Syria, was arrested and forced to testify against his fellow party members. Once a leading journalist and co-owner of the Daily Press Corporation, Mahayri was publicly ridiculed by the courts, and his influence greatly diminished as he became ostracized from Syria's political sphere.[38] He was eventually sentenced to a long spell in Damascus' Mezzeh Prison.

The crackdown on press freedoms spread across the political spectrum. Even non-SSNP outlets fell victim to the Baathist–Communist witch hunt. Husni al-Barazi, who owned *al-Nas* (the people), an anticommunist outlet, was forced to close after an editorial discussed the alleged torture of SSNP suspects and connected the mistreatment to the Baathist Speaker of the Parliament, Akram al-Hawrani. Other newspapers and outlets quickly learned to adhere to the official government line concerning the Malki Affair and the military tribunals.

Army Chief of Staff Shuqayer suggested that the party was dominated by sectarian minorities, such as Alawites and Christians, and therefore sought to isolate Syria from the rest of the Arab World through their plan to eventually establish a pan-Syrian state as stipulated by the party's ideology.[39] Many Alawites who were not members of the SSNP fled to Lebanon since they feared the growing extent of the purge. This period marked the emergence of Syria as a mukhabarat state. Abdul Hamid al-Sarraj, who had been appointed as head of intelligence in March 1955, a month prior to the assassination, was tasked with investigating and implementing the purge of the SSNP.[40] Imprisonment and torture were tools used by the Syrian Intelligence, known then as the Deuxieme Bureau. Badi Makhlouf, Abdul Munim Dubussy, and Fuad Jadid protested at their trial that their confessions had been extracted under torture, describing secret interrogation sessions involving severe beatings and electric shocks.[41]

Makhlouf, a first cousin of Anisa Makhlouf (the future wife of Hafez al-Assad), said the torture was not even comparable to what the early Christians had suffered from under the Romans.⁴² Despite his defense, Dubussy and Makhlouf were both executed by firing squad on the morning of September 3, 1956. A progovernment editorial described death as a "mercy" for the "enemies" who had "bound themselves to the colonialists."⁴³ Fuad Jadid was sentenced to life imprisonment. He reportedly had his death sentence reduced since his brother Ghassan had been killed in a hail of machine gun fire in Beirut. Other SSNP members, including the poet Mohammad Maghout, were swept up in the mass arrests and suffered torture and long-term psychological torment. In the final year of his life, he told the outlet *Al-Hayat* in 2006, "something inside of me was broken that hasn't been repaired until this day," going on to explain that it was in prison he discovered fear.⁴⁴

Ghassan Jadid and Salah Shishakli tried to strike back from Beirut. In what would become known as "The Iraqi Plot" due to the support of the Iraqi government, they allied themselves with a number of other military exiles and tried to coordinate the overthrow of the Damascus government in the winter of 1956. The plot also had the support of the CIA and British SIS, which gave the plan the codename "Operation Straggle."⁴⁵ They used Salah's family connections in Hama to devise a strategy. These SSNP meetings included Ghassan Jadid, George Abd Messih, Iskandar Shawi, Said Taqiyaddin, and Salah Shishakli. Adib Shishakli also joined the conspiracy and urged them to seek support from Baghdad. When Shishakli returned to Beirut to discuss the coup plot with the SSNP against the Syrian regime, his old friend and associate Hawrani was allegedly one of the names compiled on the hit list for the SSNP's assassination squads.⁴⁶

In the spring of 1956, Ghassan and Adib met with Iraqi army officers in Geneva, Switzerland, and again held a series of meetings in Beirut, during which Adib backed out of the plot. Seale relayed that Adib may have feared reprisals against his extensive family still within Syria and that Salah Shishakli "tried in vain to prevent his brother's precipitate departure."⁴⁷ The United States had its own doubts about Shishakli. A State Department assessment of him from June 1956 noted his lack of support and distrust due to his relationship with the French and the "conservative" SSNP.⁴⁸

Despite this, the plot continued to move forward without the former dictator. The SSNP was entrusted to handle the security and ground operations, with the Iraqi government stating that the party was a "group of adventurers" and were the lone political force with the "courage" to take on the Syrian regime.⁴⁹

Ghassan Jadid would take Homs and Salah Shishakli would secure Hama.[50] The SSNP began assembling a task force of three hundred fighters at a party training camp in Beit Meri in the hills above Beirut and sought to secure weapons from Baghdad. The SSNP's secret operatives retrieved weapons parachuted in remote locations and smuggled in through Beirut airport. However, Iraq's General Talib Daghistani had his misgivings. Even though Iraq had mobilized troops on the Syrian border, he sensed the internal dysfunctions among the coup-plotters and was further turned off from the enterprise by the British–French alliance with Israel during the October 1956 Suez Crisis unfolding in Egypt.[51] Likewise, the United States was angered by the British "double-crossing" over the Suez Crisis, and the plot eventually fizzled out. Meanwhile in Syria, Sarraj would use the uncovered coup as further propaganda to bolster his security forces and continued his campaign of tracking down and eliminating the SSNP members who had escaped Syria.

Ghassan Jadid was one of the first ones to fall within Sarraj's intelligence spiderweb.[52] Sarraj's agents tracked down and killed Ghassan outside the SSNP party headquarters in Beirut on February 19, 1957. Two SSNP members drove to the site of Ghassan's murder after hearing the news. Police and civilians had surrounded a building where the assassin, Izzat Sh'ath, was hiding. One of the SSNP members then infiltrated the building and shot dead Ghassan's assassin. Fadlallah Abu Mansur, who by 1956 had retired from the Syrian army, would take over as the party's defense chief after Ghassan's death and would go on to have a major role in planning operations against Syria's regime in the following years.[53] The assassin's killer, Aziz Ziub, was consequently arrested by the Lebanese authorities and held in Roumieh prison for six months.

Another component of the show trials was the allegation that the SSNP was working in concert with the Americans and Western intelligence. This was manifested prominently in the "Sharabi letters," an alleged correspondence between Issam al-Mahayri and Hisham Sharabi, who had left the Middle East for life in Washington, DC, and worked as a professor with the Institute of Languages and Linguistics at Georgetown. Dr. Sharabi had served as an editor for the SSNP periodical *al-Jil al-Jadid* (*The New Generation*) before seeking refuge in the United States. The letters supposedly revealed that Dr. Sharabi had helped Mahayri obtain a visa to travel to the United States with the goal of organizing an anti-leftist movement in Syria to counter the Soviet's presence in the Middle East. This evidence allowed Sarraj to claim that Syria had been able to defeat an imperialist conspiracy that was being facilitated by "indigenous anti-communist elements." A memo by the US State Department from July 1955 lamented the prevailing views of the Syrian public and the efforts of the Syrian political establishment that the US government was using the anticommunist SSNP in order to undermine Syria's sovereignty.[54] It read in part:

> References in SSNP indictment US policy and US officials ... have been used by anti-western newspapers in attempt show link between [the] SSNP and USG. Without accepting all details, many Syrians [are inclined to believe] some bases for charge exist on theory "where there's smoke there's fire." Climate has thus been created which is favorable increasing pro-Communist agitation (ostensibly on behalf "martyr" Malki). ... in indictment of alleged letters from SSNP members in US is clear attempt implicate USG ... after my objection to Prime Minister when allegations US involvement first appeared ... [Government of Syria] officials have privately assured Embassy they see no basis for charge US involved but GOS public attitude demonstrates either (A) complete ineffectiveness stop civilian officials; or (B) their genuine belief that, while positive proof lacking, there is credible evidence USG connection SSNP; or (C) both. Extent to which this "evidence" accepted may be indicated by fact that portions Sharabi's alleged exposition US policy ... A thread of consistency in GOS actions re Malki murder is effort destroy [the] SSNP. Attempt to establish relationship between [the] party and USG is intended to serve that purpose.

Although the Syrian government made liberal use of Western-linked conspiracy theories to assert its own political control, there were plots that aimed to topple the newly emerging order in Syria. A few included plans to return the exiled Shishakli to power. It was revealed that immediately after his departure, Shishakli tried to reroute the plane to Beirut when his supporters urged him to return. This effort, however, was stymied by the US State Department, and his plane was denied a landing permit at the Beirut International Airport. A State Department telegram from January 1956 expressed the fears of a Shishakli–SSNP coup against the regime in Syria:

> Anti-west Syrian officers made great effort in Malki pseudo-trial to show that the US encouraged SSNP to overthrow GOS, and their efforts have had some effect locally. Should SSNP now attempt coup in Syria and fail, regardless of real US attitude US will inevitably be blamed, with unpredictable consequences. It is therefore in US interest either to discourage SSNP from any attempted coup or to insure coup's success. The anti-Communist record of ... [the] SSNP and of Shishakli give them outward basis for cooperation in anti-Communist coup in Syria. Estimate of the motivation of different elements, however, should include further information about Shishakli in last two years. Appraisal of leadership of SSNP, a quantity unknown to Embassy.[55]

The fallout for George Abd Messih continued into 1956 when the party's new president, Assad al-Ashqar, sought to bring Abd Messih before the SSNP's Higher Council, but he refused to take part and was expelled. Abd Messih subsequently left with a faction of his loyal followers to Lebanon, effectively creating the first split in the party in October 1957. It was this faction that became known as the Intifada (or uprising). One party historian wrote:

> The smaller of the two branches supported [Abd Messih] under whose watch the Syrian events transpired. It was a rigidly doctrinarian group, removed from any political involvement, and a faithful custodian of the older SSNP traditions. The larger group was more politically dynamic and more open to experimentation and new approaches. Consequently, however, it was more vulnerable to infiltration by agents of Western intelligence agencies and political adventurers. This group dominated the political history of the SSNP for the following decades.[56]

The purges continued into 1959, partly because the SSNP was implicated in other conspiracies that were hatched by the Western powers, such as the so-called "The Iraqi Plot" of 1956. A state security court in Aleppo sentenced fifteen SSNP members to five to fifteen years in prison for their involvement in an "arms plot."[57] A few pictures from the period show the normally well-kept Mahayri with facial stubble strolling in the infamous Mezzeh Prison courtyard with members of the Armenian nationalist Dashnak party in 1957. Issam al-Mahayri would eventually be released in a deal (according to one SSNP member to "save his own neck") with the Syrian government and later head a pro-Syrian government faction of the SSNP. Malki's funeral took place on April 23, 1955. His assassination propelled him to a level of veneration and praise that was unprecedented in Syria. The sculptor Fathi Kabawah was commissioned to design Malki's statue in Damascus. Streets, buildings, and schools were named after the fallen champion of Arab nationalism. Riad al-Malki also authored a biography of his brother. Malki, as a martyr, became the embodiment of pan-Arab nationalism that cemented the Baath into Syria's political and social fabric for a generation and fixed the country onto its course for an eventual union with Egypt. Sultan Pasha al-Atrash wrote a memorial for his fallen comrade in *al-Jundi* (*The Soldier*) magazine in the summer of 1955:[58]

> There is no civilization that had more victims and martyrs
> like our beloved Arab civilization.
> If peoples' lives end with death
> the martyr's life begins with death.

That was the fate of the immortal
Adnan al-Malki, who lived two generous lives,
a short life hard lived until his last breath,
and another long lived in the peoples' consciousness.

Therefore, Adnan did not die
and here he is personified in the leader;
Col. Shawkat Shuqayer and in every
comrade of his fellow free officers,

but also in every Syrian citizen,
because in every one of those
Adnan, in his beliefs and values,
Adnan, in his determination for liberation and development,
Adnan, in his keenness for Arab unity.

There is no harm for us in these circumstances,
If we lost Adnan yesterday—although it was a huge loss—there is no
harm in sacrificing more like Adnan tomorrow.
Because they are eternal in the consciousness of the nation forever.

Thus, the SSNP briefly touched the upper rungs of power in Damascus and dramatically fell from grace. The party's association with Shishakli and the failure to survive in the onslaught of pan-Arabism in Syria would haunt the party for years. Its pan-Syrian ideology failed to resonate with Syrians outside of its close-knit elite party. In addition, it was unable to escape the stigma and public suspicion of its perceived association with the West, despite its long-running anticolonial credentials. However, it was ultimately the Malki Affair that left its deepest legacy for the SSNP in Syria, relegating it for decades to the role of an aggressor that had struck out at the Syrian people and was thus justly punished. Still, the show trials and systematic purge orchestrated by the Baathists in the wake of the Malki Affair would not be the last of the suffering felt by the party. With the final years of the 1950s, SSNP re-emerged in Lebanon where they engaged in a short-lived alliance with the Lebanese government in another effort to ward off the tide of pan-Arabism. However, this gambit would be the last time the SSNP sided in a Levantine confrontation as a solely right-wing, anticommunist, reactionary movement before it began its transition to the side of the left.

5

In the Shadow of Nasser: The SSNP and the Arab Cold War

On July 22, 1959, a military parade unfolded in Cairo, marking the seven-year anniversary of "Revolution Day," the coup that brought Gamal Abdul Nasser and the Free Officers to power, ending Egypt's British-backed monarchy. Cairo now towered over the Arab World as the capital of the United Arab Republic (UAR), a federation between Egypt and Syria that was established on February 22, 1958, the result of the period of political maneuvering that followed after the fall of Shishakli. The city was a showpiece for a number of diplomats and military figures, including delegations from the United States and the Soviet Union. The Soviet hardware that paraded past the crowd included BTR-152 armored personnel carriers, ZPU-4 and Zvezda 37-mm anti-aircraft guns, the T-34 main battle tank, field howitzers, the SU-100 tank destroyer, and the IS-3 Josef Stalin heavy tank. Mi-4 Hound helicopters, MIG-15 fighter aircraft, and Ilyushin Il-28 Beagle bombers flew overhead.[1] Anwar Sadat, an Egyptian military officer who was the UAR's secretary to the National Union, spoke at the podium on the reviewing stand. Situated just one seat away from Nasser, the giant of Arab nationalism, was a slender, dark-haired figure in a white suit.[2]

Akram al-Hawrani represented the union's other half and had long been active in Syria's class struggles, forcefully advocating for the rural peasants against the country's wealthy land owners. He had a nationalist streak as well, championing Arab self-determination, bolstering the Baath Party to power, and blasting foreign interference in Syria's internal affairs. The two men together in Cairo symbolized the height of Arab unity and military power in the aftermath of the 1956 Suez Crisis, which had occurred almost three years earlier. The confrontation, triggered by Nasser's decree nationalizing the Suez Canal, was followed by a joint British, French, and Israeli attempt to overthrow Nasser, but pressure from both the Soviet Union and the United States reversed the results of the short-lived intervention. Egypt and Syria together appeared on the verge of realizing the Arab World's destiny to confront and defend their nascent union from Israeli and Western imperialism. The SSNP, although ideologically opposed to Nasser, joined the chorus of those who condemned the invasion as a "tripartite aggression" against Egypt, and said Cairo was "capable of defending itself in a guerrilla war lasting twenty years."[3]

Aside from the geopolitical implications of Nasser's regime and the UAR on the world stage, this period was also marked by a profound split within the region. Regarded by some as the Arab Cold War, the Middle East found itself divided between the traditional pro-Western monarchy regimes of Saudi Arabia, Jordan, Iraq (until 1958), and Pahlavi Iran against the anticolonial, revolutionary regimes that desired socialist economies coupled with Arab nationalism, such as Egypt and Syria.[4] A regional bulwark rose up in response to the tide of Nasser's charisma and power. The SSNP had challenged Nasser's Arabist allies, the Baath, in Syria and had lost dramatically. The SSNP was now sidelined in Syria and played its part in the background of this regional struggle in part due to its hostility to communism but also to ensure its own survival against the threat posed by its ideological rival.

As SSNP members fled Syria in the post-Malki Affair crackdown, they regrouped in Lebanon. The party had the protection of the pro-Western Lebanese President Camille Chamoun. Chamoun himself was ardently opposed to Nasser and did what he could to limit Egypt's growing regional influence in Lebanon. The Syrian government tried in vain to corral Beirut into suppressing the SSNP in Lebanon and extraditing its members who were involved in the Malki plot back to Damascus. However, Chamoun viewed the SSNP as a useful tool given their experience in Syria and the party's hostility toward communism. In return, the SSNP was able to find relative safety in Lebanon from the reach of the Syrian and Egyptian intelligence agents. This refuge did not last for long, with the currents of the region reaching Lebanon's shores after the UAR's founding. Arab nationalism had awoken in Lebanon, and it confronted the pan-Syrian and Western forces in a fit of fury.

Although revolutionary and staunchly anticolonialist, the SSNP now had to make do with the Western powers during this critical period, the British and the United States in particular. This temporary alignment and period of scheming left the SSNP with a lasting stigma of serving as a Western agent, an accusation that would haunt the party in the Arab World long after the intrigue of the 1950s. For the remaining party members in Syria, the impact of these accusations, both real and perceived, saw thousands of SSNP partisans withering away behind bars in the Mezzeh Prison for the latter half of the 1950s and 1960s. The party's chief in Syria, Issam al-Mahayri, remained locked up until his release in March 1963.[5]

This chapter discusses the years 1958–62, a period that dramatically changed the SSNP's fortunes. The chain of events would culminate in the party's failed coup on New Year's Eve in December 1961, the results of which saw the movement begin to shift from its birth place on the political right to its current position on the left. Another factor that would change is its position on pan-Arabism. In stark contrast, the SSNP had earlier sided with the Lebanese government and Kataeb Party during the 1958 crisis to counter the threat of the Nasserists during the inter-Lebanese confrontation. The decade of the 1960s saw the SSNP from the suppression of Lebanese Muslim rebels to the party enduring an intense bout of persecution itself. By the 1970s the SSNP found common cause to go on and join the coalition of the champions and protectors of dispossessed Muslims, most importantly the Palestinians, in Lebanon. While the SSNP had always voiced its support to the Palestinian cause, it was the final years of the 1960s that would see the party land in the pan-Arab camp as its primary ally during the 1975 civil war. The Progressive Socialist Party (PSP), headed by Kamal Jumblatt, would aid in the SSNP's transition as it sought out new secular allies in the late 1960s and early 1970s.

The United Arab Republic

The impact of the creation of the UAR cannot be overstated on the Arab Cold War. For the first time since the end of the Ottoman Empire, two Arab countries, long dominated by foreign powers, had been politically and militarily forged together under an umbrella of solidarity and nationalism. It spanned two continents, linking North Africa to Western Asia; its ancient twin capitals, each a jewel of Arab culture and history, radiated a newfound sense of empowerment. The UAR adopted a new flag featuring two green stars, representing Syria and Egypt's unity. However, for the SSNP, the union was the product of a promise build on a false premise. Based on the theories of Antoun Saadeh, the Egyptians were not destined to be included in the Greater Syria scheme. The SSNP stood firm against the grain of this overwhelming wave of pan-Arab euphoria, eschewing popularity, opposing the UAR, and positioned itself as a primary opponent of Nasser.

It was the Syrian Baath and their alliance with the Syrian Communist Party in the late 1950s that was chiefly responsible for lifting the UAR off the ground.

Nasser initially had little interest in formalizing a union. In addition, he was unwaveringly opposed to communism and wary of the Baath Party's coalition partners. Throughout the 1950s and 1960s, over a thousand communists and leftist intellectuals filled Egypt's jails.[6] The Baath Party founders, Michel Aflaq and Salah al-Din Bitar, were heavily influenced by communism during their time as students in Paris, but they ultimately rejected the ideology in favor of left-wing nationalism that stressed Arab unity. Syria's communists were politically sidelined and driven underground. Other communist members, such as the Lebanese Farajallah el-Helou, were outright killed. He had risked an undercover journey to Syria in secret in 1959 and was apprehended by a joint effort carried out by the Lebanese and Syrian Deuxieme Bureau on information gained from a communist defector. He died from torture, and his body was allegedly dissolved in acid. It is likely that the Baath and Nasser knew their union would be endangered by Syria's Western-oriented neighbors, and this hostile environment would only serve to enhance the political status of the communists and Soviet interests in Syria.[7] Therefore, Nasser and his allies sought to squeeze this potential competitor out of the scene. Communist leader Khalid Bakdash and the party's entire Central Committee left Syria for exile in the safety of Eastern Europe, and the party subsequently headed into years of persecution, infighting, and irrelevancy.[8]

Furthermore, Egypt's leader had no tolerance for any organized political party activity under his reign as chief of the UAR. As part of the agreement for establishing the union, all organized political parties were outlawed. The Baath Party disbanded itself at Nasser's behest. The Baath's decision to self-ban in 1958 and subjugate themselves to Nasser only exemplified the power, momentum, and determination of their quest to unite the Arab homeland. In the years leading up to the UAR's founding, Hawrani and Syria's feared intelligence chief, Abdul Hamid al-Sarraj, squared off against Syria's indigenous political opponents, which, in the wake of the Malki assassination, predominately consisted of the SSNP.[9] It is a stroke of irony that the SSNP's primary Syrian nemesis was something of a political sibling to the party since Hawrani had his own distant connections to the SSNP. As a young man, he joined Antoun Saadeh's party in 1936. However, he left only after two years[10] and likely viewed his time with the pan-Syrian movement as an opportunity to cement his anti-imperialist credentials, a legacy he later used to bolster his political career.[11] It was perhaps the party's militant nature that initially appealed to Hawrani; he did after all take part in the anti-British, pro-German Rashid Ali Revolt of 1941 in Iraq.

According to Patrick Seale, Hawrani allegedly covered up his earlier activities with the SSNP by establishing a leftist party, the Arab Socialist Movement.

Once he left the SSNP, Hawrani did not have any long-term ideological ties to the pan-Syrian party. He felt the elitist-oriented movement was too dogmatic, intellectual, and cumbersome to grow into an effective mass political organization.[12] It was his army connections and Arab nationalism that determined his political fate in Syria's future. Still the SSNP may have left a deeper impact on Hawrani's character than previously thought. Along with the SSNP's desire to end foreign domination in the Levant, it also espoused a radical vision of reform and sought to eradicate feudalism and to establish a secular and socially progressive state.[13] Hawrani embarked on grand schemes to radically alter Syria's political character, and his ideology was not built on the direct influence of Marxism but rather through his own values and interpretation of Arab culture, religion, and perhaps drew on his political experience during his time with the SSNP.[14] The pan-Syrian party had regarded feudalism as a foreign invention that would keep the Arab World socially regressive, and it was Hawrani's war on feudalism that forever changed Syrian society and politics. For the US diplomats in Lebanon, Hawrani's name repeatedly came up in meetings with local power brokers as a potential solution to stem the tide of communism in the Levant. A wealthy landowner remarked to US officials in November 1957 that Hawrani was "no fool, and knew that he had nothing to hope from the Communists." Jumblatt himself also floated Hawrani as an alternative to the block the Soviets influence in Syria.[15]

Despite the triumphs, the UAR experiment would not last. The political repression felt by Syrians under Nasser was far more intense and suffocating than anything previously felt under Shishakli. The Baath and Communist parties were outlawed, and some of its members found support from segments of the Syrian army to implement a coup that toppled the government in Damascus, breaking apart the UAR on September 28, 1961. However, amidst this chaotic environment, there was still a faction within the Baath Party that remained loyal to the idea of preserving Arab unity at any cost. This wing came to resent the party's secessionist faction. Hawrani's political support from within the Baath Party was destroyed when he signed on to the secessionist constitution that formally took Syria out of the UAR. With his name attached to the secessionist movement, Hawrani was never able to politically recover. Historians have suggested that Hawrani was within a hair of becoming Syria's Fidel Castro, but it was not to be. He later sought to re-establish his Arab Socialist Party, but as the neo-Baathist commenced their interparty purges, Hawrani left Syria again for good, living his remaining years in exile in France until his death in 1996.

The breakup of the UAR left Arab nationalists across the region reeling. Nasser retained the UAR name for Egypt and ostracized the new regime in Damascus. Syria was slammed by the Palestinian-dominated Arab Nationalist Movement as a "feudalist-bourgeois alliance." In July 1962, Nasser called for Arab unity and began to focus on empowering the smaller, but agile, hardline nationalist organizations. This in turn gave rise to many of the guerrilla groups, such as the Marxist-Leninist Popular Front for the Liberation of Palestine (PFLP) that appeared in the late 1960s and remained active throughout the 1970s and 1980s.[16]

Created by the British, the Central Treaty Organization (CENTO), or Baghdad Pact, was formed in 1955 and created an anticommunist crescent linking Iran, Iraq, Pakistan, and Turkey. Geostrategically, together they faced up at the soft underbelly of the Soviet Union. The United States jumped in later and joined the Baghdad Pact's military committee in 1958. Nuri Pasha al-Said, the prime minister of the Kingdom of Iraq, was crucial for keeping the Middle East version of NATO tied together. A trusted confident of the British and fierce opponent of Nasser and the Syrian Baathists, Said sought to solidify Iraq as a central outpost for the West and a place where the region could seek to undermine and confront the Nasser menace. However, the Iraqi Hashemite monarchy was deeply unpopular among regular Iraqis. The UAR had astonished and galvanized a new generation of Iraqi political activists and military officers who were tired of the incompetence and corruption of an increasingly shaky regime. Prime Minister Said gambled to keep the forces stacked against him at bay, and a federation with the brotherly Hashemite Kingdom of Jordan was established. A union with Jordan might do well to ward off Nasserism in Iraq. Lebanon, for its part, failed to join Baghdad Pact, but the SSNP still encouraged the Lebanese government to take security measures against Nasser, such as suggesting the country should join the Iraq–Jordan Arab Federation. The party wrote in *al-Binaa* in June 8, 1958:

> Jordan has saved itself from the claws of Nasser and Communism by joining the Federation. As for Lebanon, we appreciate its circumstances and conditions and, therefore, support maintaining its independence within its current liberal state entity. Yet, this position need not rule out devising some new form of Arab and Fertile Crescent cooperation to protect and strengthen Lebanon's independence. There could be no better approach for this than to conclude a defensive alliance with the states of the Federation through which Lebanon could find the strength

and backup it requires after having met from the Arab League only wishy-washy bromides, immobilize, and blind stupidity.[17]

The Iraq–Jordan Arab Federation quickly proved futile. The Nasserist fever had reached segments of the Iraqi army and the Iraqi Baathist movement had also begun to take shape. An army general named Abd al-Karim Qasim and his deputy Colonel Abdul Salam Arif drove their military convoy from their base east of Baghdad through the capital, ostensibly toward the Syrian border in support of Jordan. However, the convoy did not leave Baghdad, stopping instead to launch a coup in what culminated in the July 14 Revolution. The entire family of the Iraqi monarchy was liquidated, and the Baghdad Pact soon lost Baghdad. Alarm spread through the West as uncertainty surrounded Qasim's new regime.

The Western intelligence agencies primarily viewed the Qasim regime as a Soviet-backed force that would align with Nasser. In actuality, Qasim's regime sought to balance its revolutionary outlook with an "Iraq First"-style nationalism that dispelled Nasser and ebbed in the "twilight zone between Communism and a shapeless, anarchic radicalism, resting on no visible organized support and held together largely by the bafflement of all potential challengers,"[18] as put by the late Middle East historian Malcolm H. Kerr. The Eisenhower administration, viewing the loss of British Iraq with a grave concern and embarrassment, decided to make a stand in Lebanon. The SSNP, with its militia mobilized and ready, was set to side with the Chamoun government and take revenge on their Arab nationalist enemies.

The 1958 Lebanon Crisis

The final years of the 1950s saw the SSNP reach a striking partnership with the Lebanese government and political elite that had never before existed. However, this friendship of convenience would prove to be short-lived. Signs of trouble were indeed looming for the party as the first major split occurred in 1957 (as previously mentioned) with the rise of Assad al-Ashqar, a Maronite Christian, to the party leadership. Ashqar had long been in favor of working within the Lebanese political establishment and was even part of the so-called Lebanon School that Antoun Saadeh had purged in 1947, a couple years before his death. Ashqar was known for his staunch anti-leftist outlook and continued to position the dominant faction of the party he won over from Abd Messih as a force against Nasserism in the region.[19]

The beginnings of the SSNP–Chamoun friendship can perhaps be traced back to the early 1940s when the former Lebanese President Beshara Khoury faced massive demonstrations, which resulted in his overthrow during the September 1952 Rosewater Revolution, which Chamoun supported.[20] Although banned, the SSNP played its own role in the background of the demonstrations. The downfall of the Khoury regime in 1952 led to Chamoun's victory in the presidential elections that followed. This opened new horizons for the SSNP. They were tentatively once again permitted back into Lebanon's political sphere. Chamoun also ordered the release of nine SSNP members who were sitting in prison with life sentences for participating in Saadeh's failed 1949 popular uprising. By 1956, the party had re-established itself in Lebanon. The mood had changed significantly in Lebanon since the days of Khoury and al-Solh. Indeed, the party won a seat in the Lebanese Chamber of Deputies in 1957. The deputy, Assad al-Ashqar, sought out an understanding with the Lebanese government, removed the word "Syrian" from the party's name, and altered its transnational character in an effort of appeasement. This riled the George Abd Messih's faction to no end, which retained the full name of the Syrian Social Nationalist Party and declared they were the true party of Saadeh's ideology. This faction, the so-called Intifada (uprising), remained small and marginalized.[21]

However, the main SSNP branch still suffered from internal disputes and disagreements over its conduct regarding the 1957 elections. One example was the expulsion of the famous *An-Nahar* journalist and SSNP member Ghassan Tueini who desired to run as an independent candidate, even though Ashqar urged him to list himself as an SSNP partisan. Tueini had earlier left the party over differences with Antoun Saadeh, but later rejoined after being roused by the party leader's death, and was one of the many SSNP members who served a jail sentence in 1949. Because of his stance on the election, Ashqar dismissed Tueini from the party. Despite this, a US embassy in Beirut dispatch described Tueini as "a brilliant young newspaperman" and, even though he was exiled from the party, his "only handicap is his past connection to the outlawed [SSNP]."[22] Speaking at an SSNP event many years later in 2004, Tueini said, "The party changed a lot after the execution of [Saadeh]." Tueini also acknowledged that the party, in his view, was not always responsible for these changes, which he attributed to the first major split and "the dictatorship" caused by George Abd Messih.[23]

The US Embassy in Beirut struggled to maintain its anti-Nasser political coalition in Lebanon. Its favored candidate, Tueini, faced a tough challenge from Nassim Majdalani, a business figure who hailed from a small but influential family in Beirut.²⁴ Majdalani was also a leader in the Progressive Socialist Party of Kamal Jumblatt. The embassy noted in a 1957 dispatch:

> The contest between Ghassan [Tueini] and Nassim Majdalani for the Greek Orthodox seat in Beirut is likely to be very close. At the moment, Majdalani is believed to be more popular than [Tueini] and may well be elected unless [the Kataeb] should decide to withdraw their candidate, William Hawi, and actively support [Tueini] whom they have opposed so far because of his [SSNP] connections.²⁵

Assad al-Ashqar, in his campaign in the 1957 parliamentary elections, managed to secure his seat in Matn, winning 9,063 votes.²⁶ However, the episode was marked by violence. In what became known as "the battle for Matn," the Kataeb, communists, and the SSNP clashed on election day with three people killed. In addition, Jumblatt traveled to Damascus to consult with Issam al-Mahayri and sought his support for the Maronite leader Raymond Eddé against Kataeb leader Pierre Gemayel.²⁷ Mahayri subsequently released a communique to the SSNP in Lebanon, urging them to throw their weight behind Eddé. Supporters of Eddé were then "mobilized by the SSNP from its Matn stronghold" in Dhour el-Shuwayr.²⁸

Another important figure in the party in Lebanon during the latter half of the 1950s was the SSNP ideologue Said Taqiyaddin, who came from a prominent Druze family in the Chouf and graduated from AUB in 1925. Referred to as a "Druze man of letters," he gained a positive reputation for his writings in Arabic and English. He spent a significant amount of his early life in the Philippines and was imprisoned by the Japanese forces during the Second World War. Taqiyaddin and his family repatriated back to Lebanon in 1948, and he escaped the purges that followed Saadeh's death in July 1949. Like many SSNP party members, Taqiyaddin was active in other sectors of Lebanese society, especially by serving as the president of AUB's Alumni Association until 1952. His duties included reaching out to former students and soliciting money for the university. One example of this was when he wrote to former SSNP member Fayez Sayegh in 1949 and pestered him about paying back his student loan.²⁹ He was a strong advocate for the Palestinians and favored the SSNP's secular and antifeudal platform. Taqiyaddin described how he joined the party:

> When a perfect stranger approached me and thrust in my hand "The Principles of the Syrian Social Nationalist Party," I discovered in that pamphlet a workable blue print for my vision; I promptly joined up. Here's an organization which is really worthy of the name. It is purposive and dynamic.³⁰

A self-styled intellectual and visionary, Taqiyaddin believed that Lebanon's system was built on unstable foundations and foresaw some of the country's future violence:

> There is little doubt in my mind that Lebanon will shortly be a target of a hurricane of destruction and will be drenched in a torrent of blood unless something is done drastically and quickly. Talk to any one of our so called leaders and the conversation usually ends in a hilarious wisecrack or a funny anecdote. Rome was at its wittiest best when on the point of collapsing, and the Arabs produced their best love poetry while they were being kicked out of Spain.[31]

Although a party comrade, Taqiyaddin never held any official title in the SSNP's organization and was described as a "consultant."[32] However, he was one of Syria's main targets for assassination, most likely for taking part in the coup meetings with Salah Shishakli in 1956. He had been sentenced to death in absentia in Damascus and constantly moved from location to location, never staying more than one night in the same place. The US Embassy in Beirut reported on a spate of bombings in October and November 1957 and noted that local press said these attacks were targeting the SSNP's offices.[33] A pro-Nasser attack on his home saw a bomb explode (with no injuries reported) in May 1958.[34] Later on, he left Lebanon and retired to San Andres, an island territory of Colombia. He died in February 1960. His daughter described him as a "symbol of what Lebanon could be if there were more dedicated idealists like him."

The main faction of the SSNP would take its place as a crucial part of the anti-leftist or anticommunist front against the Baathist–Communist coalition in Syria, as well as during the advent of the UAR. A communique from the SSNP in 1958 illustrated the defensive nature of the pan-Syrian movement's thinking:

> Nearly four years ago, Egyptian apparatuses, backed by International Communism, began to prepare and direct a number of police actions in the Republic of Syria, aiming at the liquidation of the mature, anti-communist, nationalist elements, which forms an invincible wall in the face of all foreign expansions in Syria…the Party…engaged in widespread battles against communist infiltration allied with Nasser's expansion in Syria, Lebanon, and Jordan.[35]

According to Andrew Rathmell, the party leadership did not actually believe it could successfully topple the Syrian regime, but rather sought to keep Damascus "off balance."[36] However, George Abd Messih's smaller faction differed, taking a much less confrontational approach. He emphasized a need to focus on ideology and told the party newspaper *al-Jil al-Jadid* in August 1958:

> It is not the duty of the Syrian Social Nationalist Movement to fight the insurgents or take part in a pointless struggle between groups and individuals in our people ... but to remain on guard and dedicated to the struggle to arouse the awareness of every citizen to the truth of the Syrian Social Nationalist (ideology). It is not its duty to support one faction against another or to fight for the victory of one group over another.[37]

After being driven from Syria in the wake of the 1955 Malki assassination and further hounded by Syrian intelligence chief Sarraj for the subsequent "Iraqi Plot" in 1956, the SSNP took its own steps to disrupt Sarraj's intelligence activities within Lebanon. In one incident, the party intercepted and held hostage two Syrian operatives who had infiltrated the SSNP-dominated village of Dhur Shuwayr. It took the intervention of the Lebanese government to strong-arm the SSNP into releasing the men after Syrian Defense Minister Rashad Barmada pressured Beirut into doing so. In addition, the SSNP had established an armed militia (which dated back to the 1930s) that allegedly fielded some 3,000 fighters. Iraq's monarchy also still maintained connections and supported the SSNP weapons and financial assistance.[38] Violence and political unrest rocked Lebanon during this period as a coalition of leftist forces and pan-Arabs sought greater influence in the country's ruling power structure. Chamoun and his supporters embraced a pro-Western outlook and kept in close contact with the Eisenhower administration. Chamoun's primary ally, Naim Moghabghab, helped formulate a united front as the Lebanese government sought to ward off their increasingly assertive foe, the Druze powerbroker: Kamal Jumblatt. The northern city of Tripoli was especially the scene of bloody clashes between the communists, Lebanese Baathists, and Jumblatt's Progressive Socialist Party (PSP).

The SSNP in 1957 through 1958 saw its back up against the wall with the onslaught of Arab nationalism. Yamak wrote:

> Its hard anti-communist line put it in the forefront of the political struggle in Lebanon. In fact, during the events of the summer of 1958, it was, along with the [Kataeb], the only organized group that supported the Chamoun regime. However, it must be noted that whereas the [Kataeb] defended the regime because of its deep-seated commitment to Lebanon as an independent political entity, the SSNP did so primarily because an independent and pro-Western Lebanon was its only refuge ... it is certainly justifiable, given the circumstances that surrounded the party during those troubled months in 1958, to maintain

that the party's actions during that period were motivated less by its loyalty to Lebanon's independence than by its desire for self-preservation. A victory by the 'rebels' would have meant its outright liquidation.[39]

In addition to this, Samir Khalaf pointed out the contrast in involvement in the 1958 crisis between the two parties and indicated the SSNP "assumed the brunt of the heavy fighting, often waging battles and provoking confrontations of their own in virtually all arenas of conflict. On the whole, the [Kataeb's] involvements were limited to Beirut and the Christian strongholds of Mount Lebanon."[40]

In May 1957, Jumblatt had declared Chamoun's government to be akin to a "police state," and fighting occurred in several towns in villages across the Chouf. Vicious battles took place in Tripoli and eventually reached the presidential palace at Bayt-ad-Deen. A detachment of loyalist Druze troops broke away from the government side as Druze leaders sought to achieve reconciliation with their co-religionists within the rebel forces, leaving the Chamounists to rely even further on the SSNP and the followers of Naim Moghabghab.[41] Baath Party leader Michel Aflaq took matters further. The US embassy expressed alarm in a June 1957 telegram commenting on an editorial he wrote in the party's organ, *al-Baath*. The embassy characterized the editorial as evidence of a popular awakening and discovery of a revolutionary tradition that forces rulers to follow police state methods of killing citizens in the streets as in Jordan, Iraq, and which "may lose king or ruler but wins people." Aflaq went on to blast the French attack on Algeria for trying to "dismember Africa" and Western imperialists for creating Israel to destroy Arab unity, and lauded the Jordanian crisis from the year prior for shaking imperialism to the point where "leaders of imperial [sic], the U.S., divulged its aggressive and imperialist character in a cheap and open manner when it mobilized funds, and its navy to withstand a small country like Jordan."[42]

In December 1957, the SSNP's office in Tripoli was attacked and burned. The Lebanese army was deployed to restore order but struggled as the city became a central hub for anti-Western, pro-Nasser activity. Mosques preached Arab unity, and many Sunni Muslims in the city advocated for Lebanon to enter the UAR. In the Beqaa Valley, the SSNP faced further setbacks. There the party had a military training camp and operated a radio station called the "Voice of Reform."[43] In February 1958, the US Embassy described the fierce clashes around the town of Zghorta, with local forces digging trenches, and remarked, "Clearly [the] government [was] confronted with serious internal security [problems.]"[44] A rebel force led by Sabri Hamadeh, the Shia Lebanese speaker of parliament close to Nasser and backed by weapons and supplies from Syria, launched a prolonged assault on the SSNP's Beqaa stronghold in May 1958. The SSNP had a sizable force in the area but, in the face of the overwhelming logistical support from the Syrian branch of the UAR to the local rebels, the party could not hold on. Its fighters were routed and many of them were tracked down and killed. Others were able to escape to government-held areas.[45] Many buildings and local economic institutions throughout Lebanon, such as the Iraq Petroleum Company, suffered from shelling and fighting with heavy weapons.

Throughout the 1958 crisis, Yamak described the party as having fought with distinction and followed and executed orders so precisely they "startled most observers." He elaborated further:

> Foreign correspondents who covered the Lebanese rebellion of 1958 were greatly impressed with the fighting ability and the discipline of the SSNP. In describing a battle between the SSNP militia and the rebels one correspondent wrote, "For the first time I have seen men going really to fight … they were civilians—members of the SSNP—who fought with faith and determination against the rebels who greatly outnumbered them." *Le Figaro* (Paris), July 2, 1958. Another correspondent reported that "…150 members of the SSNP, supported by seventy Lebanese gendarmes, attacked [the town of] Ainab and engaged the rebels in a battle. In less than an hour the rebels were forced to retreat." *The New York Times*, July 4, 1958.[46]

However, violence continued despite the US efforts of diplomacy. The Sunni leader, Prime Minister Rashid Karami, selected several prominent opposition figures for the Lebanese government's cabinet, and the kidnapping of an editor from the Kataeb Party's newspaper, *al-Amal*, only added toward the tension. The Kataeb and the SSNP disobeyed orders to stand down, and fighting lasted well into October 1958, which some historians called "the most violent phase of the conflict."[47] Ultimately, Chehab's administration decided to form a government that would include Lebanon's rebel factions. In October 1958, a session of parliament saw Kamal Jumblatt decry the Christian-dominated elite class and demanded a greater representation. Chehab promised compromise, reform, and stability.[48] In 1960, Lebanon began to tentatively recover and the economy endured a boost in the country's commercial, financial, and tourist sectors.

However, before the final demise of the UAR, Nasser still targeted the SSNP for scathing criticism, such as he did in an early 1960 speech in Aleppo, Syria. "We all know how colonialism used to rely on a little group which denied its Arabism and its country, calling itself the 'Syrian Nationalists.'" Nasser went on to describe the party as being guilty of taking money from Western powers and said "if colonialism depends on groups like that ... we can sleep quietly because we know them already."[49] The SSNP in turn blasted Nasser for his "rancorous factious accusations" and said the UAR was "fabricated and improvised," going against the very "nature and logic of history." It concluded, "[the SSNP] expects the bond of union to part, as happens when ambitions clash and intentions are exposed." The SSNP also lamented that Nasser's "positive work" went against the interests of Syria and Egypt.[50] More broadly, anti-Nasserism continued to play out in Lebanon with assaults on his supporters. Tensions would continue after the crisis into the 1960s. On March 5, 1961, a convoy of Arab nationalists was on its way to Damascus to show support to Nasser when it was attacked as it passed through the village of Kahale.[51]

The 1961 New Year's Eve Coup

It was not long after the 1958 crisis that the conditions for a coup plot in Lebanon began to take shape. The United States brokered a power-sharing agreement between the Lebanese General Fuad Chehab and Rashid Karami. After the intervention of the US military and the end of the 1958 crisis, Lebanon once again underwent a political transformation under the regime headed by General Chehab. The SSNP was by now well acquainted with Chehab, having supported him during the Rosewater Revolution that toppled President Khoury. The general had refused the president's order to deploy the army to intervene against the widely popular demonstrations. Said Taqiyaddin had spoken positively of Chehab during this time and later wrote in 1957 that he believed Chehab would emerge to guide Lebanon through the crisis and succeed.[52]

However, the feeling of warmth wasn't entirely mutual. Fuad Chehab's own military experience included his pursuit of the SSNP in the summer of 1949 when he commanded troops during the government's crackdown on the party that followed the Jummayziah incident. The new president's strategy for stabilizing Lebanon sought to accommodate and include the various rebel factions into the government, something the SSNP opposed. Chehab also ignored the SSNP's demands to retaliate against members of the Lebanese civil service who were sympathetic to the rebels.[53] The party also felt marginalized and ostracized in the Lebanese political sphere, having made little gains for its role in supporting the government in 1958. Furthermore, under the Chehab regime, the SSNP faced a renewed bout of intimidation, arrests, and police raids on its offices.[54]

The government tightened the screws where it could, even beyond the scope of the SSNP. The Lebanese newspaper *An-Nahar* featured a political cartoon that depicted Lebanon as a province of Syria. This led to the government to suspend the paper for ten days in May 1961.[55]

One rising SSNP member, Inaam Raad, did not win in the Lebanese parliamentary election of 1958. This was allegedly due to the Lebanese security forces' attempts to hinder his campaign. President Chehab jailed many of Raad's supporters during the day of the election and also tried to block his campaign's convoy from reaching his village in Ain Zhalta. The same obstructions occurred again during the election of 1960. These electoral losses left the party with a deep sense of humiliation. Raad himself began to form a favorable view of the Soviet Union. Believing the Lebanese government and the United States were responsible for the country's troubles and for supporting Israel, he wrote articles in *al-Binaa* to advocate these views.[56] As will be seen, under his later leadership in the 1970s, Raad became instrumental in the SSNP's transformative shift toward the political left. Soviet Ambassador Nicola Crabvin began holding meetings with Raad and established ties with the party.[57]

Abdullah Saadeh (no relation to the party's founder) took the helm from Abdullah Mohsen as the SSNP's president on July 28, 1960. Dr. Saadeh was from the Greek Orthodox community, hailed from northern Lebanon and once worked as a medical doctor in Saudi Arabia where he helped found two hospitals, one in the city of Jeddah and the other in Dhahran. He was known for his oratory and open criticism of the Lebanese government. The SSNP under Dr. Saadeh's leadership viewed the government as having failed to radically reform the old guard and being too accommodating with the structure of the confessional system fostered by the National Pact and had not properly reformed the country in the wake of the violence of 1958. He outlined his views of the challenges facing the party in his memoir:

> When I assumed the presidency of the party, its internal situation was critical. All the complications of the crisis in 1958 and the contradictions they had bequeathed between the party and the [Muslim] groups on the one hand, and the reservations in Christian circles that were entailed on the other side, were bearing down with all their weight on the party despite the major role it had played in the past. Having fought with fervor in 1958, the party members were disturbed by the unfolding complications derived from that conflict and by the intractable Christian and Muslim groups and their struggle for political power in Lebanon, not to speak of the quiet but unremitting way the regime was continuing to wear down the party with its discreet oppression.[58]

Dr. Saadeh adopted a hostile stance toward Chehab's government saying, "We believe that Lebanon today needs a genuine revolution, unlike that which flared as a bloody dispute between feudalists or as violence between sectarian groups, but rather, a constructive social revolution that would not demand a bloodbath as its price, but rather growth and consciousness." In return, the Lebanese government blocked Dr. Saadeh from speaking at a commemorative event celebrating the life of Said Taqiyaddin.[59] This shifting stance of the government toward the SSNP occurred as Chehab's government tried to maintain cordial terms with the UAR. Nasser had identified the SSNP as one of the "leading groups of Lebanon fighting the UAR union," and pro-Nasser press in Beirut regularly published stories attacking the party. According to Adel Beshara, these events brought about the highest level of tension and mistrust between the SSNP and the Lebanese government since the days of Antoun Saadeh's struggle with the Khoury regime in the late 1940s.[60]

A cabal of officers within the Lebanese Armed Forces had been wary of Chehab's political ambitions as early as 1956. The junior officers included Captain Shawki Khairallah and Nabih Ni'meh, who were entrusted by Dr. Saadeh, and Captain Fuad Awad, who became affiliated with the party in 1947. The group of army officers began meeting regularly with the SSNP to discuss the possibility of a coup in Lebanon. In September 1961, a coup in Syria abruptly took Damascus out of the UAR, an event that boosted the morale of the Lebanese coup plotters. Captain Awad may have had his own reasons for bringing down Chehab. The two men were somewhat close —Chehab had praised Awad on more than one occasion over his military peers—but when Chehab, on an unannounced inspection visit, scolded Awad, even slapped him in front of the other officers, for a scuffle over how the tanks were deployed in Tyre (Awad's station at the time), Awad did not take it lightly. The incident may have been the drive behind Awad's motivation to carry out the coup, of course, along with being affiliated with the SSNP. However, Awad maintained some relative distance from the SSNP since he was not ideologically involved or, as he put it, even "politically compatible with the party." Later in life, Awad often remarked that he was never completely in line with the SSNP, but never attempted to fully disassociate himself from the party. His family believed that he was more involved in the party's underground operations and that perhaps he had been forced in that direction rather than by his own choice."[61]

The SSNP's top leadership bodies, the Council of Commissioners and Supreme Council, debated the matter at Assad al-Ashqar's home.[62] The SSNP felt trapped and, as a secular party, locked out of the Lebanese confessional system.

Although the party's leadership acknowledged that a full-scale revolution against Chehab was out of the question since the majority of the Lebanese population did not seem to mind his policies, the current trajectory of the government was having an overtly negative impact on the SSNP. They believed that time was of the essence. However, a group of SSNP leaders still felt the plan was too risky and feared the conditions for a backlash were high and resigned in protest.[63] Regardless of these concerns, the Supreme Council tentatively gave the green light to Dr. Saadeh to move forward with the operation.

In October of 1961, the first of several meetings between the junior army officers and Dr. Saadeh occurred in different locations, including a rendezvous inside of a car. Secrecy was of the upmost concern since Chehab's security apparatus was closely monitoring the party's movements. Party members were deployed on secret diplomatic assignments to Jordan and Iraq to gain support for the coup. The SSNP dispatched its own representative, the party's spokesperson, Inaam Raad, to Baghdad in order to ascertain whether Iraq's strongman, Abd al-Karim Qasim, would back their gamble. Adel Beshara noted in a 1997 meeting with Raad in Melbourne, Australia, that Raad had used his cover as part of a delegation of Lebanese journalists with the Correspondence Association to Baghdad and met with Qasim in person.[64] Despite these efforts, none of the regional countries agreed to support the coup plot. The SSNP also tried a rapprochement with the new anti-UAR secessionist regime in Syria, as well as tried to win the freedom of their party comrades still languishing in Syrian jails in the aftermath of the Malki Affair, but failed to secure either goal.[65]

The coup itself can be described as a "comedy of errors." The plot was both elaborate but poorly planned. It involved kidnapping President Chehab from the presidential palace, seizing the broadcasting station, capturing the Ministry of Defense, detaining several key political and military figures, and, in the event of a major setback, the conspirators would retreat to Assad al-Ashqar's home village of Dik al-Mahdi in the Matn District.[66] December 31 was chosen as the date of the coup since many senior military leaders and army officers would be on leave to celebrate New Year's Eve. The plan was now in motion. The SSNP and its army allies went all in with a dramatic and risky gamble to change Lebanon's political dynamics in their favor. At 2:15 a.m. on the 31st, Captain Awad left his base in the southern city of Tyre and led his company to Beirut by feigning that Kamal Jumblatt and pro-UAR elements in the army were staging a coup. At first, the operation seemed successful. Several loyalist army officers were arrested and telecommunication lines linking Beirut to the south were severed.[67]

However, the plot started to collapse after about ten hours into the operation when the SSNP and army teams attempting to capture the Ministry of Defense were met with significant resistance from loyalist forces. A battle erupted as the Chehab-aligned troops held the upstairs levels and the rebels held the outside square and the ministry's ground floor. The rebels tried to talk the army officers upstairs into surrendering but failed to win them over. Furthermore, the plan to kidnap Chehab also fell through when two rebel squads failed to link up on time and lost a precious thirty minutes, thereby alerting the guards at the palace that a coup was underway. When the rebel forces at the Defense Ministry found out the president had not been secured, they tried to retreat but were largely cut off from escape with the arrival of government reinforcements.

Captain Awad knew the coup had failed. He wrote in his memoir:

> There was no unity of leadership. The [SSNP] leader thought that I could deliver power to it on a silver platter. And I in my turn was far more confident than I should have been in the armed civilian squads, which had been assigned some tasks. Up until late afternoon, Sunday 31 December, Dr. Saadeh still supposed that I had the Defense Ministry in my control, although I had left it after ordering my troops to surrender.[68]

By 7:00 a.m. of January 1, 1962, the army issued a radio statement indicating the rebel's coup attempt had failed. The full extent of the plan began to reveal itself. Some of the Lebanese army troops aligned with the rebels had not even known the true nature of their orders. In addition, some members of the SSNP had already informed the Deuxieme Bureau of the plot in advance. Dr. Saadeh's driver, Riyad Darwish, and SSNP veteran Fadlallah Abu Mansour had been promised clemency in exchange for information. Ultimately, the coup's failure led to a renewed effort by the government to completely repress the SSNP in Lebanon.

Second Purge in Lebanon

The SSNP tried to hold out in Dik al-Mahdi but eventually surrendered to the Lebanese army units that surrounded and shelled the area. A report from the *New York Times* described the events on January 3, 1962:

> Lebanese security forces completed today the occupation of the mountains northeast of Beirut, where insurgent Right-Wing forces were believed strong. The village of [Dik al-Mahdi], which was shelled yesterday was entirely subdued,

according to an official announcement. About 400 more persons were arrested in the last twenty-four hours. The arrests of 1,195 were announced yesterday. Most of them were members or followers of the Popular Syrian party (a common misnomer for the SSNP), which has been officially dissolved in Lebanon. A communique said six members of the Rightist group were killed when they tried to escape during a search following Saturday night's unsuccessful coup.[69]

Although George Abd Messih's Intifada faction had kept its distance from the coup, it allowed the main branch SSNP members to find refuge and protection from arrest in Abd Messih's home village of Beit Mery.[70] Meanwhile, the Lebanese government hailed the savvy of its intelligence services. One photo caption described Colonel Antoun Saad, the chief of the Second Bureau, as "the fox" of the Lebanese counterintelligence. It remarked that "as early as September 1961, his flair and perspicacity allowed him to be informed of the next coup d'état by the [SSNP]…he attacked his prey with rare rapacity. Lebanon is still alive thanks to the modesty of this Lebanese intelligence service officer who worked silently to preserve the country's life."[71]

Shawki Kairallah was arrested in Beirut on January 11, wearing a disguise of dark glasses with his mustache shaved off.[72] Over 4,000 people were arrested in the security sweep. Awad was captured on January 20 hiding in the trunk of a car in the southern city of Sidon at a military checkpoint.[73] Despite the victory, President Chehab was rattled by the coup attempt. The Lebanese government and the local press casted a wide circle of blame for the plot, even beyond the SSNP, alleging the British and their Jordanian allies, or Iraq, were also complicit.[74] Jumblatt placed the blame for the coup on the British, alleging the coup was carried out in conjunction with the British fleet's maneuvers.[75] However, the Royal Navy had orchestrated drills in the Persian Gulf, not the Mediterranean Sea. The UAR also blamed the British. The staunchly pro-Nasser journalist Mohamed Hassanein Heikal published an article in the Egyptian newspaper *al-Ahram* on January 5 that slammed the British as part of an elaborate conspiracy, involving "the three musketeers," the SSNP, Hashemite Jordan, and the Baghdad Pact.[76] However, Western ambassadors were quick to point out the allegations were false. No evidence ever surfaced of any involvement by the British or the other Arab states in the coup attempt.

The evidence against the SSNP itself was damning. Subsequent publications blasted the party as a conspiratorial group of misfits with deep roots across the whole country. A French-language map presented the total number of SSNP followers in Lebanon as 25,000, plus an additional 3,500 followers overseas. The map's breakdown put 4,500 members in northern Lebanon, 5,000 in Mount Lebanon, 5,500 in and around Beirut, 6,250 in the Bekaa Valley, and 3,750 in southern Lebanon.[77] Security officials also released images of the rebel's captured weapons, which included a large batch of Sterling submachine guns, MAS-36 French carbines rifles (which were widely used by the French during their colonial wars in the 1950s), Bren machine guns, along with crates of ammunition containing British 303-caliber bullets.[78]

The indictment released by the Lebanese government listed the conspirators as four army officers, two retired officers, ninety soldiers, twelve policemen, 323 civilians—including twenty Palestinians and fifty-four Syrians. From this group, thirty-eight army personnel and 262 civilians were charged and found guilty, eleven had been killed during the coup attempt, and the others "granted a stay of trial."[79] Judge Emile Abou Kheir intervened to classify the coup attempt as a "political crime," a move that the military tribunal was opposed to since they were seeking the death penalty for the top conspirators. President Chehab sided with Judge Kheir and, at the conclusion of the trial in November 1963, the party men were sentenced to hard labor in prison.[80] One SSNP member remarked that his father stood outside with hundreds of others in several feet of snow in the open-air football stadium in Beirut after being rounded up by the Lebanese security forces.[81] Indeed, a British embassy dispatch, discussing the aftermath of the coup, noted the lack of available space in Lebanon's prisons and said, "In the absence of proper facilities to deal with the present huge influx of prisoners, a small arena at the Beirut athletic grounds has been turned into an emergency detention center. Conditions there are, according to rumor, appalling."[82]

The party in Lebanon was again driven underground. Its membership allegedly dropped from 25,000 to just a few thousand after the coup attempt. During the 1964 elections, they were unable to field any candidates, but some sources indicated the party maintained a close relationship with Dr. Albert Mukhaiber, who secured a seat representing the SSNP's stronghold in North Matn.[83] The security purge was so extensive that other political movements also fell victim to Chehab's crackdown, including the Islamic Tahrir Party and the Lebanese Communist Party.[84] The SSNP would eventually emerge from prison in the late 1960s, shedding much of its hostility toward communism, and, with the region reeling from the defeat of the conventional armies of Jordan, Egypt, and Syria in the Six-Day War of 1967, worked to implant itself in the rising militant movements. It was here the SSNP found a common ground upon which to bridge the gap between its Syrian nationalism with Arab nationalism, paving the way for an understanding with the ruling Baath Party in Damascus. As the

Arab Cold War faded into the distance, the SSNP leaped onto the bandwagon of revolutionary fervor, locking arms with the Palestinian guerrillas, and the stage was set in Lebanon for the Middle East's next round of terrible conflict in 1975, one whose scale and destruction would dwarf the 1958 crisis and last for fifteen long years.

Figure 2 Antoun Saadeh, the SSNP's deeply revered founder. He was executed by a Lebanese firing squad before dawn on July 8, 1949. Public domain.

Figure 3 Antoun Saadeh with his followers in 1949. Photo courtesy of Sami Moubayed.

Figure 4 Party members wait for the arrival of Antoun Saadeh's plane in Beirut on his return from exile in March 1947. George Abd Messih is underneath the flag wearing the white keffiyeh. (This image from Alamy is also featured on the book's cover.)

Figure 5 Issam al-Mahayri (right), the first SSNP member to obtain a seat in Syria's parliament, 1954. Photo courtesy of Sami Moubayed.

Figure 6 The party suffered a harsh crackdown in Syria after the 1955 assassination of Adnan al-Malki. Here is Issam al-Mahayri (second from the right) in Mezzeh Prison in Damascus, walking along with fellow inmates who were members of the banned Armenian Dashnak Party, 1957. Photo courtesy of Sami Moubayed.

Figure 7 "Antoun Saadeh – March 1, Birth of the National Consciousness." The party's founder's profile featured in this wartime poster from the 1970s, along with an outline of Greater Syria. Courtesy of www.signsofconflict.com and Abboudi Bou Jawde.

Figure 8 Waseem Zineddine, known by his nom de guerre, Abou Wajib (the father of duty), mysteriously killed on May 23, 1975. Courtesy of www.signsofconflict.com and Abboudi Bou Jawde.

Figure 9 SSNP martyrs who fell in the battle of northern Matn, December 1986. Courtesy of www.signsofconflict.com.

Figure 10 SSNP comrade Sanaa Mehaidli, the Bride of the South, widely believed to be the first female suicide bomber, who carried out her attack on April 9, 1985. A poster honoring her memory in Lebanon's Chouf mountains. The SSNP's logo (top right) is featured with the insignia of the Jammoul resistance group (top left) formed in response to the Israeli intervention in Lebanon. Photo courtesy of Paul Keller.

6

Broken Country, Fractured Party: The SSNP and the Lebanese Civil War in the 1970s

Amid the ruins of war-torn Beirut, the SSNP maneuvered within the violent ebb and flow of the country's civil strife. With the number of dead ranging from 120,000 to 150,000, the wanton destruction of Lebanon's infrastructure and political order transformed the party as much as it transformed Lebanon itself. A chain of historical events in the Levant also shaped the SSNP's trajectory. The defeat of the Arab forces in the 1967 Six-Day War brought about an intense shock to the party. In addition, President Hafez al-Assad cemented his power in Damascus with the so-called Corrective Movement, the intra-Baathist coup of November 1970. During the war's latter phase in the 1980s, Assad sought out to procure his own use of the SSNP as part of his geostrategic gambit against Israel.

Inaam Raad, along with Abdullah Saadeh, led the party's main faction through Lebanon's fifteen years of brutal civil war, a period that left a permanent mark on the SSNP as it engaged in urban fighting, guerrilla warfare, suicide operations, and assassinations. The 1970s saw the party endure several splits and form new alliances, a trend that was part of the SSNP's recalibration on the traditional right-left spectrum toward the left. Raad came to represent this new calculated leftist tilt and the formation of a military alliance between the SSNP and the Palestinian Liberation Organization (PLO). The civil war era, in many ways, embodies a murky period of history for the SSNP, with the details on the internal party feuds, splits, shadowy operations, and instances of violence remaining thoroughly unexplored in Western research on the party during this era. To the party's critics, the West, and Israel, the 1970s and 1980s also marked the SSNP's upmost embrace of radicalism and, in their view, the continuation of the SSNP's embrace of its violent nature, either directly authoring or taking part in high-profile assassination plots and acts of terrorism.[1]

The SSNP that revived following its spell in prison was a party that was both reborn and able to retain its core irredentist character all at once. A gap of a few years from the late 1960s to the start of the war in April 1975 gave most of the party leaders time to reconnoiter their new world before the country was plunged into the most destructive conflict it had faced in the modern era. With the Arab Cold War behind it, the SSNP embraced its place in the pan-Arab landscape while still retaining its Syrian nationalist character. It was perhaps curious that the SSNP, long viewed up until this point by outside observers as a right-wing, anticommunist force that had resisted the region's prevailing decree of Arabism, now aligned itself squarely with the leftist coalition of the Lebanese National Movement (LNM) and the PLO. The SSNP subsequently surfaced from its torrid experience of political persecution during the years of the 1960s and attempted to shed the reputation that had long hampered their popularity with the majority of the Arab street.

Prewar Activities

During the 1960s, Beirut had become a haven for leftist intellectuals and political activists fleeing persecution from authoritarian regimes around the region.[2] At the start of the decade, Lebanon's youth embraced Arab nationalism and were especially active. Student demonstrations and strikes in support of Arab nationalist causes elsewhere in the Middle East were commonplace. AUB students, in particular, took the lead in orchestrating politically motivated demonstrations such as the celebration of the Algerian independence movement (December 1960), marking the anniversary of the United Arab Republic (February 22, 1961), and protesting the Lebanese government's violation of the sanctity of the Palestinian refugee camps (March 1963).[3] It was within this environment of protest, strife, and solidarity with the plight of the Palestinians that the SSNP found its footing.

In addition, by the early 1970s, the state security architecture established by President Fuad Chehab during the 1960s had withered significantly. The Chehabist era had been successful in stymying the activities of Lebanon's political parties that existed outside of the mainstream. After Chehab, the Lebanese government's ability to balance the sectarian groups and regional interests had declined.[4] It was under President Suleiman Frangieh that the Lebanese government's attempt to merge the country's divide failed.

In 1969, the SSNP, while still officially banned after the 1961 New Year's Eve coup debacle, found a way back into Lebanon's turbulent political climate. It was the Progressive Socialist Party (PSP) of Kamal Jumblatt that was instrumental in revitalizing the SSNP prior to the Lebanese Civil War. Described as "baffling enigma" and an "aristocratic power broker" by the *Washington Post* in 1977,[5] Jumblatt's party was undergoing its own period of renewal and strength. From 1965 onward, the Druze-dominated movement had seen its membership increase from not only within the working class and the economically disenfranchised segments of Lebanese society, largely Druze and Shia, but also recruiting Lebanese Sunnis. The PSP had positioned itself as an "agent of change." In addition, the PSP witnessed the Baath Party's successful power grabs in Iraq and Syria and recognized the anti-imperialist sentiments popular in the region as a harbinger for Lebanon.[6] However, it was the alliance with the Palestinians that made the PSP the dominant power broker on the Lebanese left. With the military might of the well-armed and politically assertive PLO fully behind it, Jumblatt's PSP fastened itself in the conflict as the vanguard of the LNM.

Pressure from the PSP eventually lessened the government's animosity toward the SSNP. In 1969 through 1970, the SSNP's partisans were released from prison and had finalized their evaluation of the party's future that they pondered during their time behind bars. The SSNP was ready to embrace both the PSP and its old nemesis, the Lebanese Communist Party, due to a convergence of ideological and political platforms. This consisted of the SSNP's interest in Arab self-determination via the Palestinian cause, which had been amplified in the wake of the 1967 war, and also the opportunity to obtain an avenue back into Lebanon's political sphere. The SSNP had its own long shared personal history with the PSP. One of the founding members of the PSP was Jamil Abdou Sawaya, who was in Antoun Saadeh's first batch of recruits when he founded the SSNP at AUB. Sawaya left the SSNP for the PSP in 1947.[7] Furthermore, the parties shared the same constituencies and both had long embraced an anticolonial, revolutionary outlook. In December 1969, Kamal Jumblatt, in his role as Lebanon's Interior Minister, gave the green light for an assortment of illegal and ideological parties to resume activity. This amnesty included the SSNP, the communists, the Arab Nationalist Movement, and the Lebanese Baath Party, along with the Armenian Dashnak.[8] In 1972, the Soviet Union awarded Jumblatt the Lenin Peace Prize for his efforts.

The party's spokesperson, Inaam Raad, was among the SSNP's ranking comrades released from prison. Born in 1929, Inaam Raad was an Anglican Christian hailing from Ain Zhalta, a village in the Chouf Mountains. As a youth, Raad asked his father to help identify a political doctrine that fought sectarianism, divisionism, and colonialism. His father subsequently directed him to the SSNP, and he joined the party in 1944.[9] In Raad's long history with the SSNP, he was among the first to welcome Antoun Saadeh off the plane on the tarmac when the party's late founder had returned from exile in 1947 where he led the "partisan cry" shouting "Long live Syria, long live Saadeh" at the welcoming celebration. He was also among the party members who were rounded up and jailed by the government in the wake of the 1949 uprising launched by Saadeh. Raad personified the SSNP's shift to the left during the Lebanese Civil War period. Raad, along with Abdullah Saadeh, who was re-elected party president in May 1969, led the main faction of the SSNP through the civil war years.

There was also a personal camaraderie that existed between Raad and Jumblatt,[10] and Raad soon found himself in the role as the vice president of the LNM. Furthermore, the SSNP had been under intense pressure from its old enemy on the right, the Kataeb Party, which continued its attacks on party members during the late 1960s and into the early 1970s. The danger was great enough that the SSNP leadership ordered its partisans to withdraw from the Kataeb-dominated areas and fully throw its weight behind the LNM's war effort.[11] This coalition of largely leftist and radical parties faced off against the Christian and conservative elements of the Lebanese political elite. A series of clashes, massacres, and retaliations escalated into open warfare in April 1975.

The origins of the SSNP's political transition trace back to the year leading up to the failed coup attempt. As mentioned in Chapter 5, Raad had previously initiated an overture with the Soviet Union prior to the 1961 New Year's Eve coup attempt. This move was not entirely unusual since an even earlier leftist trend had existed within the party, mainly with the so-called Lebanon School, a faction within the party more focused on socioeconomic issues, advocating for the SSNP to set aside its irredentist Greater Syria mission, and investing more attention to the people's immediate needs. Raad had written an article in the SSNP's organ, *al-Binaa*, titled "Regarding Closer Relations with the Soviets," published on December 18, 1960, which he later said had struck the party "like a political bombshell."[12] In his article, Raad laid out his view that the United States had foregone the Arabs in support of Israel and argued "the enemy of my enemy is my friend" in favor of aligning the SSNP with the Soviet Union. This was a stark departure from the party's earlier battles fought by both intellectuals and in the streets with the Lebanese Communist Party. Furthermore, he stressed that Israel was on course for developing nuclear weapons, and, therefore, the "Jewish danger" (*khatr al-yahudi*) was a far greater threat than communism. He acknowledged that there were inherent contradictions between nationalism and communism, but stated the two did not necessarily have to adopt or compromise their beliefs, but rather, the SSNP should take advantage of the Soviet Union's standoff with the United States and use it to the party's benefit. The SSNP could not continue fighting the old battles of the 1950s but had to adapt and fight the threats they faced in the new era.[13]

Prior to the 1961 coup attempt, Soviet Ambassador Crabvin visited the offices of *al-Binaa* and asked Raad whether the opinion he expressed in the article was his own or the party's official position. Raad coyly replied, based on his conviction that such relations would benefit to the party, "Do you not see that this is the official party newspaper, so do I have a personal opinion beyond that of the official party position?" However, the Soviet diplomat asked another party member the same question, who replied that Raad was merely the newspaper's editor and that the party's High Council had not made any declaration of this sort. Raad dismissed this answer as "a technocrat lacking political savvy."[14]

The SSNP's High Council subsequently reprimanded him for promoting a political course of action that had not been discussed or decided upon, which was a violation of the party's constitution. Raad acknowledged the High Council was technically correct, but insisted it was the right position politically and looking ahead. The party's president, Abdullah Saadeh, upon his return from a trip abroad, voiced his support for the Higher Council's reprimand, but agreed with Raad that the article was an important political breakthrough and an opportunity. They decided to "leak" the content of the article to the Soviet Embassy, claiming it was the official party position in the hopes of moving the potential relationship forward. Abdullah Saadeh did not mention this event in his memoir, but on a section dealing with the party's relations with the United States after 1958, he suggested the United States was pushing the party too hard to take on the Lebanese communists, which Saadeh resisted, arguing the Americans were trying to become too involved in the internal political affairs of the party and the country, which the party rejected, even going as far to state that, while the SSNP was against communism, the Lebanese communists were also their fellow citizens.[15]

In addition, many of the prominent party members jailed by Chehab during the 1960s wrote the so-called prison letters. Some of these letters offered insights into how the SSNP would reorient itself upon obtaining freedom. One letter, written in 1966 by Raad, outlined the SSNP's worldview and how to realize its central mission of achieving Greater Syria within the region's anti-Western front. He wrote that an Arab union could be reached between Baghdad and Damascus, followed by forging an economic-military alliance with Lebanon, Kuwait, and Jordan. The new Fertile Crescent entity would rely on the strength of the Iraqi military and eventually reach a military alliance with Cairo. After putting "the last dagger" into the Sykes–Picot Agreement, sectarianism in Lebanon would be abolished and social equality would allow the region's people to find loyalty to their nationalistic trend. Raad said the United States and its support to Israel had led to the deterioration of the situation in the Fertile Crescent and remarked that the Soviet Union had changed a lot since the totalitarian days of Stalin, becoming a supporter of world peace, which made it a potential supporter and ally to the Fertile Crescent's new political union.

In the summer of 1969, Assad al-Ashqar and Dr. Abdullah Saadeh traveled to Amman to build relations with the PLO and check on the SSNP's status in the kingdom. The SSNP thus established a relationship with a forty-year-old Palestinian leader named Yasser Arafat. Arafat's Fatah movement had gained significant traction in the aftermath of the 1968 Battle of Karameh in Jordan. The Israeli military had achieved its goal of forcing the PLO from the villages near the border, but a high number of Israeli casualties and a strategic retreat left the Palestinians with a morale boost. Saadeh conferred with the Fatah Party heads Abu Iyad, Khalid al-Hassan, Abu Yusif al-Najjar, and Abu Hassan. At first, the Palestinians offered funding and arms to help the SSNP orchestrate a coup in Beirut, but Saadeh, likely reflecting on the dismal experience of the party's failed coup in 1961, demurred, instead stressed the importance of the PLO as a national liberation movement.[16] This meeting formed the start of SSNP–PLO relations. The SSNP formed two committees and had its armed members fall under Fatah's military command.[17] The Palestinians were later expelled from Jordan to Lebanon during the PLO's violent confrontation with the Jordanian government in the Black September incident of 1970.

By the end of the year, the SSNP formalized its new position at a major conference. In December 1969, the SSNP members convened at the Melkart Hotel in Beirut and adopted a platform that recalibrated their worldview toward Arabism and support for the region's leftist revolutionary movements, namely the PLO, all while still retaining their brand of Syrian nationalism. The Melkart Conference, the first party conference in almost a decade, was an attempt to democratize the SSNP based out of a conviction that the party's failures in the 1950s and 1960s derived in part from a disconnect between the party leadership and the base. The congress remains one of the most controversial moments in the SSNP's history, even to the point where some of its party comrades consider it a "blasphemy."[18] This attempt to "democratize" was considered by some to be a challenge to the party constitution as ratified in the 1930s, and they deemed the new amendments to be a deviation from Antoun Saadeh's original intent and teachings. A new national council was established and filled with representatives from the *munafidhiyyat* (administrative regions) to serve an advisory capacity. In addition, Antoun Saadeh's Seventh Decree, essentially the provision that authorized a committee to select an Amin (the party's highest rank), was cancelled. This was a similar measure the SSNP's Intifada faction had done during the party's first break in 1957. Furthermore, the party officially declared its socialism. Raad later wrote:

> There's a question that might've been asked, were the prison articles (written by the SSNP leaders while in jail during the 1960s), an indicator of the Melkart conference, or did the party determine its leftism and direction in 1960–1961? I want to be honest; the Melkart conference was a massive turning point in the party's history. Even if we were to appreciate the role of certain individuals, their role was only a contribution to the Melkart Congress, not the events in the building itself. I'm proud of my role in Melkart and its preparations, but I do not claim that I came up with Melkart. It was the Social Nationalists who came up with Melkart, and it was President Dr. Abdullah Saadeh who called for the Melkart Congress along with the very important Supreme Council which adopted and approved the congress. The party also made a rule that we should not omit or pass anything without carefully reflecting on it. Melkart was held with no constitutional authority and had no power or authority, it was just a consultation convention, but it was the Supreme Council that respected the general will that Melkart had expressed, and made its recommendations as an approach in the constitution and an approach in both intellect and politics. Respecting the general will is the foundation of the constitution and that is an important rule that the Supreme Council, headed by Amin Dr. Muneir El-Khoury, that I was honored to be a member of, enshrined.[19]

However, the party did not declare itself to be a Marxist organization. Raad wrote of three trends (*tayyarat*) within the party at the start of the 1970s: one faction held the president of the party responsible for the debacle of the 1961 New Year's Eve coup, wanted Saadeh tried, and were firmly committed to maintain the party's constitution without any amendments; the second group called for a progressive revolutionary approach and the need to amend the constitution and was inclined to re-elect Saadeh as party president; the third, a weak but "loud" faction that pursued its own opportunistic interests.[20] A second conference was held in April 1975, called the Deauville Congress, which occurred one month after Raad became the party president. This conference sought to clarify whether authority stemmed from the Supreme Council or the Amin (trustee or president). The result was the "democratization" and the adoption of the Nationalist Council, which made the Amin and members that the executories elect, and the Nationalist Council elects the Supreme Council from within its body of members. The Supreme Council, in turn, elects one of them to become the Amin. Thus, the conference subsequently restored the rank of Amana.[21]

With its new platform formalized, the SSNP sought out Arab allies from the regional power brokers, primarily Syria and Libya. The LNM leadership first met in Algiers to lay out their agenda and grievances. As the SSNP was integrated into this structure, the party's leadership was also tasked with seeking out the blessing of President Hafez al-Assad in Syria. This involved responding to an invitation from the Syrian government to visit Damascus, a mission that was fraught with tension as the SSNP was still technically banned inside of Syria. Given this dynamic, the Syrian contacts were delighted in enacting a measure of psychological torment on the SSNP delegation. Raad described the apprehension they felt, remarking that, for the SSNP partisans, the journey to Damascus was a perilous one:

> This was our first visit to Damascus since the 1955 assassination of Malki. We left for Damascus and some interesting and strange events unfolded. My name was still included on the list of those sentenced during the Malki case … to 15 years in prison, including an additional seven years of exile. The SSNP was guaranteed that a delegation from the Baath National Command would meet us at the border in order to escort us and register our cars for the journey to Damascus. However, they were late by three hours and we were greeted by the Syrian border guards. The Lebanese delegation was taken to the captain's room and we had a long and interesting conversation. From time to time, the border guard captain would ask me about myself and the party.[22]

In addition, the SSNP began to seek out ties with the revolutionary regime in Libya. Raad recounted his first meeting with Libyan strongman Colonel Moammar Gaddafi in his memoir. In 1975, Kamal Jumblatt received an invitation to send a delegation from the LNM to Tripoli, in which Raad took part. Raad recalled, "[The Libyans] knew we were a nationalist party struggling against Zionism to recover the full national territory of Natural Syria and that we were a radical party that worked favorably to Arab interests. They knew all of this and that we were a fair and honest party." Abdullah Saadeh was also supposed to attend this meeting, but he stayed in Lebanon to attend the funeral of his son, Nicola, who had been killed in the fighting in Beirut's Dahieh district. Although Inaam Raad had undertaken several earlier diplomatic missions for the party, his meeting with Gaddafi was not entirely easy. Gaddafi, now six years into his rule over Libya, had fostered a platform of Arab nationalism that was strongly rooted in Sunni Muslim identity. Raad, a Christian, in a move he later considered to be undiplomatic, urged Gaddafi to reconsider the important role of Arab Christians in the region's anticolonial revolutionary struggle.[23]

The Syrian government also approached the SSNP's smaller George Abd-Messih (Intifada) faction about falling into the left-wing nationalist alliance. In 1975, Syrian Foreign Minister Abdul Halim Khaddam met with a delegation from the Intifada faction in Sabki Park located across from the foreign ministry building in Damascus. Assad's foreign minister offered the Intifada representatives arms and funding, but was thoroughly rebuffed. As with the position of nonviolence that the SSNP Intifada struck during the 1958 Crisis, they held firm again during the 1975 civil war. The SSNP figures answered without hesitation:

> This is not our war; this is the war of others unfolding on our land. We are distancing ourselves from this war. Our mission is purely advocacy for the ideology of Syrian Social Nationalism, which the leader of our country, Antoun Saadeh, believed in. We will not become involved in a war that we consider to be an external one taking place on our soil.[24]

Khaddam sat silently and ended the meeting. When the party members went back to their vehicles, they were surprised to see that the air had been drained from all four tires of their cars. Khaddam's office secretary laughed and said there must be some children playing in the area.[25] However, the SSNP Intifada members knew the message from Khaddam was clear: "I did not like your answer."[26] The full scope of the power the Syrian regime projected on the entire SSNP and the Lebanese battlefield soon revealed itself.

Descent into War

With the outbreak of the Lebanese Civil War on April 13, 1975, the SSNP took part in several key battles and assisted the LMN with securing control over Muslim West Beirut. The coalition of leftist Arab forces in the LNM was stacked up against the Western-backed Christian Lebanese Forces (LF). One former Kataeb fighter relayed the sense of siege felt by the Maronites.

> Kamal Jumblatt had all of the forces he needed aligned with him. He thought he could break the Maronites. It was revenge, a historical concern of the Druze

remembering the 1800s of the Christian attacks on the Druze. He thought he could now raise the status of the Druze in Lebanon.[27]

As the violence unfolded throughout 1975, the LNM was brought closer and closer to outright victory. The SSNP took part in the Battle of the Hotels, which lasted from October 1975 to March 1976. However, Syrian President Hafez al-Assad grew wary of the LNM's ascent to power. Jumblatt infamously met with Assad on March 27, 1976, a meeting that failed to secure Syria's support for the LNM. Instead, Syria worked to enhance its own leftist movement within Lebanon—the National Lebanese Front. This coalition included the pro-Syrian branch of the Lebanese Baath Party and the Lebanese Nasserists. The Baathist government in Syria also began to explore the idea of pan-Syrianism, which ran counter to its own longstanding ideology of Arabism. Syria's Defense Minister Mustafa Tlass actively fostered this trend, and an SSNP figure from Lebanon, Shawqi Khahallah, was allowed to promote the ideas of Greater Syria on state radio in Damascus.[28] However, even though relations between Raad and the Lebanese Baath Party head Assem Qanso were cordial and functional, the latter regarded Raad with a dose of suspicion due to his close ties with the Palestinians.[29]

The Syrian government increasingly sought to cultivate influence over a pro-regime faction of the SSNP they could count on. The old party veteran, Issam al-Mahayri, who, after his spell in Mezzeh prison, was now staunchly lined up by the Syrians, and Elias Gergi Qanayzeh[30] were the top choices for this role.[31] Prior to the entry of the Arab Deterrent Force (ADF) into Lebanon in 1976, which consisted mainly of the Syrian army, the SSNP split into two parts. Raad's faction, called Markaz (meaning center), was against the entry of the Syrian army and viewed Assad's intervention as a betrayal of the Palestinians. Assad al-Ashqar and Issam al-Mahayri were in the other wing that was later designated Khawarij (meaning *those who left*, inspired by the Islamic terminology *Khawarij/Kharijites*) that aligned itself more closely with the Syrian regime. The Khawarij felt that, by aligning with Damascus, the anti-Zionist forces united against Israel with the Syrian Baath were better suited to protect the long-term interests of Natural Syria. The Markaz faction under Raad believed that the Syrians were simply utilizing the SSNP, along with the other Lebanese parties, as a pawn in its larger geopolitical confrontations with Israel and would eventually settle for establishing a peace treaty. Qanayzeh was one of the SSNP's elder members and served as the president of the Khawarij faction.[32] Issam Mahayri, who was overseas, returned from South America in 1977 and became the leader of Khawarij, effectively replacing Qanayzeh. The SSNP's Khawawij faction's headquarters were in Jal al-Bahr, Tyre, while Inaam Raad and Abdullah Saadeh's Markaz was headquartered in Verdun, Beirut.[33]

Another important SSNP figure was Waseem Zineddine, known by his *nom de guerre* Abu Wajib (the father of duty). Zineddine's story highlights the violent scope of the internal struggle the SSNP endured during the 1970s. A stylized poster featured a black silhouette of a serious-looking, bearded young man with glasses atop a red background. Struck down in his prime, the image of Zineddine was reminiscent of the infamous picture of Che Guevara, projecting a revolutionary aura. Zineddine was a 27-year-old, well-respected intellectual within the party and informally headed the pro-Syrian faction until he was shot dead outside of the party's newspaper office on May 23, 1975. Zineddine's story was one early sign of how the inter-SSNP violence wreaked havoc within the party during the civil war. Zineddine came from a Druze family in the village of Qobbei in Baabda and joined the SSNP while it was still banned in 1965. He did his doctorate at the Sorbonne, married a French woman, and returned to Lebanon in 1974. Zineddine held a press conference at the SSNP's "House of Students" and declared that his faction was the only legitimate representative of the party, which he called "The General Executioners Movement." He was described by his party comrades as "the man who knew Antoun Saadeh's ideology the best."[34] Syria stands accused of carrying out his killing.[35] However, the mysterious circumstances of the assassination were deeply troubling to Mahayri, who voiced concern about a "fifth column" operating within the party and wanted to hold Zineddine's killers accountable. Supporters of Mahayri speculated that Raad was more likely to have a motive for Zineddine's murder.

Still, pressure came down from Syria to put aside the differences and unite the party. Mahayri announced to his Khawarij followers that they would enter negotiations with the aim of rejoining Markaz. However, there were some in Mahayri's group who opposed this hasty unity. One such member was Nassir Rammah, who wanted to deal with four issues: First, to handle the party's contradictions in the wartime alliances, namely between the pro-Syrian and pro-PLO SSNP factions; second, to establish clarification regarding the ideological dissimilarities considering that the other faction (Markaz) had adopted "problematic" theories such as Arabism and socialism; third, to hold those in both factions accountable who had financially benefited from the civil war, used the weapons and money provided by the allies, and misrepresented the social nationalists with their immoral actions. Finally, the most important point: prosecuting those who ordered the killing of Zineddine, along with those who had participated with the other LNM factions in assaulting the headquarters of the Khawarij faction, terrorized the nationalists, and violated the sanctity of their homes. This division continued from 1975 to 1978 and escalated into fighting between the two factions until Syrian Army Chief of Staff Hikmat al-Shehabi came to Lebanon in 1978. He stayed in Beirut for ten days, and the two factions were eventually reconciled with a tenuous reunification.[36]

One SSNP member recounted the views of the party splits between the Syrian and Palestinian factions at the rank-and-file level:

> I witnessed most of these upheavals but I was not clear on their final objectives: I was not wholeheartedly active in the internal politics of the party; I was following orders that never came my way. I was definitely pro-Inaam Raad in my orientation and attended most of his gatherings, was included in the small clique, and many times assembled in his home close to the AUB campus. I sensed that the pro-Syrian regime faction of the SSNP was not credible because the current Syrian Baath regime was viewed as a sectarian Alawi faction imposing their dictatorship on the entire Syrian people. And frankly, the Syrian Baath never communicated their national strategy clearly and we were reduced to accepting the tactics of the Syrian regime on face values that were contrary to the objectives of the forces of change in Lebanon.[37]

Outside of the party, the internal rifts were of little consequence. A former Kataeb fighter remarked:

> Kataeb thought the SSNP was even worse than [the Palestinians] because they had betrayed Lebanon. They had a higher standing with the Syrian regime. However, they started splitting over the policy of siding explicitly with the Syrians. George Abd-Messih favored more autonomy. He ended up being banished, sidelined, and placed under house arrest.[38]

The PLO faced its own crises. In 1974, a Palestinian coalition of radical factions broke off in a challenge to Arafat's Ten Point Program, which had been formalized in Cairo in June 1974. The so-called Rejectionist Front was backed by Iraq, and tensions within the Palestinian movements would persist through to the 1980s. This trend also reflected the issues of sponsorship from the Arab states. Central among the Palestinian factions were the Popular Front for the Liberation of Palestine (PFLP) and the Abu Nidal Organization. The PFLP's leader, George Habash, studied at American University in Beirut and was heavily inspired by two left-wing Arab nationalist intellectuals, Qustantin Zuraiq and Sati al-Husri.[39] The Abu Nidal Organization, which did not have a concrete ideology, carried out attacks in over twenty countries over the course of the civil war and killed nearly 2,000 people. The Abu Nidal group was strongly affiliated with Baathist Iraq and Gaddafi's Libya.

The Markaz faction still struggled with the ideological difference of internal two camps: the first group, called the conservatives, was against Abdullah Saadeh and amending the constitution and his efforts to make it more democratic; the other, called the reformers, supported Saadeh and his moves to amend the party's constitution. It was out of the reformers' group that a cultural Marxist trend grew within the SSNP. The reformers were against the conservatives in the party but were relatively small and insignificant. Saadeh wrote that this group of Marxist cultural sympathizers had come under the influence of George Habash and the Communist Workers Party. Raad himself was not part of the Marxist cultural sympathizer group, but gave it verbal and moral support. However, in this group, a few future party leaders, including Gebran Araiji and Sarkis Abu Ziad, attempted to steer the party even further to the left than what Raad had desired. This was described by some historians as the so-called Maoist faction of the party.[40] However, other historians affiliated with the SSNP denied there was any official Maoist faction. This characterized that neither Sarkis nor Araiji showed any interest in Maoism, but were rather involved in a crusade to steer the SSNP away from the rightist position of the 1950s.[41]

The brutal realities of the sectarian nature of the war reached the SSNP at the village level. The infamous Aintoura massacre occurred on March 26–28 in 1976 at the foot of Mount Sannine in North Matn and is widely remembered by the party as a tragic moment of the war's sectarianism. Remarkable is the fact that the SSNP partisans killed in the village of Aintoura were Maronites. There had been strategic disagreements within the LNM that insisted on consolidating the Aley/Souk Al-Gharb offensive line as priority, while the SSNP viewed that the Metn region was the most important region to defend and concentrate the LNM's forces. Consequently, Kataeb managed to enter Aintoura, lined up twenty-three mostly young members of the SSNP, and shot them against the church wall.

Two articles discussed the nature of the massacre. A piece by *al-Binaa* was pervaded with a strong sense of betrayal. Although it notes the town's strategic location in the North Metn, it nevertheless puts forward the idea that the village was considered a safe haven from the fighting for all of its sons: Kataeb and Social Nationalists alike. The fact that the youth of the village were murdered by their fellow townspeople was a shocking betrayal, and one they say was ordered from the top of the Kataeb. Furthermore, it was reminiscent of the fatal moments and steadfast ideological conviction of the party's founder. It wrote, "The bodies of the elders, young men and women, lying in front of the church, died without surrendering or compromising their convictions. It was a stand of glory and honor[42] following the example of their leader, Antoun Saadeh."[43] The other article by *al-Akhbar* also discussed the massacre and stood out in particular since the title used the term "khawarij" to describe the SSNP members, meaning in this context that the SSNP Maronites had taken a radical step away (and against) from their religious community by joining the SSNP. This term dates back to the Maronite's early propaganda against the party. The article also placed the blame for the massacre on Amin Gemayel and, in sync with the ideology of the SSNP, laments the "tyranny of sects" that enabled the Maronites to kill their own people simply because they were deemed outside of the fold by embracing the SSNP.[44]

As the war segued from the late 1970s into the 1980s, a slew of assassinations took place that permanently altered Lebanon's political landscape. In March 1977, LNM leader Kamal Jumblatt was assassinated in a drive-by shooting. Rumors pointed that the orders came from Hafez al-Assad's influential brother, Rifat. The SSNP's ability to acquire weapons during the conflict also fluctuated. The party's militia was often equipped with outdated or antiquated firearms. One SSNP member cynically recalled:

> During the civil war, the party had only 60 pieces of Simonov (Soviet AVS-36 rifle) and the only source for arms supply was Abu Ammar (Arafat's noms de guerre) who lavishly offered very outmoded arms like the Browning and Schneider. Yasser Arafat allegedly stopped supplying the party with these "ancient arms" because Raad, ever the nationalist, had refused to sign on a petition condemning the abduction of Colonel Morgan by a Palestinian organization on the basis that these activities bear no responsibilities to the LNM. The only time the SSNP was able to receive decent arms was when Libya agreed to supply and train officers for the party.[45]

East Germany was allegedly another supporter of the SSNP during the civil war. The PLO's leader, Yasser Arafat, had developed a close relationship with East Germany's Erich Honecker.[46]

The final years of the 1970s again saw the civil war metamorphize. The so-called Hundred-Days War erupted between the Syrian army and the coalition of primarily Christian militias under the leadership of Bachir Gemayel and the Kataeb forces. With the Christian parties aligned into the Lebanese Front, they began to challenge the ADF and its security infrastructure in the shattered country. In February 1978, a splinter faction of the Lebanese Army objected to the Syrian checkpoints and a new round of intense fighting broke out. The Kataeb, with support from Dany Chamoun's Tigers Militia, responded against the Syrians. President Assad's troops took over parts of East Beirut, including the Rizk Tower in the Achrafieh district, and the fighting lasted until the fall of 1978 when the Arab League and the Syrians agreed to withdraw from East Beirut and re-established a shaky ceasefire. The Israeli Defense Forces (IDF) had also entered the war in response to raids and acts of terrorism conducted by the PLO and PFLP. Operation Litani led to the IDF's creation of a security zone and Saad Haddad's South Lebanon Army (SLA). The brutal fighting in the south pushed almost 300,000 mainly Lebanese Shia refugees north to Beirut. A traumatized and radicalized displaced population would soon find solace and political power in a revitalized Shia Islam.

With the start of the 1980s, the secular-leftist LNM was wrecked with defeats, first, suffered at the hands of the Syrian intervention in 1976 and, subsequently, by the Kataeb and IDF. Furthermore, bloody inter-Christian combat saw Gemayel vanquish his primary rival, Dany Chamoun. The Christian militias, united under Gemayel by the summer of 1980, set the stage for the next round of fighting against the secular-leftist Muslim factions during the 1982 Lebanon War. For its part, the Iranian Revolution of February 1979 ushered in a new era. These new religious-fueled ideologies offered a serious competition that sapped recruitment and would greatly restructure the anti-imperialist front during the remainder of the civil war.[47] The Lebanese Shia were heavily integrated into the LNM, but gained a reputation as common "foot soldiers" and "cannon fodder," which later led to a widespread sense of disenchantment with the secular left-wing nationalist camp that, by the dawn of Ayatollah Khomeini's Islamic Revolution in Iran, had steadily gravitated away from the secular parties toward the pronouncedly Shia militias, Amal, and later on Hezbollah.[48] The Israeli invasion of Lebanon in June 1982 added a new dimension to the civil war, a narrative of injustice and occupation that energized the secular-left a bout of foreign support and ideological revival. With the IDF now fully engaged in the Lebanese conflict, the LNM reorganized itself into an underground resistance force called the Lebanese National Salvation Front (Jabhat al-Muqawama al-Wataniyya al-Lubnaniya), widely referred to by its Arabic acronym *Jammoul*. It was here the SSNP, eclipsed by the larger religious parties, made its mark with some of the war's most notorious acts that solidified the pan-Syrian movement's place in the anti-Zionist camp in the postwar era.

7

Guerrilla War to Politics: The SSNP's Role in Lebanon's Politics

The 1980s primarily saw the scope of the Lebanese conflict turn into a battleground between Hafez al-Assad's Syria and Israel headed by Prime Minister Menachem Begin. The tempo of violence by all sides was severely heightened by the geopolitical nature and consequently altered the SSNP as the war winded down by the end of the decade, leaving the party with a resistance legacy that it would use in the postwar era to bolster its support with its popular base into the 1990s and 2000s. This stemmed from the Israeli military's June 1982 invasion that significantly revived the SSNP's credentials as an anti-imperialist force. Meanwhile, the party's involvement in assassinations and suicide attacks during the 1980s solidified its reputation in the West as a sinister troublemaker, a reputation that lingered long after the civil war ended.

Although the SSNP was able to carve out a place for itself in the campaign of resistance that drove out the Israeli military and its South Lebanon Army allies from the so-called security zone in May 2000, the party still retained a strong negative stigma within Lebanese society that were either anti-Syrian or nonpolitical altogether. Like the milieu of political groups with armed militias, the history of the SSNP during this period became part of the Lebanese "collective amnesia" that existed after the war.[1] Much of the party's activities, violence, and politics in the 1980s remain off-topic and highly controversial in modern Lebanon's political and social discourse. In addition, Antoun Saadeh's party continued to suffer from internal splits as it felt its way forward into the postwar era.

The 1980s and Guerrilla Operations

As with most armed conflicts, political messages and informational warfare were utilized by all sides. The SSNP's propaganda during the course of the Lebanese Civil War emphasized its status as one of Lebanon's oldest political parties, along with its credentials as an anticolonial, anti-Zionist force. Homage to Antoun Saadeh himself was revived outside of the SSNP, perhaps in part due to the sectarian nature of the civil war and in part due to the blow Arabism suffered as a result of the 1967 Six-Day War, along with the death of Nasser in September 1970. The face of the party's late founder, frozen in time from the moment he stood before the firing squad at the age of forty-five in 1949, featured prominently on the party's wartime posters. One image from the 1970s commemorated Saadeh's birthday: "1 March. The birth of the national consciousness and the will for victory."

In other themes, the ever-distant irredentist goal of unifying Natural Syria was also heavily presented. Another poster marked the party's fifty-third anniversary in 1985 and depicted the sun rising over the mountains. However, in place of the sun was the party's zawbaa logo, with powerful rays extending out. It read "53 years for the renaissance and unity of society and for liberating the nation from the Zionist and foreign occupation." According to Zeina Maasri, the concept of the nation alluded not to Lebanon but to the long-lost Greater Syrian nation. To the SSNP, the Lebanese Civil War was only the latest example of the tragedy of Syria's division into separate states.[2] Therefore, it positioned its quest for establishing Natural Syria into the narrative of its place within the resistance to Israel's military intervention in Lebanon. This phase of the civil war also saw new tactics that had long-term repercussions in modern warfare that would extend into the twenty-first century. The guerrilla actions, which widely included the use of suicide attacks, became the SSNP's focal point of propaganda during the 1980s, a legacy that lived on in party lore well after the war concluded. In an interview with the PFLP's bulletin in 1980, Raad remarked:

> We maintain that the Saad Haddad symptom in South Lebanon, or the [Bashir] Gemayel symptom with the Israeli tanks in East Beirut, are not symptoms that can be defeated militarily, but should be defeated socially and politically, mainly through offering the alternative. If here you have a minority of Christians allied with the Palestinian Resistance, this is not something that took place haphazardly, but due to conviction and political analysis and ideology, as a result of about 50 years of political struggle.[3]

Adel Beshara explained how the mysticism surrounding Antoun Saadeh played its own role in the promotion of suicide attacks:

> Using his execution as a symbol of resistance, they instigated the elusive phenomenon of suicide bombings as an alternative form of guerrilla warfare and as a secular rather than a religious experiment. One after the other, young men and, for the first time, young women, appeared on pre-recorded video footages recalling Saadeh's martyrdom and life struggle and urging others to follow in his footsteps.[4]

On June 6, 1982, Israel launched its invasion of Lebanon. With the defeat of the LNM and the subsequent Syrian and Israeli intervention, the SSNP, the communists, Lebanese Baath Party, Nasserist groups, and other remnants of the secular-leftist factions reorganized and formed the guerrilla force called the Lebanese National Resistance Front, better known by its Arabic acronym *Jammoul*. Founded in September 1982, the front's scope was primarily to target the Lebanese Forces, South Lebanon Army (SLA), and the Israeli Defense Forces (IDF), the latter that had extended its military zone up to West Beirut.

From 1982 to 1987, the SSNP took on an active role engaging in guerrilla tactics and suicide attacks on the Israeli military and its Lebanese allies, the SLA. The SSNP's participation as guerrillas on the front would remain a prominent feature in its political prowess long after the war, with the party regularly displaying the Jammoul flag at military demonstrations and celebrations, a display that helped cement the SSNP's standing in the anti-imperialist and pro-Syrian power structure in the postwar era. Despite this, the party at the end of the decade would be eclipsed by the fast-rising and vastly more popular Iranian-backed Islamist party, Hezbollah. In addition to the competition fostered by the revival of religious militant politics in Lebanon, the SSNP in the 1980s was again wrecked with internal turmoil that ultimately relegated the party to a far smaller role in the immediate postwar years.

On September 14, 1982, Habib Shartouni, in collaboration with Nabil al-Alam, the head of the party's security office, orchestrated the assassination of Bashir Gemayel in a massive car bombing at the Kataeb Party's office in Beirut. US President Ronald Regan called the incident a "cowardly assassination" and a "shock to the American people and to civilized men and women everywhere." He said, "We condemn the perpetrators of this heinous crime against Lebanon and against their cause of peace in the Middle East."[5] Former Lebanese Prime Minister Shafik al-Wazzan described the incident as a "criminal conspiracy against Lebanon."[6] The assassination marked the party's direct opposition to the desires of the United States and Israel to steer the direction of the Lebanese Civil War. The high-profile killing also helped propel the view that the SSNP was acting at the behest of Syria. The death of Bashir Gemayel, a controversial Lebanese politician, was also manifested in the controversy of his killer, Shartouni, who survived. The assassin was a Christian Maronite from Aley who had attended several SSNP demonstrations and joined the party in 1977.[7] One SSNP member spoke of the incident, "I know the precise details of it and they are terrifying. Habibi Shartouni had always been a close friend of mine who slept in my house many times. Shartouni remained in Al-Romieh prison until he was freed during the waning months of the Lebanese Civil War." It was not long before Kateab carried out its own dastardly retaliation, with its militia fighters brutally massacring up to an estimated 3,500 innocents in the Sabra and Shatila Palestinian refugee camps for three days, all while the Israeli military stood by. Thus, the SSNP, in its moment of heroic zeal, became anchored to the story of one of the most devastating sectarian crimes in the Lebanese conflict.

In July 2012, Habib Shartouni conducted an interview with *al-Akhbar*, indicating he was still alive and in hiding. He expressed no regret for his involvement in the assassination and framed his motive in patriotic terms.[8] In October 2017, the Lebanese High Court sentenced Shartouni to death, a move that prompted demonstrations for and against the measure. Nadhim Gemayel, Bashir's son, lauded the verdict as a step toward justice. He said, "It is very important for all the country and for the state of law of Lebanon since none of all the terrorist attacks that happened in Lebanon in the last 40 years, none of them have been judged or elucidated. So it is very important for us to know that, in Lebanon, justice can prevail." However, the SSNP's dean of culture, Khalil Khairallah, retorted it was a political gimmick staged ahead of the parliamentary elections, "There were many, many massacres in Lebanon. Some of the actors of these massacres are still alive now. Why can't we judge them? Why only Habib Shartouni, and why now? Because this sentence had the chance to unify [the pro-Western] parties in the coming elections."[9] The controversy over the assassination continues. In October 2017, a Lebanese court handed the death sentence to Shartouni, who remains at large.[10]

Hafez al-Assad had his own family ties to the SSNP. Since he was from the minority Alawite community hailing from Latakia, the party was likely present all around him during his youth and political formation. Furthermore, his wife's family, the Makhloufs, was deeply associated with the party and would have made his courtship with her much easier if he had abandoned Baathism for the ranks of the Syrian nationalists. However, his impoverished childhood, his time in the Air Force, deployment to Egypt, and the heavy influence of Zaki al-Arsuzi made him a lifelong Baathist, a decision that would propel him to power through the 1960s. It is likely that if he had joined the SSNP, Assad would have never reached the presidency in Syria. The Baath Party in Syria had already shifted toward a Greater Syria scheme under Salah Jadid when his coup ousted Amin al-Hafiz's faction of the Baath Party in February 1966.[11] The lure of the SSNP's brand of Syrian nationalism was evident in Assad as early as 1975. In the final meeting of the Baath 12th National Congress on July 24, 1975, he gave a speech:[12]

> You know the special circumstances that we went through in 1963, with the absence of the (Baath) party from the Syrian streets, which was filled with Nasserism at the beginning of the revolution (the March 8 Revolution of 1963), and, in order to consolidate the revolution we had to give importance, at a fast pace, by concentrating the party's authority in the armed forces. Not only to hand our comrades sensitive leadership joints but to also educate the army on the party's ideology, and in this context, I asked the great Arab philosopher Zaki al-Arsuzi to visit us in the airbase that I was heading, and upon gathering the soldiers, commissioned and non-commissioned officers, to see him, I remember that he touched on the subject of the Fertile Crescent during his speech. Believe me comrades, I simmered while sitting in my chair, and felt as if this beautiful image of Zaki al-Arsuzi was besmeared with something. I said to myself he should not pollute himself by talking about the Fertile Crescent, because that term refers to an old colonial project.

> This incident I mentioned more than once to the leadership and wondered on more than one occasion, was it justified that I faced Arsuzi's speech with such feelings? My assessments is that the superpowers' strategies back then had an interest in forming the Fertile Crescent project, and had an interest at another time in forming the project of a unitarian entity called Greater Syria. However, this naming is naturally not an invention but was the original reality, the rise of a Greater Syria state, and because the colonial countries back then had an interest in it, we had strongly opposed these projects without fully considering our own interest in it.

> ... Imagine if that Greater Syria existed today, would that be in the interests of the French or the English? Of course not. In addition, it would have been different for Israel, that is, if Israel was even founded. ... Oh, how we wished we were living in Greater Syria. How we wished we were living in the Fertile Crescent's state, our capabilities would have been much larger and we would have been better able to face colonialism and Israel. And I say again, we cannot consider a unity between Syria, Palestine, Jordan and Lebanon, that is if we can

even call it unity, since it was historically one existing state, to be in the interest of the English forever. No, because it is our own essential interest.

Later on, during the celebration honoring the members of the Sixth Conference of Arab American Institutions and Associations Union in Damascus in October 1, 1983, Assad said, "Colonialism didn't only exploit us, but it also ripped us into statelets as you can see, and you know there was no [individual] Syria, Lebanon, Palestine or Jordan, we were all one state, one political entity, and all of this land was called Syria until colonialism came and founded Jordan, gave Palestine to the Jews and founded the state of Greater Lebanon." Abdullah Saadeh wrote that his first official meeting with Hafez al-Assad took place on December 18, 1979, and that earlier discussions were handled by Foreign Minister Abdul Halim Khaddam.[13] For its part, the SSNP softened their stance against Arabism. The SSNP had never entirely wished to isolate Natural Syria from the rest of the Arab World. In one pamphlet from Antoun Saadeh, he wrote, "Those who believe that the Syrian Social Nationalist Party seeks Syria's withdrawal from the Arab world, because they do not distinguish between the Syrian national awakening and the pan-Arab cause, are grossly mistaken. We shall never relinquish our position in the Arab world, nor our mission to the Arab world."

The so-called Mountain War unfolded from September 1983 and lasted until February 1984. This sub-conflict, sparked by the entry of the Lebanese forces to the Chouf, saw an estimated 2,000 SSNP militia fighters taking part on the side of the PSP and PLO. In February 1984, the SSNP also took part in an intense battle, alongside Amal and the PSP, which wrestled West Beirut from the Lebanese army. The *New York Times* wrote:

> Moslem militiamen completed a takeover of predominantly Moslem West Beirut, and the United States Embassy evacuated nonessential staff members and families. Fighting broke out along the so-called green line that divides Christian East and Moslem West Beirut. Lebanese Army units began breaking apart along religious and political lines.[14]

One of the most infamous attacks authored by the SSNP was the "Al-Wimbi Operation" carried out by Khaled Alwan on September 24, 1982. There were three Israeli officers sitting at the Wembi cafe in the Hamra area, insisting on paying the bill in Israeli shekels. Khaled Alwan, who was sitting at a nearby table, approached them, pointed his 38-caliber pistol at them, and fired. The incident allegedly was the start of Jammoul's operations against Israel. An SSNP member named Maan Hamieh told the Lebanese outlet *Daily Star* in 2000,

"Beirut was helpless. There was no resistance to the Israeli invasion. In line with the party's national principles, Alwan acted on his behalf and arranged to shoot Israeli soldiers because he couldn't bear seeing the enemy enjoying their time in our country."[15]

Alwan himself was killed two years later by a militant affiliated with the Progressive Socialist Party. Alwan's killer, Hisham Nasireddine, was not close to Walid Jumblatt but rather acted as an internal challenger within the PSP. He allegedly killed Alwan and set his car on fire to make it look like he died in a car accident. According to SSNP lore, Nasireddine was not a Mossad agent who sought to help Israel avenge the Wembi cafe attack, but was rather killed Alwan for a later incident he was involved in. Alwan had been arrested in June 1983 for an assassination attempt on the former Libyan ambassador to Lebanon, Abdulqadir Ghoqa.[16] Ghoqa was tasked with heading Libya's Popular Committee for Arab Fraternity Bureau and helped coordinate Libya's supplies to the factions of the Lebanese National Movement. Alwan confessed to the shooting but said it was not done on behalf of the SSNP, which condemned the attack and called to punish those behind it. Alwan escaped from prison in March 1984, and it was only after his death that the SSNP revealed he had been behind the Wembi attack.[17]

The SSNP also retained a militia presence in the Bekaa Valley. In 1985, the Israelis carried out air strikes against the SSNP in Bekaa. The *New York Times* reported the party's headquarters, located only ten miles from the Syrian border, was destroyed with two of its fighters killed and four people wounded.[18] This was in retaliation for seven car bomb attacks on Israeli forces. The Israeli Air Force later targeted the SSNP in 1988 in the village of Beit Lahia, also in the Bekaa Valley, which destroyed a "one-story structure" and damaged four houses.[19] In June 1986, the party's militia took part in battles in the Bekaa region in the town of Mashgara against Hezbollah with nine fighters killed and ten wounded. Seventeen others were kidnapped.[20] The SSNP turned to the Marada Brigade in battles with the Lebanese forces in Byblos and Bifkaya in January 1986.[21] In December of that year, they participated in the final rout of the Islamic Unification Movement's Tawheed militia in Tripoli. After the Syrians arrested a Tawheed commander, they retaliated by attacking and killing fifteen Syrian troops manning a checkpoint. This led to a coordinated assault by the SSNP, SAA, Baath militias, the Lebanese Communist Party, and Ali Eid's Arab Red Knights (also known as the Pink Panthers) militia. The latter group was the armed wing of the Arab Democratic Party, a Lebanese Alawite-dominated unit with ties to Rifaat al-Assad, which sprang up late in the war with influence and presence throughout Lebanon.[22]

1985 beckoned in a dangerous time for the IDF's mission in Lebanon. The Israeli forces positioned themselves in southern Lebanon and established the SLA, headed by Antoine Lahad. Subsequently, the "martyrdom operations" began against the Israeli army and the Lahad forces. Along with the Communist Party, the SSNP and other embarked on a wave of missions from which their attackers knew they would not return. The first suicide operation was carried out by Rushdi al-Sayegh on March 13, 1985, who blew himself up next to an Israeli convoy. The second attack that gained the most notoriety was the one carried out by Sanaa Mehaidli in April 9, 1985. Then an operation by Khalid Azrak on July 9, 1985, blew up a car with a thousand tons of TNT in an Israeli convoy standing at the SLA checkpoints. Afterwards, Ammar al-Asr, who hailed from Banias, blew himself up at an Israeli roadblock on November 4, 1985. One party member relayed through an intermediary how the SSNP's suicide attacks differed from the attacks carried out by the Islamist militant groups:

> All of these martyrs did not want paradise or nymphs in the sky. They were all secular, some of them were atheists and some were believers, but what they all shared was their belief in the Syrian nationalist ideology, and in their belief in the sanctity of the earth and that dying for others to live is the noblest end and holiest of causes.[23]

The pro-Syrian SSNP also fought against Hezbollah in battles in the town of Mashgara in the Bekka Valley in June 1986.[24] In February 1987, fighting broke out in West Beirut, with the SSNP supporting the PSP along with the LCP and the Mourabitoun in five days of successful combat against Amal, forcing the Shia militia to retreat. On the war's tenth anniversary, the Christian Voice of Lebanon radio said most of the fifteen dead in the village of Yuhmur (twenty-eight miles southeast of Beirut) were SSNP members. This came as Israel carried out a wave of searches for insurgents in Shia villages across the south.[25] According to Edgar O'Ballance, the LCP held its fifth party congress and was attended by Jumblatt and an unnamed member of the Soviet Central Committee.[26] Likely referring to Husayn Muruwwah, he also noted that an LCP member had been assassinated on February 17. Amal attempted to attack the party's headquarters, a move that drew in the other leftist factions in support of the LCP. These events led to the Syrian takeover of Beirut in the final years of the civil war.

The final years of the civil war saw a new powerful figure rise through the ranks of the pro-Syrian branch of the SSNP. Assaad Hardan was born in 1951 to a Greek Orthodox family in Rachaya al Foukhar in the Hasbaya district of

Lebanon's Nabatieh Governorate. He joined the SSNP in 1968 at age of seventeen. Hardan's family had a long history in the party. He is related to the SSNP hero Nawwaf Hardan, a famous writer who became active in the party's early years and grew into a leader in the SSNP's militia in Marjeyoun. Later on, Nawwaf's house in Rachaya al Foukhar was blown up by the Lebanese authorities after he fled to Damascus following the Antoun Saadeh's 1949 uprising.[27] Assaad Hardan studied at the Lebanese University and allegedly struggled academically and failed to graduate. His first name, Assaad, is not to be confused with the Arabic word for lion, but rather means "the happiest." Hardan came to represent a Machiavellian and controversial leader in the party. To the party's critics, Hardan was a dastardly figure who was allegedly behind the SSNP's most heinous acts of violence and manipulations to align the party for its postwar future with the Syrian regime. However, for Hardan's supporters, it was under his guidance that the SSNP strengthened its relations with the Lebanese Hezbollah and Damascus, thereby securing a place for the party in Lebanese politics in the post-civil war era. They also credit him with facilitating the SSNP's dramatic return to Syria, obtaining legalization, increasing recruitment in Syria over the years, expanding into Jordan and Palestine (especially in Gaza), as well as being behind the formation of the Eagles of the Whirlwind to fight with the regime's warring coalition in Syria.

The party continued to face a slew of internal challenges that morbidly took the form of assassinations. One of the major setbacks that occurred on June 3, 1985, was the assassination of the SSNP's defense chief Mohammed Salim.[28] The party's security boss hailed from Sarafand, Lebanon, and joined the SSNP while studying in France in 1969. He became active in the party and, in 1970, headed the SSNP's branch at the Jesuit University upon his return to Lebanon, quickly moving on to run the party's military training courses in Sidon in 1972. Salim was one of the founders of Jammoul and also instigated the use of suicide bombing during the Israeli occupation of southern Lebanon. According to party lore, Salim was instrumental in positioning the party within the vanguard of the "national struggle" against the Israelis. However, Salim's position within the SSNP defense apparatus was apparently fraught. Although affiliated with the party's pro-Syrian faction, he still held the Palestinians in high regard. Orders came in from Damascus for the SSNP to move its militia to Tripoli to participate in fighting the PLO to force them out of the city. Salim was authorized to execute the commands, but refused to do so. This disobedience resulted in Assaad Hardan dispatching a patrol to arrest Salim at his home. When Salim tried to resist, an inter-SSNP battle ensued. Hardan's patrol opened fire using a DShK 1938 "Doshka" heavy machine gun and RPG. Salim then attempted to escape through the first-floor window, but fell and broke his leg. One of his attackers then found him and executed him at point-blank range. The prevailing conviction among those familiar with the incident is that Hardan's team was actually tasked with killing Salim, not to arrest him. This is perhaps the origin of the longstanding assertions that Hardan and his followers are a Syrian intelligence faction in Lebanon.[29]

Another such incident befell one of the party's beloved intellectuals. Habib Kayrouz, a young and charismatic leader, was gunned down while he was getting a haircut on Hamra Street on October 21, 1987. Kayrouz was a Christian from Yahchouch in Lebanon's Keserwan District and was highly active and respected as a prominent information official within the party. Interestingly, many of his own family members were in the Kataeb Party.[30] Kayrouz was well known for his artistic abilities, producing many drawings, including ones that featured the party's zawbaa logo with geometrical designs, as well as poetry writings. He headed the main SSNP's broadcast department, oversaw the university students' branch, and worked as an editor in the party's *al-Binaa* newspaper. The killing was allegedly carried out by four Palestinian militants armed with assault rifles. The primary motive contends that Kayrouz had been marked for death by the PLO since he was affiliated with the pro-Syrian branch of the SSNP and was close to Issam al-Mahayri.[31] A video of the funeral showed Mahayri and Assaad Hardan with their arms held aloft in the party's ninety-degree salute as they circled Kayrouz's open coffin during his funeral surrounded by wailing mourners. It was a scene that had become familiar for the party members. However, another theory is that his death was the result of an internal power struggle. Given the fact he was killed in the SSNP's own territory, it has been alleged that Hardan sought Kayrouz's removal since it was rumored he was being groomed to become the party's next leader.[32]

Meanwhile, the Syrian forces asserted their dominance over the renegade Arafat, amassing an array of pro-Syrian militias and anti-Arafat Palestinian forces against the PLO. Despite this, Inaam Raad's faction of the SSNP sought to maintain its relationship with Arafat's Palestinians. His faction of the party supported the Palestinian cause and refused to participate in the War of the Camps waged by Assad's coalition against the PLO.[33] The fighting around the refugee camps lasted on and off from May 1985 to July 1988. In February 1987, the SSNP and the Lebanese Communist Party sided in the fighting with the Druze PSP after Amal took over West Beirut and had laid siege to the Sabra and Shatila and Burj el-Barajneh Palestinian refugee camps in the outskirts of Beirut. Although the anti-Syrian factions were successful in dislodging Amal, the

Syrians found other ways to assert their authority over Lebanon. Pro-Khomeini elements, which later became Hezbollah, began training in the Bekaa Valley with security provided by Damascus and financial assistance from Iran.[34] The Iran–Syria partnership did not always run smoothly. The War of the Brothers between the pro-Iran Hezbollah and the pro-Syrian Amal lasted from 1988 until 1990. Meanwhile, the SSNP still retained ties with some of the other Palestinian factions, most notably the PFLP. In July 1986, they carried out a joint operation, which commemorated both the martyrdom of Antoun Saadeh and the PFLP's intellectual leader, Ghassan Kanafani, who was killed by the Mossad with a car bomb on July 8, 1972. The maritime raid they had planned ended in failure, and the PFLP-SSNP team was killed by Israeli naval forces at sea.[35]

Abdullah Saadeh passed away in 1987. On November 22, the internal bickering led the SSNP to encounter another split, with one faction led by Inaam Raad (which was called the Supreme Council) and the other led by Issam Mahayri.[36] This pro-Syrian faction, led by Mahayri, became known as the *Tawari* or "Emergency" faction, a nickname that came from the party faction's official designation, *Majlis al-Tawari*, or the Emergency Council. The full extent of foreign influence on the SSNP's internal strife is unclear. There are longstanding rumors that both the Israeli and the Syrian intelligence were trying to divide the SSNP during the 1980s.[37] Libya also asserted its influence over the party. Moammar Gaddafi continued to provide all forms of support for the SSNP with money, gear, and arms. In addition, he opened training camps for the party's cadres in Libya, from which they returned as hardened fighters. The training taught them how to carry out raids and incursions. However, in a situation reminiscent of later Levantine participation in Libya's 2014 civil war, some of the SSNP fighters took part in Gaddafi's 1987 war in Chad. Allegedly, an estimated 250 SSNP combatants took part in this faraway African conflict.[38] This left a bitter legacy among SSNP purists, who felt these foreign adventures were completely contrary to the Syrian social nationalist ideology and brought about charges that the party had improperly engaged in "mercenaryism."[39] The Supreme and Emergency split lasted until 1998.

During the 1980s, the SSNP became noticeably selective of with whom and where it would undertake a violent action. Around the time of the attack on Israeli ambassador Shlomo Argov in London, the SSNP was approached by the notorious Abu Nidal Organization to join them in initiating operations against the Israelis. However, the party's militia declined to take part.[40] It is possible that the SSNP had weighed Abu Nidal's ties to Iraq and kept their distance as the party went increasingly under the tutelage of Assad's Syria. With Damascus aligning with Revolutionary Iran, Baghdad's avowed enemy, the bitter inter-Baath Party feud between Iraq and Syria was in full swing. The SSNP likely sought to keep itself out of the fray to incur lesser wrath of either Assad or Saddam Hussein. By 1989, Abu Nidal himself was placed under house arrest in Libya at the behest of the PLO, as the Palestinians sought to better position themselves in order to engage in diplomacy with Israel.[41] The SSNP also allegedly planned an operation in the United States, which was foiled by law enforcement. Three party members were arrested crossing into Vermont from Canada with a bomb. The FBI said they had planned to carry out an assassination in New York City.[42]

In October 1990, the final battles unfolded that led to the shape of Lebanon's postwar environment. General Antoine Lahud's faction of the Lebanese army, backed by Syrian troops and other pro-Damascus militias, including the SSNP, carried out an offensive against General Michel Aoun's forces in Beirut. The agreement between the SSNP and the Syrian forces was to attack Baabda Palace and arrest Michel Aoun before his escape and retreat to the French embassy. In addition, the SSNP would be at the forefront since they were familiar with the area, which enabled them to carry out scouting missions. Their forces would also attack Roumieh prison to free Habib Shartouni, a goal that the Syrian military administration approved. Following several hours of heavy artillery, along with diplomatic pressure from the French, Aoun ordered his soldiers to surrender to the authority of the Syrian forces.

Postwar Lebanon and Syrian Occupation

The convoy stretched along the highway leading out of Beirut. SSNP party comrades stood at attention on the roadside, displaying the party's ninety-degree salute as they held the black-and-white flags emblazoned with the red zawbaa. The funeral procession traveled up to the mountains into Aley. The cars meandered through the Druze towns and carried the body of party leader Inaam Raad to his final resting place in Ain Zhalta.[43] Among the crowd gathered at the funeral was Walid Jumblatt, the son of Raad's late comrade-in-arms, who now headed the PSP. The SSNP's old ideologue and wartime figure was laid to rest. Raad's funeral in 1998 marked a new chapter in the party as it left the Cold War behind and prepared to enter full speed ahead into the twenty-first century. The SSNP now had to put the conflict behind it and engage in Lebanon's sectarian system. This was a challenge as a party that was regarded as "cross-sectarian" and secular, like the Lebanese communists and Baath, it remained small and struggled to gain a wider appeal in Lebanon's postwar era.⁴⁴

The end of the civil war also signaled an era of Syrian security, economic, and political dominance over Lebanon. In May 1991, President Hafez al-Assad, together with Lebanese President Elias Hrawi, signed the Treaty of Brotherhood, Cooperation, and Coordination in Damascus. It was made clear, in the view of the two countries' leadership, that the Lebanese and Syrians were one people and "nothing would ever drive them apart."⁴⁵ The SSNP's Nasri Khouri headed the Syrian–Lebanese Commission and the party secured victories in the 1992 election, gaining six seats in the Lebanese Chamber of Deputies.⁴⁶ By 1996, the SSNP had achieved a slight increase in sectarian diversity among its party leadership, with three Orthodox Christians, two Maronites, two Sunnis, two Druze, one Shia, and one Catholic present on the executive committee compared with its leadership demographics from 1948 to 1958.⁴⁷

Sporadic clashes with Israel continued throughout the 1990s that saw the party sustain casualties. During Operation Grapes of Wrath that unfolded between Hezbollah and Israel in April 1996, seven SSNP members were among those killed in an Israeli air strike on April 12 in the Lebanese village of Sohmor in the Beqqa Valley. The splits within the party continued to endure after the end of the civil war. Regional developments helped exacerbate these internal policy and ideological differences. One such example was the 1991 Gulf War in which Damascus positioned itself on the side of the Western-led military coalition against Saddam Hussein's Iraq. The SSNP's Intifada faction continued its long-held policy that the conflict was "a war of others" being fought on the soil of Natural Syria, essentially that Iraq was the same as Syria or Lebanon. A young SSNP member from Hama named Ali Haidar made this position clear and issued a statement denouncing the participation of the Syrian armed forces in the alliance to liberate Kuwait from Saddam. This landed him in trouble with the party elders, and he was subsequently "abandoned" by Issam al-Mahayri, who dispatched a Syrian intelligence agent to tell the Intifada faction members that Mahayri had disowned Haidar and he was not representing the party. However, the Intifada faction remained very small and kept to itself on the sidelines. The even larger divisions that occurred to the party's main faction in 1987 continued well into the 1990s.⁴⁸ The SSNP-Emergency faction won five seats in the 1996 parliament, and Raad's faction did not obtain any seats during the election.⁴⁹ The so-called Emergency Council and the Supreme Council finally achieved unification on November 5, 1998, in the aftermath of the Lebanese elections. Mahayri was subsequently replaced with Ali Qanso as the party's president.⁵⁰

Within Syria, the final decade of Hafez al-Assad's rule still kept tight reigns on the party's activities. In particular, members of the Intifada faction were not properly aligned with the Syrian government. One Intifada comrade in Syria described his experiences during the 1990s:

> I was arrested in 1995 and 1996. At that time, I was not holding any positions in the party. The first arrest was because I was promoting the party in college, and the second one was because I was transporting internal party correspondence from Lebanon to Syria. I was arrested at the border with the documents in my custody. Both times I was held for a few days, beaten, warned, and released after that. I did not meet any other party members in jail, but I know of a few other members who were arrested. After the year 2000, none of our party members were arrested.[51]

As 1990s saw the party being positioned as an agent of Damascus, the 2000s brought about the withdrawal of Syrian forces from Lebanon. The Syrian government subsequently began to rely on the SSNP's symbolism even more. The party's flags became a more prominent icon of pan-Syrianism and the notion of "Greater Syria" to focus on Syria and Lebanon's interconnected destiny. This was one of the first times the Assad regime would put its former rival to political use, and rather ironically, the SSNP flag was seen during government-organized protests in Adnan Malki Square by Western observers.[52]

By the end of the 1990s and with the arrival of the early aughts, the SSNP in Lebanon continued its transition from a relic of the Cold War and civil war into a traditional Lebanese party. The pan-Syrian movement simultaneously sought to curb dissent over Syria's dominance in Lebanon while fostering a new generation of leftist-oriented party members. This trend was perhaps best manifested by the election of long-time party leftist Gebran Araiji to head the party's main faction in 2001. As noted in the previous chapter, Araiji was among those who Raad had allowed to foster a Marxist trend in the party during the 1970s and 1980s. The election was triggered after Ali Qanso resigned in order to take up his position as Lebanon's minister of labor. The SSNP's Higher Council held a secret meeting and secured Araiji's position with more than two-thirds of the votes. Araiji lauded Qanso's accomplishments, "despite the obstacles and challenges the party and its president confronted during this time" and urged "all Lebanese to unite and avoid divisive issues." Furthermore, he emphasized the need for Lebanese–Syrian unity "against the threats facing the region" and proclaimed that bilateral relations "should only be discussed by their respective governments and were not an issue for the people."[53]

Araiji retained popularity and boasted support both inside and outside of the party. The SSNP's main faction was optimistic during this period since it was anticipating a shift in the Syrian regime's official position toward the party, which essentially meant legalization. Although the Syrian Baath Party had long softened its attitude toward the SSNP, the pan-Syrian movement still remained officially banned inside Syria. In preparation for its entry into Syria's political sphere, the SSNP's main faction under Araiji was expected to implement internal reforms and increase the role of youth in the party.[54] Along with Sarkis Abu Ziad, Araiji was close to Raad and shared his leftist views. Araiji had previously twice sought to head the party but first withdrew in favor of Raad. The second time he lost to Qanso.[55] However, Araiji's reform efforts fell short and he resigned just a few years into his term due to internal disagreements with Assaad Hardan.[56] Sarkis went on to hold several senior posts in the party, most notably as the SSNP's dean of culture, and is still active and heads a cultural center in Beirut, called Alef. Araiji died on January 9, 2019.

Antoun Saadeh is buried in the Mar Ilyas cemetery in Beirut. The party's members pay annual homage to their martyred founder with ceremonies and large red garlands in the shape of the SSNP's signature logo. The yearly visits to the party's founder tomb remained steadfast even as the situation around the party and the wider region began to rapidly change. The era of Syria's military occupation in Lebanon came to an abrupt end. International pressure had been building on Syria to allow free and fair elections in Lebanon and to remove its military presence from the country. The UN Security Council adopted resolution 1559 in September 2004, which saw massive rally of pro- and anti-Syrian forces in Lebanon. SSNP President Araiji met with Lebanese President Emile Lahoud and insisted the rallies reflected the nation's unity for closer ties with Damascus.[57] Massive demonstrations occurred after the assassination of former Prime Minister Rafiq Hariri on February 14, 2005. During the final years of the civil war in the 1980s, Hariri had cultivated a close relationship with Hafez al-Assad and his associates. Heavily involved in the reconstruction of postwar Lebanon, Hariri's government sought a balance with both Syria and Lebanon. However, it was during the transition of influence to Hafez's son Bashar in the late 1990s that Hariri began to lose influence with the Syrian government.[58] As the last Syrian troops traversed the Masnaa border crossing in April 2005, the SSNP's flags proudly flew alongside the flags of Syria as the crowds greeted the returning soldiers.[59] Following the withdrawal of Syrian military and intelligence forces from Lebanon, there was a bout of security reorganization among the country's political factions. The void left behind led to a heightened state of Lebanon's sectarian and political tensions. The SSNP sought to shore up support for the Syrian government in Lebanon. It was not long before the reactions to the withdrawal began to reverberate throughout the Lebanese arena. Historians noted, "Pro-Syrian militias such as Baathists in the Beqaa, [the SSNP] in Beirut, Alawite gangs in Tripoli and even Amal, prepared intensively for urban fighting."[60]

While Vladimir Putin's Russia offered Damascus some diplomatic support during this period, by blocking moves for sanctions in the UN Security Council, the Russians largely adopted the view that the Assad regime had miscalculated with Hariri's assassination and did little to help Syria maintain its military foothold in Lebanon.[61] More consequential for the party, the SSNP's reputation continued to cause fear throughout the general Lebanese population. During the bombing campaign that commenced after the Syrian army's withdrawal, rumors alleged that former militia members from the party were constructing car bombs in an underground parking garage in Rue Jeanne d'Arc in Beirut's Hamra neighborhood.[62] Lebanese security forces initially sought out a handful of pro-Syrian figures as suspects. Pro-SSNP MP and owner of the party's *al-Binaa* paper, Nasser Qandil, was arrested and quickly released at the Lebanese–Syrian border in late August 2005.[63]

Apart from being aligned closely with Syria, the SSNP tread forward in Lebanon's political scene as a close partner of Hezbollah. The secular party had its own familial links to the Party of God's leadership. Hezbollah Secretary General Hassan Nasrallah's father, Sayyid Abdulkarim Nasrallah, in an interview with Lebanese journalist Ghadi Francis on OTV's show *Seemline* explained how he was once a member of the SSNP. Abdulkarim Nasrallah said his thought on Greater Syria mirrors that of Antoun Saadeh and argues that, while SSNP is not religious, it also does not oppose religion, and this is what appealed to him. He said he was part of the SSNP's leadership in the city of Tyre; however, following the 1960s dissolution of the party, he was no longer interested and became focused on his family. During the interview, he quoted Saadeh verbatim to echo the SSNP's closeness to his political thought of resistance. Abdulkarim remarked, "the leader says 'the blood that goes through our veins is not ours, its the nation's deposit in us. Whenever it is asked for, it finds it.' " After he started a family, he no longer passed on the SSNP's ideology to his family and left it behind and allowed his children to learn the "science of the Hadith." He believed his children should have the freedom to choose what they want, like when he was a child, "no one pushed" him to become a nationalist; therefore, he did not push his children to any particular path.[64]

The 2006 Israel–Hezbollah War unfolded in mid-July and wrought a vast amount of devastation to Lebanon's infrastructure, with over a thousand civilians killed. "Similar to the period after the Iraq war, [Assad] was again perceived in the region as the only Arab leader—together with Hezbollah leader Hassan Nasrallah—who successfully upheld the flag of resistance on behalf of Palestinians facing the Israeli enemy," remarked Syria observer Carsten Wieland.[65] In the aftermath of the Israeli–Hezbollah conflict, the SSNP became the target of Lebanese government scrutiny. The pro-Western government of Prime Minister Fouad Siniora sought to confront the pro-Syrian Lebanese factions wherever it could. On December 22, 2006, the Lebanese security forces raided the homes of SSNP members in the Koura district and displayed crates of aging weapons in front of the media, many of which were likely leftovers from the civil war.[66]

With the tensions rising between the pro- and anti-Syrian sides, it was not long before the SSNP found itself caught up in another dangerous internal standoff. The May 2008 clashes in Lebanon were the results of a confrontation that had been brewing since the Hariri assassination, the subsequent Syrian withdrawal, and months of political deadlock. The pro-Syrian forces sprang into action when the government removed the Hezbollah-affiliated head of security from the Beirut International Airport and attempted to shut down the militia's telecommunications network. The SSNP was once again pitted against their fellow Lebanese citizens and simultaneously grasped victory and suffered painful losses. The party was featured prominently in the raid on an office belonging to Saad Hariri's political party, the Future Movement, in Beirut, with armed assailants outside the doors, and a masked figure clad in black sporting a red whirlwind armband was photographed rummaging through a desk, AK-47 held aloft. But the party also gained new martyrs during the conflict. In northern Lebanon, the crisis boiled over into bloody clashes between Sunni militants and the pro-Hezbollah camp. Eleven SSNP members were massacred in the northern town of Halba by the anti-Syrian factions when a crowd stormed the party's office. The fallen included an Australian who was visiting. The party's martyrs were commemorated by the party in the aftermath of the clashes.[67]

Hezbollah and the SSNP were able to rout the pro-Western militias of the Future Movement due to their better training and equipment. In addition, the Lebanese Armed Forces were better integrated into Hezbollah's communication and command structure, allowing the pro-Syrian movements to vanquish their opponents.[68] Druze leader Walid Jumblatt, whose PSP militia fought alongside the Future Movement, remarked, "We avoided civil war." He expressed hope that the negotiations that unfolded in the aftermath of the clashes would lead to a national discussion on the weapons held by the country's non-state actors.[69] In a sense, the 2008 victory was the final twilight of Assad's prewar Syria, described as a "golden period" where Damascus was able to reassert itself both within the region and on the international stage.[70] In June 2008, Assaad Hardan made a speech to indicate the party's alignment with pan-Arabism. He said, "Our party has found in Damascus the beating heart of the nation … we call on all great Lebanese to realize the truth of the positive role of Syria in preserving Lebanese unity and Arabism."[71]

As the Syrian Civil War unfolded in Lebanon's neighbor, trouble was brewing just below the surface for the Markaz faction. Signs of internal upheaval began to bubble up when Assaad Hardan tried to orchestrate a third term for himself as the party's president in 2016, but he was removed from office. Antoine Khalil, a former MP, objected to this move and blocked Hardan's ambitions. Hanna al-Nashef was elected as the party's president in November 2017. After Ali Qanso died in the summer of 2018, internal grumbling began to rise to the top. Several members threatened to resign from the Higher Council in October 2018. Amidst these internal power-plays, other personal disputes spilled out into the open. In 2019, a famous SSNP member, Charles Ayyoub, also the owner of the *Ad-Diyar* newspaper, found himself expelled from the party.[72] Ayyoub later tweeted that Hardan had threatened to kill him.[73]

However, Assaad Hardan still remained a prominent figure in the party and leveraged his role in parliament to try to keep the SSNP relevant. Following the 2018 parliamentary elections, he slammed the sectarian character of the Lebanese government. The SSNP's MP also engaged in infrastructure development projects in Lebanon. One was asphalting the roads between Aintoura and northern Matn. This is a part of the SSNP's rehabilitation efforts for the roads in a number of towns and villages in the south. In June of 2018, the roads of Hula in Nabatieh were asphalted and rehabilitated, a project allegedly funded solely by MP Hardan. By late June, the roads reached the Kfarchouba and Kfarhamam villages in the Arkoub region of Hasbaya. In September, the roads connected to Khalwat al-Bayada, the Druze sanctuary and theological school in Hasbaya. In October of that year, an 800-meter-long road was constructed between El Faouqa in Nabatieh and the road of Khalwat al-Bayada, and many other roads were constructed and asphalted in Hasbaya. The villagers of Kfeir reacted by hoisting a banner, which read, "Thank you to his respected excellency Minister Assaad Hardan for his contribution to paving some of the town's roads. The people of Kfeir."[74]

Antoun Saadeh's party in Lebanon looks destined to remain on the fringes of Lebanese politics. However, the future may provide some opportunities for the SSNP to capitalize on the domestic scene. If the party is able to resolve its infighting and perhaps unite with Intifada, no doubt a tall order since they have effectively been split since 1957, it would perhaps be able to make some in-roads in regard to expanding its recruitment and calibrating its message to a wider generation of Lebanese youth who are disgruntled with the rampant corruption and cronyism that has dominated the country since the end of the civil war in 1990. Furthermore, there is a growing sense of antisectarianism and appetite for a secular society among the young and increasingly politically active. The antigovernment demonstrations that resulted in the resignation of Prime Minister Saad Hariri in late 2019 saw the party placed in a precarious position. It wanted to adhere to its message of a revolutionary renaissance that would completely restructure Lebanon's politics and society, while still maintaining the balance in favor of the pro-Damascus and Iran coalition currently led by President Michel Aoun.

Assaad Hardan voiced his concerns in December 2019, "Discussions touched on the worrisome situation in Lebanon. We are eager to deflate the tense political rhetoric in Lebanon."[75] The SSNP has charted a difficult situation during the 2019–20 Lebanese antigovernment protests. The party's position on antisectarianism and reformist platform should solidify itself with the anticorruption movement. For instance, Salim Saadeh, an MP affiliated with the Markaz faction and the son of Abdullah Saadeh, posted online messages in January 2020 regarding the need to establish a civil state based on social justice. The pictures include his late father, thereby directly allowing Salim to channel his father's role as an antigovernment revolutionary in the 1961 New Year's Eve coup attempt.[76] However, Salim himself was attacked and beaten by antigovernment protesters in February 2020. He subsequently shared social media images of himself in a hospital bed before cheerfully apologizing for his delayed return to the parliament due to "health issues."[77] Following the incident, he received a hero's welcome in his home district of Koura.

The SSNP in Lebanon continued to find itself in the awkward position of championing a complete overhaul of Lebanon's sectarian system and being trapped as a component of that very same system. As the country grappled with the Covid-19 global pandemic, the capital faced its gravest catastrophe yet. On August 4, 2020, a large stockpile of ammonium nitrate sitting in the Port of Beirut detonated after a fire had broken out earlier. Over two hundred people were killed and over 6,500 injured by the blast's shockwave that shattered windows over six miles away. Among the fatalities was an SSNP member serving in the Lebanese Army Sergeant, named Hasan Tay, from the village of Nabi Osmane.

The party urgently issued a public statement in the aftermath of the blast, calling for Lebanese citizens to donate blood, and its young men and women took to the streets of Beirut, armed with brooms and shovels, to clean up the city's debris.[78]

Interestingly enough, the SSNP took a nuanced position regarding the role of Lebanon's old colonial master. The Lebanese people, fed up with the entrenched corruption of the ruling class, began to call for a greater French involvement in implementing political change. French President Emmanuel Macron arrived on the scene in Beirut on August 31 in the aftermath of the disaster.[79] The differences in the party's factions over France's newfound involvement in Lebanon were stark. The Markaz faction's dean of foreign affairs, Caesar Obeid, mused on a pro-Hezbollah channel that France could possibly play a role in helping Lebanon, despite the objections of the presenter.[80] However, the Intifada were unwavering in their position toward foreign influence in the Levant. The Intifada's dean of radio, Elie El-Khoury, blasted foreign interference as responsible for the Balfour Declaration, the Sykes–Picot Agreement, the oppression of the Ottoman Caliphate, and pointed out that Lebanon's devastation would continue until the barriers that divided the country (Greater Syria) were removed.[81]

However, the SSNP, like much of its history, perhaps faces the largest risks and rewards, not from politics but from war and violence. As Lebanon's woes continue, the party still becomes caught up in the violence that occasionally plagues the nation. One evening in late August 2020, a car drove up to the town of Kaftoun in the Koura district, and the vehicles' occupants were challenged by several armed SSNP members on a nightwatch patrol. The car's passengers opened fire and drove off into the night, leaving three SSNP comrades dead. Their funerals were live-streamed on LBC International, with a crowd of mourners sitting on white plastic chairs next to coffins draped with the party flags before a stage of Orthodox priests.[82] A banner hung over the large crowd that stretched along the road to Koura. It read: "Long live my dear comrades and loved ones, Fadi, George, and Ala." Among the speeches made during the funeral, the party's painful history of sacrifices was sorrowfully recalled, with reference to the SSNP's suffering during the days of the dreaded Abdul Hamid Sarraj's Second Bureau.[83] The scene was sadly familiar for what had already been occurring for the party's militia members in neighboring Syria. With the outbreak of conflict in Syria in 2011, the dangers and opportunities for Antoun Saadeh's party subsequently presented themselves amid a devastating war and humanitarian disaster in Syria. For the SSNP in Lebanon, new political openings arose in Syria, but at a cost the party's comrades were well acquainted with.

8

Battles and Ballots: The SSNP and the Syrian Civil War

The coffins were carried through the streets of Syria's towns and villages. Crosses, flags, and portraits of Syrian President Bashar al-Assad were common features among the funeral processions. However, in lieu of the twin green stars of the Syrian national flag on the coffins were the black flags baring the SSNP's striking red zawbaa. As Syria's terrible civil war expanded and unfolded throughout 2012 and beyond 2013, images of the party's fallen began to flood the social media. In some instances, online images released by the party's media outlets also showed the fallen family members receiving not the Syrian flag but the SSNP's party flag.[1] The SSNP's deceased militia fighters appeared in martyrdom posters indicating the name of the member and their date of death. The story of SSNP's sacrifices, propaganda efforts, and political activities within the Syrian Civil War best indicates the party's current status within the graces of the Syrian government, a place fraught with both perils and prizes.

The emergence of the SSNP in President Assad's warring coalition during the Syrian Civil War brought the party out of a slumber and back into the consciousness of Western observers. The 1990s and 2000s had relegated the old pan-Syrian movement to relative obscurity. Widely regarded in the West as small, irrelevant, marginalized, and a tool of the Syrian government in Lebanon, the SSNP largely retained the reputation it had forged through its suicide bombing campaign during the later phase of the Lebanese Civil War. However, it was subsumed by the far more visible and powerful Lebanese Hezbollah in the Levant's pro-Syrian political sphere. Headed by the charismatic cleric, Hassan Nasrallah, the Lebanese Shia party had indeed established itself as the primary force in Iran and Syria's Axis of Resistance bloc along the eastern Mediterranean coastline. As discussed in Chapter 7, Israel's Grapes of Wrath campaign in April 1996, along with the 2006 July War, had brought Hezbollah to the fore during this period. Now fielded in Syria to fight the anti-Assad rebels, the Lebanese

Islamist party took on a new role, positioning itself as an essential vanguard for preventing the fall of Assad's regime, professedly fighting terrorism and protecting vulnerable Syrian sectarian communities.

As the yellow flags baring the green Kalashnikov assault rifles dotted the Syrian battlefields, the SSNP's swirling red zawbaa stood out among the array of pro-regime militias. Riding the tide with Hezbollah, the SSNP's militia, the Eagles of the Whirlwind (Nusur al-Zawbaa) had a new mission: to protect the purportedly secular regime and defend the country's territorial integrity. After fifty years of political exile, the pan-Syrian movement had not only returned to the Baathist state, it was now carrying arms on behalf of the Assads. The Syrian conflict represented both a dramatic opportunity and an extreme risk to the party. In late 2011 and early 2012, the days of the Assad family's rule in Damascus appeared to be numbered. Furthermore, the Baath Party itself had suffered a political blow and was weakened and undermined.[2] The SSNP was now well positioned to prove its value to Assad's fledging government. If Assad was toppled, the SSNP's dream of establishing Greater Syria, which always seemed so distant and remote, was now imminently threatened. The potential for a political partition of Syria would also run contrary to the party's wishes. Whether or not a pro-Western liberal or conservative Islamist government assumed power in a post-Assad Syria, the prospect of a new regime intent on cleansing away the old order made the party fear a new round of persecution for its activities and membership. The tiny SSNP blip that now flickered on the Syrian political scene for the first time in over fifty years would be snuffed out in its infancy.

Early Syrian Civil War 2011 Protests to 2014

The SSNP's Intifada faction had taken part in earlier opposition activism during the short-lived Damascus Spring in June 2001 and the years that followed and even participated in the peaceful protests that occurred in 2011. However, the party distanced itself once the events turned violent.[3] To the SSNP, the very survival of Syria itself was at stake. In the party's view, the threat of Islamist rebels storming Damascus and the possibility of Kurdish secessionism were real. The potential fall of the Assad regime would signal a new order that would plunge the future of the SSNP into the unknown. Leaving the SSNP with Lebanon as its sole island to operate, as so often shown, would put Saadeh's party in great danger. Without both Lebanon and Syria, the party would not have a refuge to swing back and forth in order to survive.

In line with its anti-imperialist nature, the SSNP also viewed the rebel movement primarily as a Zionist and Western conspiracy aimed at overthrowing what was truly an independent and sovereign nation within the modern-day international system that had for decades resisted Western money and military power. The party's propaganda during the war years fervently worked to assist the regime's narrative of this conspiracy. In mid-2011, thugs affiliated with the SSNP and other pro-Syrian groups brutally attacked peaceful anti-Assad demonstrators in Beirut. One activist was quoted in the aftermath of violent street clashes saying, "We didn't provoke them. As they chanted 'We sacrifice ourselves for you, Bashar,' we chanted over them, 'We sacrifice for you, Syria,' and then they attacked us." However, the SSNP denied that it was involved. SSNP spokesperson Bilal Bou Dargham said, "The SSNP wasn't involved in the incident last night. Some members of the SSNP youth were involved in the pro-regime demonstration because it was close to where they work." He further explained that the protesters had not allowed sufficient notice for the Lebanese Interior Minister to provide enough police protection to separate the two sides. "We don't have a problem with people going out and demanding reform or anything. In Lebanon everyone has the right to say their opinion while respecting the opinions of others." However, the activists bitterly complained the Lebanese police did nothing to properly document the incident.[4]

For the Syrian opposition, the SSNP was another cog in the Syrian security apparatus that could even reach the rebel fighters and democracy activists who had sought safety in Lebanon. One Syrian opposition figure representing refugees in Lebanon, Ahmed Moussa, told the *New York Times* in February 2012 why they preferred the northern city of Tripoli to Beirut: "It is safer for us to work here because we have popular support and because Hezbollah and the Syrian Social Nationalist Party do not have much influence here."[5] The violence did eventually reach Tripoli, with fierce sectarian clashes erupting between pro-Assad Lebanese Alawites and anti-Assad Sunnis engaging in gun battles along the city's Syria Street, the so-called Bab al-Tabbaneh–Jabal Mohsen conflict

The Amana Split

It was not long before the SSNP's main branch endured a new fissure. In 2012, roughly a year after the Syrian conflict began, Markaz once again split into two, this time with a small faction seemingly designed to operate solely within Syria. The exact reasons for this division are not entirely clear. This was supposedly not about a Syrian party having branches outside of the country, but rather a party that was "based" outside of Syria, issuing orders to its branch inside Syria, essentially amounting to a form of "foreign influence." Thus, the so-called Amana (Trusteeship) faction was officially formed under the leadership of party elder Issam al-Mahayri, now in his nineties, before being handed to the Syrian SSNP politician named Joseph Sweid.

The details behind the Markaz-Amana dispute allegedly stem back to the decisions made in Damascus, apparently without the input of the SSNP headquarters in Beirut, but as will be discussed in the final chapter, the responsibility and the subsequent power struggles behind this split were the work of President Assad's cousin, Rami Makhlouf. The SSNP in Syria was already essentially operating as Markaz's branch there but ostensibly, because of the law banning foreign political parties, Issam al-Mahayri and the leadership in Damascus opted to register the Amana faction as an independent party altogether. The Amana faction was also officially known as the SSNP in the Syrian Arab Republic, or SSNP-SY. The personal and political disagreements that emerged as a result of this decision effectively split the largest faction of the party. It is likely the fissure was needed in order to allow Markaz the ability to legally deploy its militia in support of the Syrian government in the conflict all while simultaneously allowing the Baath Party to keep the party under more political control.

Joseph Sweid, a Greek Catholic party leader and Syria's minister of state since 2011, has also been a member of the People's Assembly since 2003 and served on the Foreign Affairs Committee. In the party, he served as the constitutional secretary of the Political Bureau. Sweid also acted in a diplomatic capacity and was instrumental in facilitating dialogue between President Assad and the Vatican, meeting with Pope Francis' secretary of state Archbishop Pietro Parolin and the Vatican's foreign secretary Archbishop Dominique Mamberti in December 2013.[6] The December discussions revolved around finding a way to end the conflict without foreign intervention. The party as a whole was active with international diplomacy, arranging many meetings with foreign officials and representatives from parties across the political spectrum. The SSNP's Intifada notably met with Germany's right-wing populist Alternative für Deutschland (AfD) party in 2018 in order to highlight the Syrian regime's intent to restore order amid the insecurity, which the AfD no doubt wished to project for a push to return the Syrian refugees in Europe back to their homes.[7]

Intifada, on the other hand, has over sixty years of a historic split with the Markaz faction, a legacy that will be much more difficult to overcome. However, Intifada's leader, Ali Haidar, who studied ophthalmology with President Assad had an advantage through their friendship.[8] As will be discussed further in Chapter 10, Dr. Haidar forged partnership with People's Will Party leader Qadri Jamil and took part in a new opposition grouping called the Popular Front for Change and Liberation (PFCL). Jamil was later dismissed by the regime from his government post in October 2013 for meeting with US officials in Geneva. Joseph Sweid had the backing of President Assad's cousin, Rami Makhlouf, became the head of the Amana branch in 2016 after Mahayri resigned to join his son in the United States.[9] Syria's parliament, the People's Council, is typically described as a rubber stamp body in the West.[10] Still, the party's parliamentary presence yields interesting information regarding the party's role that is permitted by the regime and the overall scope of the SSNP's political activities in Syria.

In the 2012 parliamentary elections, SSNP obtained six seats:

1. Ilyas Shaheen (who also became the president of the Amana faction), from Homs
2. Sawsan Sayyed Wahba, from Idlib (faction unknown)
3. Ali al-Sheikh Haidar Bin Ismail, from Hama, Intifada [11]
4. Mustafa Abu Souf, from Aleppo, Amana
5. Necmedîn Şemdîn, from Damascus, Amana
6. Nawras Mirza, from Hama, Amana

The 2012 Syrian legislative elections were held on May 7. An article in *An-Nahar* magazine from May 8, 2012, wrote there was "a new split in the SSNP" and noted that Mahayri (then the SSNP's president of the Political Bureau in Syria) had presented papers for the registration of the SSNP under the new Syrian partisan law. The same day, *al-Hadath News* contacted Shawqi Riyachi, then the dean of broadcast of Markaz, denied that a split had occurred and said the party's leadership in Beirut had simply ordered Mahayri to register the party in Syria. Information about the split remained vague until June of 2012 when Amana held the so-called Regenerative Congress in Damascus, which in effect legitimized the split. Since Mahayri was head of the Political Bureau of SSNP in Syria, those who ran as SSNP candidates in elections were loyal to him, especially since he was SSNP's (other than Intifada) only representation in Syria. This also meant that his candidates likely had received votes from SSNP members who may have not realized their votes were going to a soon-to-be new faction of the SSNP. By 2016, with the new schism fully apparent, Markaz began setting up its own branches all over Syria and developed its own separate support base, and in the 2016 election, it swept the SSNP's seats in parliament.

List of the SSNP MPs—2016 parliamentary election:

1. Ahmad Marei, from Aleppo, Markaz
2. Inas Mohammed Khair al-Mallouhi, from Tartus, Markaz
3. Bashar Yazigi, from Homs, Markaz
4. Sameer Hajjar, from Damascus, Markaz
5. Sameer Naseer, Latakia, Markaz
6. Mazin Azzouz, from Hama, Markaz
7. Talal Houri, from Idlib, Markaz

Despite these advances, it was not long before Markaz found the Baath were still up to their old tricks. In the 2018 municipal elections, the SSNP's Sweida and Homs branches withdrew their participation when the Baath opted to squeeze the other parties out of the National Progressive Front's lists. The party branch in Sweida issued a statement on social media denouncing the government's moves and said they were making a mockery out of the party's contributions to fighting terror in Syria.[12] The regime's attention soon fell on the other factions in Syria. As abruptly as it appeared, the Amana's candlelight was snuffed out by President Assad. Amid a government crackdown on financial corruption that targeted his cousin, the faction met its untimely end. As of October 2019, the Syrian government ordered for the Amana faction to be disbanded and the faction's members were supposedly integrated into Markaz.

The Eagles of the Whirlwind

As the civil war accelerated between 2011 and 2012, the Syrian government began to adamantly reach out to its allies. Damascus was under the threat of being toppled by the various rebel groups that had sprung up around the country and had successfully taken control of several regime military bases and urban areas. Russia was not yet on the scene, and Hezbollah still had yet to reveal itself as fully being involved in the Assad regime's military efforts. Pro-government militias, such as the National Defense Forces (NDF), were formed and deployed in both offensive and defensive capacity. In addition to the above actors, the Syrian government called in an old favor from the main branch of the SSNP in Lebanon. The party would go on to take a key role as the Syrian Arab Army suffered from defections and defeats in the early days of the war. The number of fatalities the party has suffered throughout the course of the conflict is difficult to verify. The SSNP reports to date that it has lost an estimated 120–150 martyrs. These include 50–80 members of the party's militia, with the rest being civilians or SSNP members serving in the Syrian armed forces. The SSNP General Executioner of Homs, Nouhad Samman, explained some of the party's military involvement at the outset of the war:

> Our party, like all the historic parties in this part of the world, has always had a militia. The SSNP militia participated in the military operations that drove the rebels out of the predominantly Christian village of Sadad, near Homs, in November 2013. The rebels had religiously cleansed the village. But once Sadad was under the control of the SSNP forces, the Christians were free to return. After the expulsion of the rebels, President Assad accepted the presence of the SSNP militia as the force to guarantee the security of the Sadad and its environs. The same thing happened in Saydnaya and Marmarita.[13]

One of the militia's first major engagements was the seven-month battle to wrestle Ma'loula from Jabhat al-Nusra. In the ancient, predominantly Christian mountain town, the Aramaic language is still widely spoken. From September 2013 to April 2014, the town was captured, lost, and then retaken in coordination with Hezbollah fighters and the NDF, along with the remnants of the Syrian Arab Army. The Eagles of the Whirlwind were also redeployed from Latakia to Aleppo to take part in the military's final offensives to recapture the devastated city in November 2016.[14] However, the party suffered significant losses. Most notable of these was the SSNP's media officer and beloved figure, Adonis Nasser, who was born in 1981 in Choueifat, Lebanon. He was the third Lebanese citizen to die in combat with the Eagles of the Whirlwind in Syria, after Mohammad Awwad and Adham Najm. Nasser had joined SSNP in 1998 and was killed in Syria in February 17, 2016. He and other Eagles of the Whirlwind militia members died in Kinsabba when their vehicle was hit by a rocket launched by the fighters affiliated with the Jaish al-Fateh militant group. Thousands attended the funeral held in his hometown. The delegation that attended his funeral included the vice president of the Political Council of Hezbollah, Mahmoud Qamati, along with representatives of the Lebanese Democratic Party, the Free Patriotic Movement, Amal, the Lebanese Communist Party, Mourabitoun, and the National Movement for Democratic Change. Muhanna Al-Banna delivered a eulogy:

> We miss meeting you at every celebration, the cubs and the flowers [the party's young men and women] miss you.

The Renaissance Camps longs for you, and the dirt's scent yearns for you.
The olive trees will ask about how you left
And we will say: Before leaving you told us
I'm the martyr, remember me when you celebrate victory.

In January 2018, the pro-Assad *al-Mayadeen* outlet released a documentary focusing on the Eagles of the Whirlwind militia. The video wields a remarkable amount of insight into how the SSNP views its place in the Syrian conflict within the scope of its ideology and contained strong themes of defending the nation, protecting Syria's cultural heritage, along with a narrative acting as a bulwark to the Islamist rebel factions involved in the conflict. Also present was the party's vision of Natural Syria and the view that the region's artificial borders were a part of the problem. Furthermore, the foreign powers supporting the Syrian rebels were part of a conspiracy to divide and weaken Syria's sovereignty, and the party was at the forefront of the effort to resist this.

One SSNP fighter described how they are fighting against division and how those seeking division "now know that there are people who are going to give everything for unity." The theme of how the SSNP has deeply imbedded itself into the fabric of Syrian society is also prevalent. Sameer Mulhem, the party's general executioner in Sweida, said, "We say that the people of Sweida are born Social Nationalists congenitally." A notion of civility and companionship emphasized the stark contrast between the SSNP fighting on behalf of the government and the barbarism of the Islamic State group. The video shows another SSNP trooper who says, "Here we have the mentality, 'my comrade comes before my own soul,' but [the terrorists] do not have this." Another militia member remarked, "Once the warrior abandons his humanity, he's not a warrior anymore, he's a mercenary." In addition, the soldiers chant for the party's long-martyred leader, Antoun Saadeh, not President Bashar al-Assad. The scene later moves to Aleppo, and a group of SSNP fighters in the background can be heard chanting:

"Whose life is it?"
"Our own!"
"For who do we live?"
"Syria!"
"Who's our leader?"
"Saadeh!"
"Long live Syria! Long live, long live, long live!"

However, despite this, the party makes it clear that it operates under the authority of the Syrian government and is not entertaining any political opportunities the

SSNP stands to gain in the event of a regime victory. The scene moves to the town of Ayn Tarma and shows Saleh Hussein, the SSNP's general executioner of Quneitra, who says: "We do not seek any political or material gain; we only seek to defend the nation." The video scene cuts to Nouhad Samman, who discussed the moment when IS came to Sadad:

> At the beginning we were in Sadad, the chief of the directorate of Sadad, Suleiman Khalil, woke me up in the morning, said: "Mr. Executioner there they are outside." I replied, "Who are they?" He said, "The militants are outside shouting 'Allah Akbar' and they are all bearded, they have captured the town hall, and I'm locked in my house." I told him "What are you saying? Stay home and lock your door, we're going to come." This was October 21, 2013.

The video interviews SSNP fighters who describe how they only had forty-six militia members on hand to defend Sadad. One of them notes they lost nine martyrs in the battle, also adding that only two of the SSNP martyrs were from Sadad, the rest were from different areas of Syria and from different religious sects.

The narrative surrounding the SSNP's role in the protection of Syria's historic and cultural sites was also a central point. The documentary illustrates how the party, in contrast to the Islamic State's efforts to destroy Syria's cultural heritage, sought to safeguard it. Nouhad Samman appeared again and said:

> From the moment the militants first arrived, we were concerned about preserving our heritage, so I went to the police commander and asked him to allow us to establish checkpoints in old Emesa (the Ancient Greek name for Homs). We had to mark old Emesa on the map because most people do not know about it, so they consulted with me in order to prevent any human errors. The SSNP set up checkpoints at Emesa's seven gates, and closed off Emesa to completely protect it. We left one gate open, and that gate was secured by our combined forces until Emesa was complete liberated and cleansed of explosives. Those heritage sites were our primary concern! I mean, this is Emesa, and it cannot be liberated without its history.

Samman continued:

> On May 9, 2014, the militants had already begun a week earlier, we saw the smoke coming out, they were burning everything, they were burning cars, documents, their offices, their courts, so they might've burned something that was very important to us. The Eagles of the Whirlwind's main task alongside the army's engineering units was to clear the district of explosives. The bombs, they

were in the hundreds, not tens, hundreds of small bombs, they had colored them red, blue, and so on, and hid them everywhere. You could open a closet and a bomb explodes … you could open a car door and it explodes.

The SSNP Homs chief concluded, "Hence, the party became a demand of the people and are now trusted to the point that they can only sleep comfortably when the SSNP are outside. That means this area is safe." Samman continued, "We left old Emesa on September 1, 2017." In the town of Salamiyah, executioner Ammar Daiyyob remarks, "We're all volunteers, we all have our own businesses and jobs, for example, this comrade is a farmer, and this comrade is a Lebanese citizen who lives in the Sham (Syria) and, to us, it is like he was born here."[15] The emergence of the party's Eagles of the Whirlwind militia in the conflict was a stunning development given how long the party had been banned and repressed in Baathist Syria. An SSNP Facebook post in 2014 remarked,

> Go back only two years, and we would not see the party's symbol or slogan except on the inside of houses and in secret. Ask the people of Homs about the Nationalists, and one of them will answer you, laughing, "I asked them for a flag of the party to hang in my house, but there were none left, so I painted the 'hurricane' on the entrance to my house myself."[16]

Still, like many of the other videos produced by the SSNP and the myriad of other fighting forces in the conflict for online consumption, its accuracy and content could not be independently verified. In the *al-Mayadeen* documentary, there are parts that appeared to depict real combat and the troops shown look much more professional and are better equipped. However, it is often not clear whether the soldiers and weapons that are shown indeed belong to the SSNP and not to another militia or the Syrian army. These combat footage inserts are from a different unit than the original documentary and are far more informative regarding the SSNP's military capabilities. Some combat footage included a Soviet-era heavy NSV machine gun on a pickup. Interestingly enough, there are some SSNP flags seen. The problem with the inserted combat footage is that these do not necessarily consist of footage of all of the SSNP troops, but most likely include other units as well. However, the flags suggest that some of the weapon systems seen in the combat footage indeed belongs to the SSNP. We never see a tank filmed closeup with SSNP identification marks. The emblem on the fighters' left arm displays an eagle with curved wings, grasping the party's logo in its talons, which looks very similar to the design used by the German 'Luftwaffe' (Air Force) in the Second World War. Many of the militia fighters appear to be wearing Israeli-style army parkas, as well as cheap military vests bought in bulk from China. Commanders depicted in the footage occasionally are seen holding Motorola civilian radios. Some appear to be wearing US Marine digital-style camouflage uniforms or US desert camo patterns. The militia fighters' training and appearance vary in professionalism and many are clearly not frontline units.[17]

The Syrian regime allegedly offered to arm Ali Haidar's Intifada faction, but he refused on the grounds that, in his role as the minister of reconciliation, he could not acquiescent the responsibility of heading an armed movement. A noteworthy incident took place involving thirty party members in Salamiyya, a strategic town located near Hama, who were besieged by IS, which was firing rockets and conducting incursions. They demanded that Haidar send them arms, which he did reluctantly, sending them thirty Kalashnikovs, along with strict rules of engagement. (1) They were forbidden from establishing barriers or road blocks around the town. (2) They could not openly carry their weapons. (3) The armed SSNP personnel could only fire if they were fired upon. Viewing these rules as absurd, the town's SSNP members allegedly returned the guns.[18] This story demonstrates that the party youth and others were fed up with Haidar's inaction and unwillingness to use violence, even to avenge the death of his own son, Ismael.[19] It was an indictment of his leadership, especially when faced with the threat of IS. The Salamiyya residents likely sourced the arms from elsewhere, perhaps even from the Markaz faction. However, the story is also yet another example of the deeply ingrained tradition of nonviolence that is woven into Intifada's fabric: that the party should stay out of armed conflict and that force is to be used solely by the state.

The Syrian conflict's numerous war crimes did not spare the SSNP's armed fighters. The party had a highly negative reputation due to its association with the regime, which thus made it a prime target for the many groups fighting in the country. One opposition media outlet, Shaam, said that the Eagles of the Whirlwind were "killing Syrians in the name of Christians" and noted the high number of Christian fighters in their ranks.[20] Another outlet wrote that the SSNP were recruiting child soldiers to fight for Iran.[21] Photos posted on opposition social media accounts showed the ID cards of several SSNP members who were fighting as part of the local defense forces in Sweida and killed by the rebel groups in August 2017. The Eagles of the Whirlwind took part in several prominent and devastating regime offensives, including the siege of Aleppo and Eastern Ghouta during Operation Damascus Steel. So far, no video or photo evidence has surfaced that indicates that the party's militia was directly implicated in any large-scale war crimes or crimes against humanity. However, given how extensively the Eagles were deployed, such crimes are certainly possible, given their close operational cooperation with the regime's forces.

The party's militia was allegedly involved carrying out an extrajudicial execution of an IS fighter in the Sweida Governate in August 2018.[22] The IS fighter was taken prisoner after an attack on an SSNP checkpoint and was subsequently hanged by the locals in the ruins of a former Byzantine church in Sweida City over a stone arch known as "the gallows." However, the SSNP's militia sought to control the narrative surrounding the hanging. For the party, it was essential to be seen as operating within the confines of the Syrian state's legitimacy, and it would set a dangerous precedent if the SSNP began meting out its own form of justice on the IS prisoners. The Eagles of the Whirlwind released an urgent statement shortly after the incident:

> Following the publication of a number of photographs and films-ulteriorly circulated on various social media platforms concerning the execution carried out in the town of Sweida, with the SSNP's flag raised above it, we wish to clarify the following:
>
> Firstly: [The Eagles of the Whirlwind's] combatants fight alongside the Syrian Arab Army, answering only to the Government's institutions, for we firmly believe in accountancy being a matter of institutional responsibility, handled solely by security and judicial authorities, upon the apprehension of terrorists.
>
> Secondly: This retaliatory method bears no relation whatever to the SSNP's [Eagles of the Whirlwind] fighters, who have striven towards the consecration of moral fighting against all forms of terrorist and armed groups that have hitherto attempted to dismantle the government's system and its social structure.
>
> And thus, based upon the foregoing, we disclaim any endorsement and/or involvement of the SSNP's [Eagles of the Whirlwind] in the execution carried out in the town of Sweida.[23]

The SSNP's militia also took part in the regime's offensive in Idlib Province in September 2018, with the pro-Damascus *al-Masdar* news outlet reporting the party's militia fielded "divisions" from the predominately Orthodox towns of Al-Suqaylabiyah and Mahardah. The SSNP's militia conducted further operations against IS in Sweida in March 2019.

When asked about the future of SSNP in Syria after the war, a young Syrian SSNP sympathizer replied:

It all depends on the international agreements. If things go well, SSNP will slowly rise to become the majority party in Syria. If it doesn't go well, the SSNP will end up getting banned. The SSNP is seeing an increase, everyday new members join. If you observe the SSNP's martyrs during the war, you'll see that nearly all of them joined post-2012/2013. As for the parliament, a united Intifada-Markaz should be able to participate … if they do participate, SSNP will at the very least double its current seats.[24]

One ally the party has potential for influence and postwar support is Russia, which has positioned itself at the forefront of the government's reconciliation efforts, even attempting to maintain a nonsectarian approach to negotiate with Syria's rebel groups.[25] Aside from the military aspects of shoring up President Assad's forces, the SSNP has also been of interest to Russian observers for political purposes as well. For instance, in 2017, senior Valdai research fellow Nikolai Sukhov explained to the Russian outlet Lenta.Ru, "The concept of the SSNP on a secular Syrian nation consisting of equal rights of nationalities and religious communities allows us to satisfy the requirements of various parts of society and preserve a single state."[26] Other Russian observers expressed interest in the SSNP's predominately Orthodox constituency.[27] Russian state-owned English-language media outlets regularly featured mentions of the party and frequently quoted Tarek Ahmad and described him as part of the opposition even though he is with the Markaz faction. In April 2017, he urged for all of the conflict's armed groups to be included in the peace talks and said that the Geneva talks to be hosted in Damascus as well.[28] In June that same year, Ahmad expressed concern that the Gulf States' diplomatic crisis with Qatar would have a negative impact on the peace talks in Astana.[29] In August 2017, he denounced the Kurdish political movements' quest for independence or autonomy in Syria's northeast and directly tied it to Israel's intervention in the conflict, remarking that an independent Kurdish entity would only foster more wars in the region.[30] Ali Haidar was closely working with the Russian military officials and was seen taking part in a press conference with General Victor Bankov at the Russian Coordination Center at the Hmeimim Air Base in December 2017.[31] On November 2, 2017, the Russian ministry of defense awarded the medal of battle honors to several of the party's militia members.[32] However, it is clear, despite these emerging relationships, the Syrian government will attempt to keep the party in check. Ali Haidar ultimately received a demotion in November 2018. Dr. Haidar led Syria's state ministry for reconciliation until he found himself reshuffled into a new body, the National Reconciliation Authority; the purpose or activities of this new body remain unclear.³³

In October 2017, a military helicopter descended on Sweida City. The aircraft was carrying the body of the Republican guard's fearsome Major General Issam Zahreddine. In the crowd, the SSNP's zawbaa flag flapped in the wind alongside the flag of the Syrian government. A member of the Syrian Druze community and a lifelong Baathist, he joined the People's Militia in the 1980s. Zahreddine's force had held out for three years in the besiege city of Deir Ezzor, sounded by a sea of Islamic State fighters. General Zahreddine was killed in an IED explosion while driving in the Deir Ezzor Province. The SSNP's showing at his funeral was a notable salute to the Baathist general. The SSNP has a significant presence in the Druze-dominated Sweida Province, where the general hailed from. Zahreddine also maintained ties with the SSNP's political leaders in Syria. For instance, he was pictured shaking hands with Bassem Radwad, a Supreme Council member affiliated with the Amana faction in Syria. Outside of coordinating military activities with the Syrian government, the SSNP had another important role to play. Dr. Ali Haidar's Intifada faction was able to position itself as a mediator between the government and certain armed rebel groups. The SSNP, with its own experience of persecution by the Baathists and its long history of being banned in Syria, just the knowledge that they too, had been persecuted, perhaps allowing the party some space when entering into talks with the rebel factions.

One Intifada member indicated that their faction of the SSNP had little contact or say in the movements or operations of the party's militia that operated under the control of the Markaz faction, "I have no idea about Markaz's forces." The party also faced some sigma and distrust from the regime's security forces for even attempting to reach out to and negotiate with certain armed rebel groups. Ilya Samman, Ali Haidar's political adviser, explained, "They hate our guts. They think we're giving comfort to terrorists. I remember a colonel telling me: 'You're worse than the terrorists. We fight but you give them a chance.' But my argument is that it makes sense to allow a couple of hundred fighters to go elsewhere and let a couple of hundred thousand civilians return to normal life."³⁴ Allegedly, due to the staunch military opposition, President Assad himself had to intervene in order to allow the ministry of reconciliation to proceed with its work.³⁵ Samman described the reconciliation process thus:

> Our party members or supporters in areas controlled by rebels would help in establishing contact between their local community and the Ministry of Reconciliation. Once the contact is established, the Ministry teams (employees

and volunteers) would take over and negotiations would start with the leaders of the armed groups in the area. When reconciliation is accomplished, the fighters who agree to give up their weapons are granted amnesty, and they can go back to their normal civilian lives if they were civilians, defected soldiers, officers, and policemen are allowed to go back to their jobs as well. The main challenge we face during every reconciliation process is the foreign fighters and the radical jihadi groups. The main challenge is to convince the local rebels to get rid of their foreign leaders and ask them—in some cases force them—to leave the area. In regards to what do most of the rebels think of SSNP, we have a serious problem. Like many Syrians, rebels do not realize that there are two SSNPs and they confuse us with the other SSNP, which is allied with the regime. It takes a lot of effort and explanation to clarify this confusion. Once this point is clear, we do not have any problems dealing with the rebels.[36]

Still, the negotiations offered some sort of amnesty to rebels who wanted to put down their weapons. Ilya Samman said:

Some agreements have broken down but there are 103 sustained reconciliations which have worked and are surviving completely. They have affected the lives of two million Syrian citizens, who have returned to their normal productive lives. More than 100,000 "wanted" people have benefited from amnesty. Usually the taswiya (settlement) is done on site in a school or other public building. We've reached agreement with the security people to do it on the spot.[37]

The SSNP's ultimate legacy regarding the Syrian conflict has yet to be determined. The party's role in helping to prop up the regime during this crucial period essentially saw the SSNP revert to its role as a counter-revolutionary force as it had acted for the Chamoun government in Lebanon's 1958 crisis. It also was adamant about ensuring the survival of Syria's state institutions and restoring the country's sovereignty over its territory. Additionally, the party's propaganda sought to bolster the Syrian regime's narrative that all of the opposition groups were terrorists. Its role in the reconciliation process is notable but, with regard to the millions of Syrian refugees who have yet to return, it is unclear how effective these efforts can truly be in healing the country in the long run, or whether the party can help integrate the opposition elements back into Syrian society. The full extent of the influence of Russia and Iran and the political future of the Syrian government will be closely watched as the war reaches either a political solution or a military conclusion. In the event of possible relapses into further rounds of conflict, the SSNP would face extreme risks and struggle to find its footing in this troubled environment in the years to come.

9

Fires on the Mountain Tops: Women, Youth, and Social Media

The women of the SSNP are one of the most interesting elements of the party that make it stand out against the many other political movements of the region. The party's women members have a long history, even from the earliest days of Saadeh's movement. Following Saadeh's arrest, Afifah paid him regular visits in jail and brought him food from the family restaurant, as well as relayed messages to and from Saadeh and his comrades. The SSNP considers Afifah to be the first female member of the party. The party's custodian, Abdullah Qubrusi (the Cypriot), later described her character, "During Saadeh's first imprisonment, she used to carry provisions to the Raml Prison in 1935, without having a breakdown or second thoughts. It's more than enough that she executed her duties in admirable preciseness, never disobeyed an order, or exposed a secret, nor abandoned a comrade in need." This trend of female participation and activism would later signify the party's stance on gender equality and inclusion in view of the hardships faced during its earliest beginnings.

The party also celebrates its women through culture and folk lore. The famous Lebanese singer Fairuz was long rumored to be a member or party sympathizer, but this has never been proven. A song written by the Rahbani Brothers allegedly came out on Antoun Saadeh's birthday. One song was allegedly about how, when Saadeh was imprisoned in March of 1936, the SSNP leadership decided to light fires on the mountain tops to honor him and declare the party's growing presence. Fairuz sang this song at the Damascus International Fair in 1960. It was never confirmed that the song was about the SSNP, but many SSNP members claim that it was. The song's lyrics:

> My loved ones mother oh mother
> Flames at the tops of mountains
> My loved ones mother oh mother
> They left to a place far away and forgot me

And their love is still on my mind
Fires at the tops of mountains
I will head to far away mountains
To stand and wave my hands
And see their tents up high
Fire at the tops of mountains"

Another play, called "Night and Lantern," did not explicitly name SSNP, but it was presumed by a number of writers and researchers (such as Fawaz al-Tarabulsi)[1] to be about SSNP's 1961 coup and was performed in Damascus at the Lebanon Casino in 1963. The play speaks about a stranger threatening a town and its prosperity and stealing its wealth. Mantoura, Fairuz's character, is a young and her task was to protect a tent that served as a shop where the lanterns made by the village's people are sold, which is their only income. A thief named "Holo" causes trouble and steal things. So one day the village's people decided to hang a large lantern at the crossroads to catch Holo. He escaped and asked Mantoura, who did not recognize him, for a place to hide him from his pursuers, and she helped. Holo eventually tricked Mantoura and stole the earnings bag from the tent she was guarding. Mantoura found out and felt very bad for failing; she turned off her tent's lantern and left the town out of guilt. When Holo saw that her tent's lantern had been extinguished, he realized how much he had devastated her and decided to return the money, leaving a message with a friend of his to tell her to not leave.[2]

In an interview with a Spanish media outlet, party member Zainab Khierbeck, who comes from a prominent SSNP family, explained that the role of women in the party was not any different from the role of men. She quoted Saadeh as saying that nationalist work was not reserved for men and that work will never be nationalist until women participate and become active members and further added that the party's women "embody all truth, goodness, beauty, freedom, strength, trust, sacrifice and work, and that is what we strive for, to be the future of all women in Syria."[3]

What draws the most attention to the party is its history of women fighters and suicide bombers. As discussed in Chapter 6, this trend was particularly active during the 1980s amidst the tense geopolitics of the Lebanese Civil War. The SSNP's decision to field women in suicide operations as a military tactic also had a long-lasting impact on the party. Perhaps the most infamous case was Sanaa Mehaidli ("Bride of the South"), who left a deep impression on a generation of Lebanese youth. *The Girl in the Red Beret* was written in 2009 by Lina Mounzer, who explained:

> I still remember the first time I saw her. I was on my way to school in Ammo Mohammad's carpool. It was a sudden jolt, so fast it took me a few hours to piece together the reason for my shock. I'd seen the posters every morning on the same drive, and the faces changed often; there was always a new one papering over the old. Then suddenly I realized what was so strange about this new face: the smooth skin, the thick profusion of hair pouring out from under her red beret, stood out amid the multitudes of beards and moustaches. She was the lone woman in a sea of men ... She had brown hair and eyes like mine, and she was beautiful. It wasn't so much her features as it was just something about her, her easy comfort in her fatigues, the confident angle of that red beret. I'd never seen a girl who seemed so much like a boy.[4]

On July 17, 1986, Norma Abu Hassan detonated her car at the town square in Jezzine.[5] She was from Zgharta and joined the SSNP in 1984. Former CIA officer Robert Baer met with her handler in 2009, who described how no one pressured her to carry out the act. He shared a note she left behind, which he still carried with him. It read, "To comrade Munir al-Jamali, from Norma Abu Hassan, Zawbaa (Storm) Norma."[6] The SSNP has also yielded female martyrs in the ongoing Syrian Civil War, albeit not in suicide operations. A female SSNP member named Jianna Khadher Eid was killed while being enrolled in the regime's National Defense Forces (NDF) militia in October 2017. The party released a poster commemorating her death, and the SSNP party's storm logo was featured alongside the Syrian national flag. Women remain at the forefront of the SSNP's militancy and feature prominently in the party's emphasis on warding off imperialism or foreign aggression. One leading female member, Randa Baa'qlini, the president's office secretary, remarked in a speech at a party rally in 2007 that the party and its members have fought bravely and will always fight.[7] Baa'qlini is a Maronite from Dhour El Choueir, and her father, Mansour Hanna Baa'qalini, was one of the party's earliest members, who joined in 1947.[8]

Inas Mohammed Khair al-Mallouhi is a deputy in the Syrian parliament representing the Tartus Governorate. She is part of the SSNP's Markaz faction, and is described by her party comrades as "an outspoken woman" and commended for having made a few "controversial but brave" statements in her political career. This included: that Russia does not have the right to write a constitution for Syria; the government is not paying enough salaries; the Syrian parliament is full of people who do not do their jobs; and, finally, she proposed that the Syriac language be studied in schools instead of French, because "the French language is useless."

A young SSNP member remarked, "the Syrian people are used to 'silent MPs,' so this is a huge change in what people are used to and they like it." Syriac is still used by some Syrian Christian sects for liturgy and as an everyday language. In Ali Haidar's Intifada faction, there are two women in the Supreme Council (the highest legislative body of the party) and three women on the Executive Board (the highest executive body of the party). The SSNP's Facebook page hailed a recent workshop titled "Strengthening the Role of Syrian Women" organized by the Syrian Cultural Foundation, held at the Pullman Hotel in Al Shahba, Aleppo. The post noted, "150 women from various political, social, cultural, economic and media activities attended the workshop."

Arwa Abu Ezzeddine, in an October 2015 interview with the pro-Assad Janoubia (South) news outlet, said she joined the party in 1986 and has been active in the central leadership since 2004. She said, "Women have played an active role since the founding of the party. ... entering the cage with the eagles there is no distinction between men and women. Antoun Saadeh played the role as a human example in society, so women can radiate within the party." There have been a number of women who played a prominent role since the early years of the party's founding, most notably Afifa Haddad and other influential members in Beirut such as Fayza Maalouf Antiba and Amina Najla Matouk.

One party sympathizer explained that the SSNP's so-called "Nationalist Marriages" were common, but they are quite controversial. In Lebanese and Syrian society, this military-like attitude attracts criticism of fascism and also because the marriage is not being done in the Islamic or Christian traditions; since there is no civil marriage in Syria or Lebanon, this marriage will not be recognized by the state, and this particular point will cause a lot of legal issues in the future for these people and their future kids. The SSNP branch in Syria debated Syrian Minister of Awqaf Dr. Mohammad Abdul-Sattar al-Sayyed in the parliament, who denied the existence of the Qubaysiat, a once clandestine Islamist movement for women founded in Damascus in the 1960s. The group was later partially decriminalized by President Bashar al-Assad in 2003.[9] The SSNP is vehemently anti-Qubaysiat.[10]

The SSNP later rejected "decree number 16," which would allegedly grant more power to the Ministry of Awqaf. SSNP MP Tala Houri gave a speech slamming the decree:

> Members of the Parliament, you are standing before a historic responsibility, to perform your duties for your country and your people who have placed their trust in you. Today, the Ministry of Awqaf surprised us with the decree number 16 of 2018, which sets out the policy of the Ministry. We have read its contents, which were published in an informal manner, and it was clearly meant to appear "righteous" when in reality, its true purpose was to interfere in the official and administrative institutions of the state and to direct the government's policy through the representatives of the ministry in the local and popular councils and the government and dominate the source of Fatwa and tie it to the Ministry, which put it into law. The Minister, who has always told us through the media platforms about this "moderate Islam" to justify and ratify the Qubaysiat organization (after the state disbanded Women's Union) and the Sunni Muslim Youth Movement led by his son, who is considered the "legitimate heir" to the Ministry of Awqaf.

He continued:

> It is not the Ministry of Awqaf's responsibility to direct the general policy of the essential Ministries of Culture, Education, Higher Education and Media; its purpose is to manage the religious endowments for the Syrians of all religious backgrounds and to supervise the places of worship and guide them in accordance with the state policy to serve the national interest which is vested in the society's unity based on social and economic justice—because religion is a spiritual reservoir of the people, not the opium of the people, because religion is supposed to honor life, the Syrian people are not a herd of sheep driven by a shepherd with internal sectarianism that appears righteous on the outside but seeks to spread ignorance among the Syrian people on the inside and lead Syrians to their destruction and ruin. We have experienced some of this during the events caused by the Muslim Brotherhood during the 1980s as well as now with the eight years of the ongoing killing and destruction of the humanity and our spiritual structure before the destruction of our economic and urban structure or our national heritage that the nation derives from its culture and talent.[11]

The SSNP continues to take a secular approach to gender issues. For instance, in March 2020, President Assad introduced a draft law to the parliament that would abolish article 548 in the penal code, which was essentially a sentence reduction for "honor killings."[12] SSNP MP Ahmad Merhi said the party would support the move and called it a major step for gender equality.[13]

Youth

There is an extremely high level of engagement and emphasis the SSNP places on youth in the Levant. The SSNP believes that the children are the region's future and invests a great deal of energy in indoctrinating them for a future based on its values. This involves keeping Syrian and Lebanese youth busy with a plethora of social and educational activities. These efforts include offering free afterschool courses for students and awarding diplomas in different fields. Other activities and outings are more community- and civic-minded. This included reforestation efforts and environmental cleanup, encouraging athleticism and healthy lifestyles by organizing marathons and sports activities. In addition, the party's efforts include fighting for gender equality and feminism, offering free shelter during storms, training civilians and party members on the use of weapons for self-defense, working with organizations to aid and cheer up the elderly, such as sending delegations to celebrate Christmas in elderly homes, and working for people with disabilities, along with the organizations that take care of them. The SSNP has a whole institution for people with disabilities. One youth remarked on why he sympathized with the party:

> I have supported the SSNP since I was a kid. I knew about this mighty party because of my family which most of them are SSNP supporters. What really captured my attention about this party was the non-sectarianism principle. When I was 12 years old, I was introduced to the party, but this principle really took my attention since it amazed me that there's something that tells us to leave religions apart and treat each other equally.[14]

One young member explained that the party is quite active in their community especially socially and noted the party frequently held social events or dinner gatherings and lectures to mark historical events. The youth said it was important to note that, even though the party was active politically, the party was really working with its community and trying to spread Antoun Saadeh's doctrine as wide as possible to its supporters and to recruit non-supporters as well.[15] A review of SSNP social media posts shows the extent of involvement of young Syrians and Lebanese. The party's Engineering and Literature student directory in Latakia held a picnic to celebrate the end of exams. At the American University of Technology, the SSNP Koura branch hosted a family dinner. A youth camp in Krak Des Chevaliers held learning sessions on the value of respecting others, protecting the environment, and the importance of order.[16] Another youth camp in Aintoura in 2018 held games and educational activities. The same year a camp in Hama held a graduation ceremony in which the city's SSNP leader, Hafez Yaqub, said, "I salute the Syrian Army and the Eagles of the Whirlwind, but I emphasize that it is you, the youth, who protect these victories."[17] In the Sweida Governate, local SSNP youth and cadres in the city of Shaqaa, wearing black, had a solemn candlelit vigil for the souls of Syria's martyrs.[18] Young SSNP cadres and volunteers handed out candy to Syrian soldiers to mark Army Day, held annually every August 1.[19]

Some of the young adults in the party had the opportunity to fight with the party's militia during the Syrian Civil War. The Ibrahim twins, brothers Ali and Aziz, fought in several combat engagements and often posted images of their exploits on their social media accounts. The Ibrahim brothers are from Tartus and studied in the economic school of Tishreen University in Latakia. Aziz is currently in Lebanon, studying political science in the Lebanese University. Ali graduated recently from the Wadi Private International University and majored in architectural engineering. Aziz explained how they became involved in the party and noted their family's long history with the party. Before their grandfather passed away, he received the SSNP's medal of persistence.

> We became part of the party from a young age because our parents raised us at home on the principles and values of the party. My parents are also in the party. And my grandfather is one of the party's strugglers from the first generation.[20]

Another element that appealed to younger members and sympathizers was the belief that the creation of a Natural or Greater Syria would help eliminate the necessity and causes of wars and violence in the Middle East. This is partially rooted in the idea that there would be no reasons for the region's countries to go to war if they were all a part of the same political and economic structure. This, along with antisectarianism, was the primary driver for young people interested in the party and propagating its ideology. Despite how antisectarianism resonates with the younger party members, some still found it difficult to explain the mission of unifying the countries that Saadeh believed to belong to Natural Syria. One young supporter explained:

> I became interested more and participated in many SSNP lectures and social activities, in my opinion, it made me a great person in this doomed Middle East to be honest. The idea of uniting Greater Syria again under a secular principle could really help our countries and lead them to become a very strong nation without any wars and conflicts, but that's really a dream now and hard to achieve such a thing, sadly. The non-political Lebanese community members do not really know about our ideology and they always think that the SSNP is a

Syrian party. By Syrian, I mean Syria, the country that we know of now, not the historical Greater Syria. This thinking makes them a bit worried and insecure about the party. However, when you tell them about the SSNP's ideology and what it stands for, they start to like the idea of the party. But others get even more worried and they tend to dislike the SSNP, especially after they learn about the idea of uniting with Syria and Iraq and the other Levant countries under one nation called Syria.[21]

Young members attend the party's dinners and social gatherings with their family. One described a festive but serious occasion that marked the party's eighty-fourth anniversary, "It is like a big dinner where some officials in the party read their speeches that covers the history of the party and the current situation in Greater Syria and Lebanon specifically."[22] Interestingly enough, there might be some divergence on the newer generation's views toward social issues that would otherwise be considered off-limit or taboo for the party's older members. For instance, an Intifada member made it clear that LGBT issues were not on the SSNP's agenda.

> As a matter of fact, SSNP has no official view regarding homosexuality at all. In general we tend to be kind of conservatives and we pay a great respect to the family values, and as you are aware, homosexuality is not socially acceptable in our culture and society. Anyway, decriminalization of homosexuality is not in discussion by any means in the Middle East.

One individual who attended the party's youth camps in the 1990s acknowledged that the party hardly takes positions on social issues but remarked that

> the conservatism is more prevalent among older generations, particularly those who grew up in the region. Ironically, because one of the tenets of the SSNP was "secularism" and ardently promoting "tolerance" among the Levant's various religious and ethnic groups, that the "tolerance" message inadvertently resulted in younger generations more susceptible to "liberal" thinking on social issues. You'll find younger generations who grew up with SSNP backgrounds actually incredibly liberal and adopting of Western-style human rights concepts, extending to LGBT.

However, they noted that these liberal views often do not translate into the wider party due to the older generation's conservatism. With regard to young people outside of the party, opposition outlets have noted that many non-partisan youths in the region have adopted a deep distrust or cynical views toward many of the old, established parties, citing a lack of freedom of expression.[23]

The former youth camp attendee further remarked, "The SSNP has successfully stifled new membership, particularly among younger generations, largely to preserve positions of influence within the party for themselves and that is why it has gone nowhere in 40 years."[24]

The changing attitudes among the party's youth could also appear to be extending toward their perception of relations with Jewish people. While still largely retaining an uncompromising approach to the state of Israel, there appears to be some level of recognition regarding the need to respect the Jewish religion and to protect Jewish cultural and historical sites within Greater Syria. However, determining how widespread these attitudes are is very difficult, and it would more likely be present among the younger members and unofficial Syrian nationalists in the party's overseas diaspora.[25]

Social Media

Like most of the political movements around the world, the SSNP has entered the age of social media with gusto. The SSNP was purportedly one of the first political parties in the Levant to begin experimenting with websites in the early 1990s.[26] With this new platform of outreach, the daily activities, opinions, internal drama, and divisions were now accessible in a way that was unprecedented. No longer were the ongoings of the party confined to the restricted access of a tightly guarded community. Now, every individual had the means of instant public communication directly at their disposal.

The SSNP is incredibly active on social media, with multiple accounts for party news, youth activities, livestreaming events, the involvement of its militia in the Syrian conflict, and releasing content and propaganda on a daily basis. Most prominent was the activities of the Eagles of the Whirlwind's military campaigns during the conflict, with a high volume of images and content released over the course of the war. In addition, political activities from each of the party's branches in different towns and cities, as well as each faction have their own social media accounts. The subtle rifts between the party's various factions also can be seen on social media. The Amana faction made a reconciliatory gesture by acknowledging the late Markaz faction's president Gebran Araiji, who died in 2018, on its Twitter and Facebook pages. They had earlier abstained from paying tribute to long-time Markaz faction leader Ali Qanso when he passed away in July 2018. Up until this point, there had been no public acknowledgments of Markaz or the Eagles of the Whirlwind militia on their social media accounts.

The party also used its Facebook page to stress its role in defending the people. For example, after Homs was cleared of rebel elements in 2014, the SSNP's Homs branch posted: "The families of Homs return to their homes and thank the party for providing security for them."[27] One observer of the party's social media accounts remarked how the SSNP's antisectarian nature had attracted new recruits amid the religious-oriented violence during the Syrian conflict, as well as the importance of Syrian solidarity framed by the Greater Syria platform.

> After all, their number one priority is survival. Judging by the amount of propaganda pouring out of SSNP portals boasting about their popularity the future appears bright (at least for the short term). New recruits sickened by the sheer amount of killing in the name of religion have found the SSNP's inclusiveness comforting. In addition, a sense of alienation precipitated by the fighting seems to have fostered a new appreciation (especially the younger generation) for the SSNP's vision of a "Greater Syria."[28]

It is the July 8 Movement that especially represents an interesting case study for the party's activities on social media. The name comes from the date of Antoun Saadeh's execution in 1949. This Facebook page belongs to an unofficial trend within the Markaz factions and has about 1,525 followers.[29] "Our movement to achieve reform and unity," blares out in large letters on the top of the page. The group, which occupies a gray area within the party, was formed in 2016 and is made up of around three hundred members, who are both current and former party members. The July 8 Movement embodies an anti-Hardan tendency and advocates reform. For example, the page posted a picture of Hardan with the caption "A corrupt person in my party. Cancer of the party."[30] In November 2018 in the town of Chtaura, the July 8 Movement held a press conference at the Massabki Hotel and declared itself to be a political faction within Markaz, called "The Social Nationalist Renaissance Movement," and is led by Rabi Zeineddine and Yousef Zidan, with Tammuz Qanayzeh as the vice president.[31] Tammuz, whose first name means July, is also Elias Gergi Qanayzeh's son. This further signifies that these internal dissenters were not minor fringe but rather dedicated party members and part of the SSNP's notable elite who were fed up with the status quo. In addition, the trend wishes to end the SSNP's long-term split. Contact was established between the July 8 and the Intifada faction; however, the reception by the latter was described as lukewarm. The movement had strong grassroots following, but this has allegedly largely tapered off.[32] Party unity remains elusive.

10

Invisible Leaders: The Future of the SSNP

A video was posted on the SSNP Amana faction's YouTube channel in July 2016.¹ Young Syrians in white t-shirts stomped in formation across the dusty parade grounds. Before them stood a crowd of the country's political and social elite. One youth steps forward and asks for permission to begin the ceremony, which is granted by the SSNP Amana faction's vice president Joseph Sweid. The national anthem of the Syrian Arab Republic blares out solemnly, followed by the anthem of the SSNP. A large segment of the gathering raises their right hands in the ninety-degree salute of the party. Other crowd members stand with their hands politely by their sides, indicating that they are nonpartisans. The young, smart-looking men and women march about the parade grounds in a military style, with each of the six formations named after a fallen SSNP martyr.² The SSNP cadets perform a demonstration that includes a mock rescue of one of their comrades captured by Israeli soldiers. The SSNP squad ambushes the Israeli military jeep and defeats their enemies, casting down the Israeli flag and replacing it with the SSNP flag in triumph.³ A song plays out in the video's background. Amana official Jamil Murad steps forward and gives a speech:

> My comrades! The leader (Antoun Saadeh) said, "Become nationalists, because the future is yours!" By choosing, 'Syria, the redeemed' as the name of your course, you have proven that your roots are deep-seated in the ground and your crowns are exalted in the sky, just like the trees of our homeland. You have proven that every one of you is longing for the hour when you give your lives so their Syrian homeland can live in glory and the cause can triumph and crush the oppression that humiliates the people. Here you are today, naming your factions after your martyred comrades, following the examples of their heroics, making them torches of light that illuminates your renaissance, for the days you live as an orderly group … a group that has to be free of the disease of the individualist tendency and opportunist opinion.

On the surface, the Amana faction looked destined to become the party's primary political force in Syria. However, it was only four years later the Amana faction was dismantled in Syria as part of a dispute between President Assad and his wealthy cousin, Rami Makhlouf. The party's separate factions all retain the same name and use the same logo, but differentiating between these factions and understanding the dynamics and politics of unification, and how each piece of the SSNP puzzle fit into the realm of the Baath, is critical for projecting the party's future in Lebanon and Syria.

The Invisible President

President Assad's cousin was heavily involved in the regime's response to the demonstrations and subsequent armed uprising. Rami Makhlouf funded the Bustan Organization's charity along with a separate militia to help bolster the regime's forces during the course of the civil war. He was frequently discussed and highlighted as an example of the loyalist figures that remained closely aligned with President Assad in the face of armed opposition. Prior to the outbreak of the conflict, Makhlouf had largely been associated as Syria's wealthiest citizen, the head of the country's telecommunications network Syriatel, and was widely cited as a source of government corruption. But what Syrian observers rarely mentioned was that Makhlouf was also described as the SSNP Amana faction's "invisible president" in Syria.[4] Even though he had no official capacity in the party's leadership, he was allegedly pushing his favored SSNP associates to land seats in the parliament. The Markaz vice president Wael Hassanieh remarked to *al-Arabiya* in May 2020 that Makhlouf had started a trend that was distinct from the Markaz's factions that held seats in the Syrian parliament. An anonymous Markaz security official told the outlet that Makhlouf had paid huge salaries and noted he was able to start recreational and social activities for the party in Syria that were unprecedented. Tarek Ahmad also pointed out that Hussein Makhlouf, Rami Makhlouf's cousin, was the dean of interior for the party, and despite this, the Markaz faction's license had been revoked, which first prompted the split.[5]

In May 2020, President Assad's cousin took the extraordinary step of posting videos of himself on Facebook to challenge the government's allegations against him. It was this inter-family clash between the titans of the ruling dynasty that dragged the SSNP out of its traditional comfort zone and into the fore. The Makhlouf family was instrumental in helping Hafez al-Assad forge his power over the country, with their connections to Syria's urban elite.[6] The SSNP's

Amana faction in Syria ultimately became a casualty of the Makhlouf–Assad feud. As noted earlier, the Assad family was connected to the Makhloufs through marriage with Hafez al-Assad's wife, Anisa. Once Anisa passed away in February 2016, Rami Makhlouf's level of access to the president began to shift. His business network fell under tighter state scrutiny. When the government opted to close down the Amana faction on October 10, 2019, Makhlouf's supporters shared an old photo of Antoun Saadeh meeting with members of the Makhlouf family in the Alawite village of Bustan al-Basha on social media.[7] The photo was taken as Saadeh made his final tour of Tartus, Syria, before his capture and execution in 1949. This was done in order to demonstrate the Makhlouf family's deep ties to the SSNP.

President Assad is evidently preparing to enter a murky environment, unsure who his new enemies are. The Syrian Civil War's aftermath will now provide the greatest challenge to Assad's extended hold on power. A devastated economy, cities in ruin, millions of refugees abroad, a significant loss in territories that are now outside of the state's control, from within the regime camp, the scent of blood is now in the water. The Syrian president is now picking up the pieces and will attempt to restructure the state, a process that is fraught with risks, along with accommodating his foreign allies, Russia and Iran. Assad's "anticorruption" drive comes as part of an effort to secure funds for the state, as well as an attempt to bolster the government's image.[8] Makhlouf's charity, the Bustan Organization, also had its own progovernment militia, roughly 20,000 strong. This armed group was banned in August 2019.[9] Regardless of how the standoff between President Assad and Rami Makhlouf plays out, the SSNP remains a part of the larger picture. In late August 2020, President Assad met with members of the Makhlouf family in order to smooth over the dispute.[10] With genuine grassroots support, the Amana members will likely be reconciled back with the Markaz faction. For now, the Makhloufs appear to be indefinitely sidelined from Syria's political elite. Whether or not they will someday re-establish their own fiefdom with the SSNP remains to be seen. What the story of the Amana faction's short life tells us is that the Syrian regime has the ability to effectively slice off chunks of the SSNP when it senses the need to divide the party and dial back the SSNP's activities and influence. The party's future will ultimately be determined by the other two factions, the Markaz and Intifada.

Within regime-held Syria, the party has a political advantage; compared to the cynical view of the Baath Party, its members are staunchly committed to the SSNP's ideology. "They really, truly, believe in it," remarked one Syrian from Latakia.[11] This means the party's platform is accessible, and its anti-sectarianism, secularism, and anti-imperialism seem more sincere and, unlike the Baath, untainted by decades of corrupt rule and cold geopolitical calculations. On the other hand, the SSNP faces significant disadvantages in a competition with the Baath Party. The Baath Party controls all mechanisms and levels of the state and is able to mobilize and curtail the SSNP's ability to compete in elections at will. Furthermore, the SSNP has little support outside of the minority sects, and it appears that the government is charting a slow but steady course for a rekindled relationship with the largely Sunni Arab World. The Assad family is also facing its own internal divisions with President Assad's wife, Asma, gaining more influence to the determent of the Makhlouf clan.

Reclaiming the Center

The Markaz (Center) faction has the most political influence and power. With the greater numbers and armed militia of 6,000–8,000 fighters, Markaz still retains the ability to operate in both Syria and Lebanon. However, the Markaz bloc is in the midst of an extensive leadership crisis. Recent years have shown the party is lurching about and changing presidents at a faster rate. Hanna al-Nashef took over the reigns in 2017 and was out by 2019. The internal party disputes within Markaz spilled out in June 2019 when President Hanna al-Nashef was forced to resign. Members loyal to Hardan accused Nashef of trying to remove the dean of defense Ziad Maalouf and gave him two options. Nashef could either resign or face removal by the Supreme Council. Nashef selected the "least bitter" choice and submitted his resignation. The statement released by Hardan's office offered assurances that everything was fine, even "better than normal."[12] Faris Saad came next and was gone by January 2020.[13] He later appeared alongside Hanna al-Nashef and other members of the July 8 Movement in a video the group posted on Facebook, demanding reform and party unity. Wael Hassanieh subsequently steered the party as the acting president. Hassanieh's role appeared official when he met with the leader of the Lebanese Baath Party, Numan Shalq, on July 25, 2020.[14] The party finally selected Rabi Noureddine Banat as the new president in October 2020 after an internal scuffle.

Hanna al-Nashef's appearance in the nearly twenty-minute-long video posted on July 29, 2020, by the July 8 Movement is striking since it illustrates that the internal trend is still active and steadfast in their determination to oppose Assaad Hardan.[15] He opens his statements by referring to the "wound of July," a direct reference to Antoun Saadeh's martyrdom, along with the "many misfortunes that have happened to our party." Nashef remarks that the party has been backstabbed many times, not only from its enemies in the outside but also from rivals within and "inside of the inside." He then issues an urgent call for a mobilization to rescue the party, noting that four party presidents have fallen within the span of four years and that seven members of the High Council have resigned in protest. Nashef says there are private interests and ambitions for controlling and dominating the party and points to a parallel command structure that has hijacked the party. He calls for unity and reform of the party, but "a reform from within the party, not from its outside."[16] Nashef concludes his statements by threatening to take action with his group and that they control all of the party's power structures. He called on the SSNP members to boycott the coming elections, if they were not delayed, labeling them as "illegitimate."

The SSNP held the internal party elections in Dhour el-Shuwayr on September 13, 2020, and it appeared that an anti-Hardan list had gained the advantage on the Supreme Council.[17] Al-Tal was on dean of defense Ziyad Malouf's list during the elections that competed against Hardan's list and won fifteen out of seventeen Supreme Council seats. However, Hardan still retains a seat and will wield significant influence. In late September 2020, Hardan's supporters accused the anti-Hardan group of pulling off a "soft coup" following the Supreme Council elections and said the elections were fraudulent.[18] Hassan Sakr, a member of the party's Central Political Bureau, appeared poised to take on the presidency.[19] He spoke to reporters:

> Trustee [Hardan] is represented by every attending member here today, he's a historical leader in this party and his status is great for us. Today he is not attending and I don't know why honestly … but he is represented by every one of us. Those who competed belonged to one team, there was competition only to serve the party, but there was no coup against anyone, it is the complete opposite.

Sakr remarked:

> the important thing is … there is a new project within the party, a new vision, new blood, people who would like to take the party to the position it deserves. Every stage has its people and this is a new stage. There's a new generation which has arrived to become the party's leadership and will surely lead this stage with its own style, performance, and capabilities.[20]

This was Sakr's nice way of showing Hardan a ledge for him to jump off.

The July 8 Movement in Lebanon will remain an important trend to monitor within the party's internal conflicts in Lebanon. Within Syria, the end of the

Amana faction signals that Markaz now has the opportunity to reorganize and reassert itself in the postwar environment. However, the Syrian parliamentary elections held on July 19, 2020, made it clear that the government is in no mood to entertain any notion of ceding legislative control to the other legal political parties. For Assad, emerging from a bloody and extremely costly civil war, along with economic ruin, international sanctions, and a global pandemic, there was too much at stake at this juncture to allow any real political rivals to gain even a symbolic toehold. But perhaps most important will be the fact that Assad's constitutional term limit as president comes to an end in 2021, an issue he will want to maintain close control over until a new postwar constitution can be engineered in order to allow him to stay on in power until at least 2035 or 2042.[21] Prior to the election, SSNP politician Ahmad Merei expressed hope that the election would help facilitate constitutional changes and adamantly described Syria as a democratic country.[22] However, it was clear that, as the elections drew close, the whole process would amount to little more than a mechanism for the Baath Party to further cement its rule.

The parliamentary election was held on July 19, 2020. It had originally been scheduled for April, but the government postponed it due to the Covid-19 global pandemic. The SSNP's winning candidates in Syria's 2020 parliamentary elections are:

Nouhad Samaan, Homs Governorate: 734,990 votes
Sameer Hajjar, Damascus Governorate: 673,226 votes
Ahmad Merei, Aleppo Governorate: 137,712 votes
Total: 1,545,928 votes

The SSNP's bloc in the Syrian parliament issued a statement on their Facebook page to congratulate the winners.[23] Two other SSNPers ran as independents: Ra'fat Bakkar, the former director of the SSNP's Jaramana Directory in the Rif Dimashq Governorate, secured 30,944 votes; and Jamil Murad, the former dean of youth and education for the recently disbanded Amana faction, for Damascus Governorate, received 154,474 votes and won himself a parliamentary seat.[24] On the night of July 20, a party member named Manuel Hanna posted a twelve-minute livestreaming broadcast of a convoy of cars driving through the streets of Homs waving the party's flags out of the windows.[25] The fact that only three candidates who ran as official SSNP members were able to win seat indicated that the party was being kneecapped. The Baath-led National Progressive Front list secured 183 seats, with 166 Baath Party members. Sympathizers said the party members privately described the situation as infuriating. Frustration had been building. Regarding corruption and government inefficacy, the former MP from Tartus, Inas Mohammed Khair al-Mallouhi, said prior to the election in June 2020, "The people have lost trust in the parliament and government."[26] She subsequently did not appear on the ballot. Other prominent party members also chimed in their disappointment. Mazen Azouz, a member of the Markaz faction's political bureau from Salamiyeh, in the Hamah Governate, called the election a "shameful night in history" and added that "there was no place for honorable people in this country, period."[27] The Markaz faction's dismal performance as a party in the parliamentary elections signaled that the Markaz had for now reached a political dead-end in Syria. As the proponents of pan-Syrianism looked about the Syrian regime's political arena in dismay, their gaze may fall elsewhere to the party's smallest faction, the Intifada.

Quelling the Uprising

On March 28, 2017, Dr. Ali Haidar, Milad Sebaaly, Ali Qanso, and Assaad Hardan gathered at the Syrian Embassy in Beirut, hosted by Syria's ambassador to Lebanon, Ali Abdul Karim.[28] During the meeting, Haidar said that he was cooperative and even put forward two members of his faction for negotiations but said that Markaz did not respond, which showed that they were not serious. Neither faction appeared to be very excited about unity since they both had their own internal issues.

Despite the long rift, some Markaz faction members still hold George Abd Messih's renegade faction in fraternal esteem and emphasized the bonds of the party's ideology. One militia member remarked:

> All of those who remain in Ali Haidar's wing are also Syrian Social Nationalists, the only ones who know the truth about Syria. The union of the Social Nationalists is a unique bond. We have contracted to rise together or fall together in a project that is equal to our existence. I hope, as they hope, that we will return to the same body. What hinders unity is administrative, rather than ideological. We are all nationalists and in the event of any entitlement it is certain that we are together regardless of wings and management.[29]

It must be emphasized that Ali Haidar's Intifada faction in Lebanon and Syria is small, numbering only from an estimated several hundreds to no more than a few thousand at most. However, as for the main faction, its numbers are difficult to independently verify, and SSNP members tend to obscure or inflate their numbers. A rough estimate puts 50,000 in Lebanon, 80,000 in Syria, 2,000 in Jordan, 1,000 in Palestine, and 500 in Iraq. Despite this disadvantage in numbers, the Intifada carries its own credibility through discipline and an aura that lacks from within their larger rival. The Intifada competes for influence with Markaz for the party's believers in the Lebanese and Syrian diaspora with thousands of members and sympathizers in the United States, Australia, Canada, and Europe. Intifada is "a quiet and stable faction in comparison to the others," remarked one party sympathizer. However, it is likely that the lines between the different factions overseas are more blurred and many members might not even know which faction they belong to. The Intifada draw their strength primarily from their adherence to Antoun Saadeh's ideology. The small faction has the benefit of being a bit more distant from the Syrian state's authoritarianism and spearheading the government's reconciliation efforts. Conversely, the branch also represents the most dogmatic interpretation of the SSNP's vision and principals, namely that they were opposed to taking part in politics, as well as engaging directly in violence. Intifada was thus able to produce a valuable asset for the regime's political aims as a force for reconciliation as the Syrian conflict unfolded.

One SSNP comrade said, "I think this war is part of an intellectual, political and civilized development in our country and this includes redefining Arabism from the standpoint of the Syrian nation first. It is what many Baathist believe today, which has been the mentality of Hafez al-Assad for a long time."[30] Another SSNP member remarked, "There are no longer any major differences between us and the Baathists. The war and the course of events have played a major role in bridging our views."[31] However, there are still differences between the Baathists and the SSNP. One Alawite from Latakia explained:

> I didn't really know much about [the SSNP] before the war, because like everyone, everything around us was about the Baath Party. When the war started, it became clear people were looking at religion more as an identity rather than a belief, and this is destructive. I am from Syria, and therefore I am Syrian first. This is what the SSNP represents and is trying to push in society.[32]

Another SSNP member from Idlib Province added, "This crisis has produced a new reality, and people are realizing that the Baath idea of Arabism has collapsed. Arabism has shown that Syrians only have the Syrians, and that they have been abandoned by the Arabs." Other new party members emphasized the need to protect Syria's sovereignty, keep the country united, and applauded the SSNP's dedication to improving Syrian society through "an entire lifestyle."[33]

Intifada was well suited for the position of reconciliation, especially given the fact that the SSNP caused a great deal of trouble in regard to the Malki Affair. Now, the Intifada had been provided a chance to redeem the party. For years, the Intifada faction of George Abd Messih remained banned in Syria. The party could not operate in the open and was prevented from publishing and conducting all types of political activity. This faction staunchly maintained that the entire plot was orchestrated by the Egyptian ambassador to Damascus, Mahmoud Riad; the Syrian Army Chief of Staff, Shawkat Shuqayer; and Syria's intelligence chief, Abdul Hamid al-Sarraj, in order to eliminate the party in Syria.[34] Abd Messih died in September 14, 1999. Prior to Abd Messih's death, the Intifada faction was headed by Dr. Antoine Abu Haidar. Abu Haidar was a Rum Orthodox from Baskinta in Lebanon's Matn District, and he remained president of the Intifada faction until November 8, 2008. He died on January 15, 2017. Dr. Ali Haidar, an ophthalmologist born in 1962 from the town of Masyaf in the Hama Governate, became the Intifada faction's leader. Dr. Haidar knew President Assad from the medical school at Damascus University, took on the key role in the tolerated opposition, as well as headed the Syrian government's reconciliation efforts during the Syrian crisis.

The Intifada faction still retains a positive image of George Abd Messih with members affectionately calling him "Uncle George."[35] The branch viewed itself as an opposition party, and its platform included the desire to bring about free elections within the framework of a secular state in Syria. In July 2011, together with the Syrian Communist Party, the Intifada forged a coalition within the scope of a loyalist opposition called the Popular Front for Change and Liberation (PFCL). This grouping eventually merged with other loyalist opposition groups to become the Coalition for Peaceful Change Forces.[36] Sitting at a press conference in March 2012, alongside Qadri Jamil, the leader of the People's Will Party, Dr. Ali Haidar, remarked:

> The political reforms in Syria are a starting point for any other type of reform. The political reform starts with a political process which may take various forms, with some details that we may accept, and others that we may refuse. After all, we accept to be part of the political process, despite all our observations, since we consider that it is the only exit from the current Syrian crisis.[37]

This shift caused a number of SSNPers to defect from Markaz to the Intifada. One Intifada member explained why he left the larger faction:

There are two parties with the same name, logo, and ideology. Both parties were active illegally in Syria. In 2005 the party I used to belong to joined the National Progressive Front. A group of SSNP members thought it did not make any sense for a political party to be led by another party, and consequently many comrades, including myself, decided to leave and join the other SSNP.[38]

Conclusion

The SSNP and its two remaining factions have their fair share of challenges ahead in postwar Syria, and yet, there is still plenty of fertile ground for the party to explore as it moves forward. First and foremost is the potential outcome of the Syrian conflict's resolution. Russia has a keen interest in propping up the SSNP as an official opposition party in a postwar Syria. The party's nationalism and secular nature, as well as its Orthodox constituency, all lend it an appeal that endears itself to Moscow's growing diplomatic and security interests in the Levant. The United States' continuing military presence and support of its proxy force, the YPG-dominated SDF forces in northeastern Syria, will be of particular interest to the SSNP since it wishes to expel the foreign presence and restore Syria's national sovereignty. Russia's entry into the Kurdish areas after the partial US withdrawal in October 2019 will also be instrumental in building these relations. The YPG also is perhaps the one political faction in Syria that has the deepest secular ideological convictions outside of the SSNP. The YPG, like the SSNP, has adopted inclusive practices that encompass many different religious and ethnic groups in its territory in the northeast.[39] For the Kurds, the Baath Party, on the other hand, has long been tainted by its decades of brutal rule, its platform of Arab nationalism, and well-founded reputation of rampant corruption through the regime's entrenched patronage networks, a fact that Syria's Kurds are keenly aware of.[40] Despite this, the SDF and the YPG's primary long-term concerns will be surviving against its primarily nemesis, Turkey.

There are many factors at play regarding Syria's Kurds, but how the YPG rises or falls will be primarily linked to the future of the United States' engagement in Syria, and the SSNP is busy exploring the paths to reconcile the Kurds with the rest of the country. The Intifada faction is said to have positive relations with the YPG and PKK. The ongoing anti-Turkish insurgency in Aleppo's Afrin District will be another factor in a complicated YPG–regime dynamic. An editorial in *al-Binaa* called the Syrian Kurds "our sword and shield," denounced federalism, and warned that the foreign powers only cared about human rights when they wanted to use the Kurds for their own agenda. It went on to recall that, after the First World War, the 1920 Treaties of Sèvres had made promises to the Kurds and the 1923 Treaty of Lausanne then betrayed them.[41] The Turkish presence in Syria may be the key component of building this YPG–SSNP relationship. However, if the United States opts to retain a long-term presence in Syria, the SSNP could become one element that the regime uses to confront and challenge the US allies in the country's northeast.

The continued involvement of Turkey and its armed Syrian groups will perhaps offer the SSNP the best chance to rally itself in Syrian nationalism with its own unique platform. The issue of reclaiming Hatay and Cilicia from Turkey has been part of the SSNP's drumbeat since its founding decades. Whether or not Damascus is able to attach itself to the anti-Turkish coalition that is emerging in the region, namely Saudi Arabia, Egypt, and the United Arab Emirates, has yet to be seen. The UAE has already established an embassy in Damascus, and the growing tensions between these countries and Turkey and Qatar could result in a net positive for the regime.[42] The SSNP's ability to ostensibly act as an opposing but, nevertheless, reliable, loyal force could allow Russia and its friendly countries to promote or push for a greater political role for the party in the postwar era. But the future role of the Arab Gulf states should not be understated. The Baath Party is hard at work, attempting to resuscitate itself, playing an increasingly active role in Syria's social and public spaces, and a new brand of Arab nationalism might be vital in establishing Syria's return to the Arab fold, and this would usher in new challenges to the SSNP as the twenty-first century continues.

This in turn overlaps into another area of contention, the future of the Israeli–Palestinian conflict. The SSNP has been a staunch opponent of Israel from its very foundation and predates the Jewish state's own existence by over fifteen years. The growing isolation of the Palestinians from the United States, the threats to annex the West Bank, and the inability to solve the conflict all offer the SSNP some opportunities for growth. Perhaps most notably will be the role of the wealthy Arab Gulf states vis-à-vis Israel. The Syrian government's own future relationship with the Gulf States, especially given that the UAE has now established formal diplomatic ties with both Syria and Israel, could put Damascus in a tough spot as it will likely rely on donations for reconstruction. Israeli air strikes look set to challenge Syria's sovereignty and will be, at best, a source of nationalism or, at worse, embarrassment for the ruling Baath. With negotiations over the future status of the occupied Golan Heights, which the United States has formally recognized,[43] governments in Damascus, whether pro-Western or not, will wrangle with the SSNP, if the party views the results of the negotiations unfavorably. The SSNP's diaspora in the United States, Canada, Australia, and Europe is highly attuned to the Arab–Israeli conflict and will be watching closely.

Lastly, the SSNP's heartland, Lebanon, will remain the home of the Markaz faction. To study the SSNP in Lebanon is to climb down the ladder of Lebanese politics until you reach a place most observers tend to avoid. Lebanon in 2020 has witnessed the most turmoil the country has seen in a long time—a crashing economy, dismal unemployment due to a global pandemic, heightened tensions from the United States and Israel's confrontation with Iran and Hezbollah, the uncertainty of relations with Syria, the antigovernment protests against the long-running sectarian system and corruption, Beirut partially destroyed in the port explosion, all of these factors would give any other radical and revolutionary party the opportunity to make some headway in the political scene. Despite all of this, it must be emphasized that the SSNP still lacks broad-based popular support, and most Syrians and Lebanese are suspicious and cynical about the old political parties, no matter their platforms.

Alas, the SSNP remains trapped, reviled as the perpetrator of violence and always on the defensive as a target of violence itself. The SSNP is unable and unwilling at this juncture to unshackle itself from Hezbollah and Damascus. The party still holds its legacy of resistance. But what is that legacy worth in the twenty-first century? Around the room, the other parties watch it with a mix of curiosity and deep suspicion. To liberals and Lebanese nationalists, it is an anathema of everything they hold dear. For the communists, an unlikely soulmate forged in years of animosity and shared anti-imperialism. For the Islamists, an authoritarian enemy. For Hezbollah and the Baath, a partner in crime. How the SSNP will find its way through a protracted internal leadership crisis, decades of party splits, and climb out of the Lebanon's entrenched sectarian divisions is uncertain. The red zawbaa spins surrounded by the blackest night. Its razor-sharp edges lash out in defiance and desperation. The SSNP was founded decades ago in a time when a great geopolitical storm was brewing on the horizons. The dream of Greater Syria, just like the utopian vision of a united Arab world, remains just as remote as it was in the wake of independence. Today, the same party established so long ago by Antoun Saadeh is caught in another storm, one that is unsure of where it will be when the dark clouds finally part. Yet, he still marches along with them, carrying the great weight of the party's long history with him, unbowing and unbroken.

Epilogue

In October 2020 the Markaz faction of the Syrian Social Nationalist Party emerged from its contested party elections with a new president, Rabi Noureddine Banat. Born in 1977 and highly educated, Banat is perhaps the youngest party member to reach the presidency. He joined the SSNP in 1998 and obtained a PhD in economics from the University of Grenoble in France. How successful Banat will be in charting a course forward for the party remains to be seen. Markaz currently faces a new split, with Assaad Hardan forming his own Supreme Council and establishing his headquarters at the *al-Binaa* newspaper. In February 2021, a small group of armed Hardan faction members took over an empty party office in the Lebanese coastal town of Batroun in the dead of night and posted a video statement online. The other faction's members reacted angrily, accusing Hardan of authoritarianism on social media. This new fissure has the potential to even overshadow the Amana split that lasted from 2012 to 2019 and could be the most critical internal crisis the party has faced in recent years.

The SSNP at this juncture is wrestling with how to unite the party and address the many economic, political, and social issues that contributed the cause of the crisis in Lebanon. Banat met with Intifada faction leader Ali Haidar in February 2021, but the visit was described as simply a diplomatic meeting, and party unity remains elusive. The SSNP must confront the stark challenge of either maintaining its comfortable role in the current political establishment, or attempting to revert to a more radical and subversive role that challenges the Lebanese system. Addressing sectarianism, civil marriage, electoral reform, and pushing for a secular state are all on the party's agenda. The option of an outside agitator is the one fraught with risk present throughout the SSNP's history, the dire consequences of which include imprisonment and death.

As this book demonstrated, the Lebanon School trend that has remained dominant in the post-Saadeh era offers the party the safer route, remaining within the existing political establishment in order to bide its time and survive. As the Intifada members have always argued, the region is not yet ready for the party's ideology. Instead, the SSNP's comrades must have an internal focus, concentrating on recruitment and returning closer to what Antoun Saadeh's vision originally intended. Despite its political positioning and compared with the other political parties on the scene, the SSNP has also largely kept its principles and ideology consistent since its early years. However, the party thus remains anchored to an inherently sectarian system, especially in terms of its alliance with the Lebanese Hezbollah and Iran's Axis of Resistance against the West. Overcoming the widespread suspicion with which the rest of the population regards the SSNP would take decades.

Across the realm of what would encompass Saadeh's plan for Greater Syria, there is an increasing recognition that regional integration will yield advances in trade, cultural ties, and economic growth. A shared prosperity could be the result of a political or economic mechanism that brings the countries of the Levant closer together and breaks down the long-despised borders. It is possible that this regional economic integration may occur without the party, leaving them behind to react in the aftermath. It is the party's idea of uniting the Levant's ancient empires that has always made it unique and outstanding in contrast to the nationalism of the other political movements of the region. It is ultimately this intellectual legacy that heavily outweighs the SSNP's real political impact. However, the region also appears to be growing further divided, with war and factions carving out territory and further compounding the breakdown of the existing states and local sovereignty. The SSNP will remain a part of this complicated landscape as the party's dreams of Greater Syria stay far off on the distant horizon, always searching and ever loyal to Antoun Saadeh and his undying quest to complete a nation.

A List of SSNP Presidents

1932–8: Antoun Saadeh (officially not a president, but the leader of the party)
1938–47: Ni'mah Thabet (not officially a president, but de facto leader while Saadeh was in exile)
1947–9: Antoun Saadeh
1949–54: George Abd Messih
1954: Issam al-Mahayri (for a few days)
1954–6: George Abd Messih
1956–7: Mustafa Dheeb Irsheed (Jordanian, died in 1957)
1957–9: Assad al-Ashqar
1959–60: Abdullah Mohsen
1960–2: Abdullah Saadeh
1962–9: (New Year's Eve coup imprisonment)
1969–73: Abdullah Saadeh
1973: Assad al-Ashqar
1973: Yousef al-Ashqar
1974–5: Abdullah Saadeh
1975: Elias Gergi Qanayzeh (pro-Syria faction)
1975–7: Inaam Raad (pro-Palestinian faction)
1977–80: Abdullah Saadeh
1980–4: Inaam Raad
1984–92: Issam al-Mahayri
1987–8: Gebran Jurayj
1988–92: Dawoud Baz
1992–6: Inaam Raad
1997–8: Mahmoud Abdelkhalek
1996–2002: Ali Qanso
2002–6: Gebran Araiji
2006–8: Ali Qanso
2008–16: Assaad Hardan
2016–7: Ali Qanso
2017–9: Hanna al-Nashef
2019–20: Faris Saad
2020: Wael Hassanieh (acting)
2020–present: Rabi Noureddine Banat

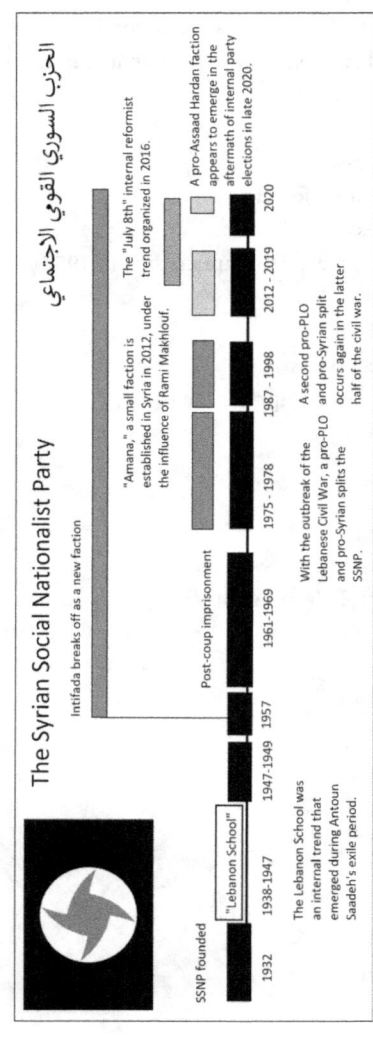

Figure 11 A graph illustrating the timeline of the SSNP's splits from 1932 to 2020.

A Timeline of the SSNP's Factions, Historic Splits, and Events

1932: Antoun Saadeh secretly founds the SSNP in Beirut in November 1932.

1936: The party operates in the open and confronts the colonial French administration, rival parties (Kateab, communists).

1938: Antoun Saadeh leaves Lebanon for self-imposed exile in the Americas (mainly Brazil).

1938–47: The so-called "Lebanon School" changes the party's flag, salute, and sharply tones down the pan-Syrian ideology. The exile period is sometimes referred to as the Lebanonization of the party.

March 1947: Antoun Saadeh returns from self-exile to Lebanon; ends the so-called "Lebanon School"; purges figures from the party; and fully restores his ideology of pan-Syrianism.

July 8, 1949: After the failed launch of the First Social Popular Uprising against Beirut, Antoun Saadeh is betrayed by the military regime in Syria, handed over to the Lebanese security forces, put on a short trial, and executed by firing squad all within forty-eight hours. The party is extensively purged in Lebanon.

1949–55: The SSNP grows in Syria, and several SSNP-affiliated army officers or sympathizers take part in the three coups of 1949.

The April 1955 Adnan al-Malki assassination brings about a harsh crackdown on the SSNP, which drives it underground in Syria and forces many members back to Lebanon. Party leader Issam al-Mahayri receives a short jail sentence, but some party members said he and a few others had "cut a deal to save their necks" by testifying against George Abd Messih.

1957: SSNP–Intifada faction, headed by George Abd Messih, is expelled by the party's Supreme Council. Other party officials who testified against him are allowed to stay in Syria. Mahayri's faction remains in Syria.

1958: The SSNP joins with the pro-Western Lebanese forces of Camille Chamoun against the Arab nationalist rebels led by Kamal Jumblatt during the 1958 Lebanon Crisis.

1961: Launched the failed "New Year's Eve" coup attempt against President Chehab at the end of December 1961. Party suffered a harsh crackdown by the Lebanese government.

1969: Many members were released under a general amnesty by the Lebanese government.

1969: The Melkart Hotel Convention occurs ahead of the Lebanese Civil War.

1970: SSNP becomes legal in Lebanon with the help of Druze leader Kamal Jumblat.

1975: The main faction shifts to the political left and joins the Palestinians and Lebanese National Movement during the Lebanese Civil War.

1976: Syria intervenes in the first phase of the Lebanese Civil War on the side of the Christians. SSNP splits between pro-Palestinian factions and pro-Syria factions.

Inaam Raad and Abdallah Saadeh (no relation to Antoun Saadeh) head a pro-Palestinian faction.

Issam al-Mahayri's pro-Syria faction, called the Khawarij faction, was led by Elias Gergi Qanayzeh.

1978: The party is reunited. Syrian Army Chief of Staff Hikmat al-Shehabi comes to Beirut and negotiates a reunification.

1982: The SSNP joins the Lebanese National Resistance Front (Jammoul) following the Israeli invasion and continues to remain active against the IDF until their withdrawal from the "security zone" in 2000.

1987: New split—pro-Syrian and pro-Palestinian

1998: Unification of pro-Syrian and pro-Palestinian factions. Issam al-Mahayri and Ali Qanso form a joint emergency committee.

2004: Syrian President Bashar al-Assad allows a limited degree of political participation for the party's branch in Syria.

2005: The party is officially legalized in Syria after a period of fifty years. The Markaz faction joins the National Progressive Front, a coalition of small leftist parties loyal to the ruling Baath Party in the Syrian parliament.

2011: The Syrian Civil War begins.

2011: Ali Haidar becomes Syria's minister of state for national reconciliation affairs.

2012: Issam al-Mahayri and Assaad Hardan split. Mahayri's faction is called Amana or "trusteeship." Hardan's faction is known as Markaz, or "Center."

2012: Ali Haidar leads the SSNP–Intifada faction in the Popular Front for Change and Liberation (a coalition of tolerated political opposition in Syria).

2014: SSNP–Intifada withdraws from the Popular Front for Change and Liberation in May of that year in order to support Bashar al-Assad as president.

2016: Parliamentary elections held in Syria. Intifada and Markaz factions both field candidates, with Markaz securing the majority of seats.

2017: In Lebanon, Hanna al-Nashef elected as president of the Markaz faction and promises to reunify the party.

2018: Ilyas Mtanious Shaheen is elected the leader of the Amana faction in Syria.

2019: A dispute between Assaad Hardan and Nashef occurs, and Nashef resigns as the president of Markaz faction. Faris Saad becomes the main party faction president. The Amana faction is disbanded by the Syrian government in October 2019, and its members presumably merged with Markaz.

2020: In Lebanon, internal disputes continue within the Markaz faction, and Faris Saad resigns as president in March. Wael Hassanieh takes over as the acting president.

2020: The party takes part in the Syrian parliamentary elections and only wins three seats. Two others win seats as independents. In Lebanon, Rabi Noureddine Banat becomes the head of the Markaz faction following contentious party elections, and Hardan splits off with his own smaller faction.

Notes

1 Introduction: The Storm in the Shadows

1 Michel Aflaq, "In Memory of the Arab Prophet," lecture delivered on April 5, 1943, at the University of Damascus, translated by Ziad el Jishi, http://albaath.online.fr/English/Aflaq-00-In-Memory-of-the-Arab-Prophet.htm (accessed January 15, 2017).
2 Leonard Binder, *Ideological Revolution in the Middle East* (New York: University of Chicago Press), p. 205.
3 Fayez A. Sayegh, *Arab Unity, Hope and Fulfillment* (New York: Devin-Adair, 1958), p. 182.
4 "Syria, A Country Study," Federal Research Division, Library of Congress, April 1987, p. 198.
5 Ernest Tucker, *The Middle East in Modern World History* (Routledge, 1st ed., 2012), p. 228.
6 James L. Gelvin, *The Arab Uprisings, What Everyone Needs to Know* (New York: Oxford University Press), p. 104.
7 Rayan al-Atrash, "Opponents of al-Assad Regime in As-Suwayda Wait for Their Freedom," *Enab Baladi*, https://english.enabbaladi.net/archives/2020/10/opponents-of-al-assad-regime-in-as-suwayda-wait-for-their-freedom/ (accessed June 15, 2020).
8 Aron Lund, "The Miserable Afterlife of Michel Aflaq," Carnegie Middle East Center Diwan, March 10, 2014, https://carnegie-mec.org/diwan/54844 (accessed March 24, 2017).
9 Rami Ginat, *Syria and the Doctrine of Arab Neutralism: From Independence to Dependence* (Sussex Academic Press, 2010), p. 212.
10 Judith Palmer Harik, *Hezbollah, the Changing Face of Terrorism* (London: I.B. Tauris), p. 11.
11 J. K. Gani, *The Role of Ideology in Syrian–US Relations, Conflict and Cooperation* (Palgrave Macmillan, 2014), p. 185.
12 Joshua Stacher, "Reinterpreting Authoritarian Power: Syria's Hereditary Succession," *Middle East Journal 65*, no. 2 (2011): 198, doi:10.3751/65.2.11 (accessed February 20, 2017).
13 Ibid., p. 27.

14 Christopher Phillips, *Everyday Arab Identity: The Daily Reproduction of the Arab World* (Routledge, 2012), p. 63.
15 Anand Gopal, "Syria's Last Bastion of Freedom," *New Yorker*, December 5, 2018, https://www.newyorker.com/magazine/2018/12/10/syrias-last-bastion-of-freedom (accessed April 5, 2017).
16 BBC News, "Profile: Syria's Ruling Baath Party," July 9, 2012, https://www.bbc.com/news/world-middle-east-18582755 (accessed April 6, 2017).

2 The Party of the Martyr: The SSNP's Beginnings in Lebanon

1 Adel Beshara, *Outright Assassination, The Trial and Execution of Antun Sa'adeh* (Reading: Ithaca Press, 1949), p. 117.
2 For example, the anti-Syrian Lebanese Druze leader Walid Jumblatt marked the 70th anniversary of Antoun Saadeh's execution by tweeting that his father, Kamal Jumblatt, had tried to ensure Saadeh received a fair trial and was given the opportunity to defend himself. See https://twitter.com/walidjoumblatt/status/1148106235343978496, dated July, 8, 2019 (accessed April 26, 2021).
3 Daniel Pipes, *Greater Syria, The History of an Ambition* (New York: Oxford University Press, 1992), p. 5.
4 Sami Moubayed, "Antoun Saadeh: The Father of Greater Syria," *Gulf News*, May 11, 2016, http://gulfnews.com/culture/people/antoun-saadeh-the-father-of-greater-syria-1.1824903 (accessed December 10, 2016).
5 D. S Margoliouth and Khalil Saadeh, *Saadeh's Dictionary: A New, Practical and Exhaustive English–Arabic Dictionary Arranged on Totally Original Lines, with the View of Giving the English Language a Much Wider Scope in the East Than It Has Hitherto Had, and of Raising Arabic into the Dignity of a Scientific Language* (Beirut: Maktabat Lubnan, 1974); Khalil Saʻadah, *Caesar & Cleopatra: An Historical Romance* (London: Edwin Vaughan, 1898).
6 Labib Zuwiyya Yamak, *The Syrian Social Nationalist Party: An Ideological Analysis* (Harvard Middle Eastern Monograph Series, Cambridge: Center for Middle Eastern Studies, 1966), p. 53.
7 Patrick Seale wrote that Khalil Saadeh had earlier studied the ideas of a French geographer named Elisee Reclus whose book, *Nouvelle Geographie Universelle* (1884), described a Syrian race that was ethnically unique from that of the Arab people. However, other researchers have seen no evidence of Reclus' influence on Khalil, nor did Khalil's Syrian nationalism have a racialist or ethnic component that suggested any distinction from the Arab nation.

8 Kamal Salibi, *A House of Many Mansions: The History of Lebanon Reconsidered* (London: University of California Press, 1988), p. 132.
9 Patrick Seale, *The Struggle for Arab Independence, Riad El-Solh and the Makers of the Modern Middle East* (New York: Cambridge University Press, 2010), p. 377; see also Asher Kaufman, *Reviving Phoenicia* (London: I.B. Tauris, 2004), p. 8.
10 Sami Moubayed, *Steel & Silk, Men and Women Who Shaped Syria 1900–2000* (Seattle: Cune Press), p. 476.
11 Patrick Seale, *The Struggle for Syria* (New Haven: Yale University Press), p. 64.
12 Yamak, *The Syrian Social Nationalist Party*, p. 54.
13 Antoun Saadeh, *The Ten Lectures Ending Centuries of Decline and Disintegration of Greater Syria*, trans. Fouzy Najd, under the supervision of the Department of Education and Fine Arts of the Syrian Social Nationalist Party (Lebanon, 2005).
14 Michael W. Suleiman, *Political Parties in Lebanon, The Challenge of a Fragmented Political Culture* (Ithaca: Cornell University Press, 1967), p. 64.
15 Yamak, *The Syrian Social Nationalist Party*, p. 55.
16 Ibid., p. 168.
17 "Report about Anṭun Sa'adah (Anton Saadeh)," October 30, 1935, History and Public Policy Program Digital Archive, Emir Farid Chehab Collection, GB165-0384, Box 2, File 1F/2, Middle East Centre Archive, St Antony's College, Oxford, https://digitalarchive.wilsoncenter.org/document/176046 (accessed October 22, 2018).
18 Seale, *The Struggle for Arab Independence*, p. 378.
19 Yamak, *The Syrian Social Nationalist Party*, pp. 131–3.
20 Seale, *The Struggle for Syria*, p. 68.
21 Seale, *The Struggle for Arab Independence*, p. 379.
22 Antoun Saadeh, "Communication to Public Opinion—Blue Declaration," June 15, 1936, http://antoun-saadeh.com/works/book/book02/128 (accessed November 6, 2018).
23 Bonnie F. Saunders, *The United States and Arab Nationalism: The Syrian Case, 1953–1960* (Praeger, 1996), p. 10.
24 Yamak, *The Syrian Social Nationalist Party*, p. 125.
25 Ibid., pp. 125–6.
26 John Pierre Entelis, *Pluralism and Party Transformation in Lebanon: Al-Kata'ib, 1936–1970* (Brill Academic, 1974), p. 47.
27 Ibid., p. 46.
28 Robert Fisk, *Pity the Nation, the Abduction of Lebanon* (New York: Nation Books, 1990), p. 65.
29 The Gemayel family had a long history of fraught relations with the SSNP. One prominent SSNP party member, Mas'ad Hajal, later recalled how he met with Pierre Gemayel's cousin, Maurice, who confessed to him that he had been a member of the SSNP when the party was driven underground. The matter caused a political

fracture in the Gemayel family. Antoun Saadeh later met with Maurice and told him to prioritize his family, but to remain with the SSNP in his heart. Hajal said that Maurice resisted this at first but eventually accepted Saadeh's advice in order to heal the family. See Hajal's biography: *Mas'ad Hajal, Lam Ubaddil … wa Lan: al-Mujallad al-Awwal* (Beirut: 2018), p. 267.

30 Salim Mujais, *Antoun Saadeh: A Biography, Vol. II: Years of the French Mandate* (Beirut: Kutub, 2009), p. 196.
31 Seale, *The Struggle for Arab Independence*, p. 380.
32 Abdullah I of Jordan, dismayed by the partition of the region after the First World War, had his own Greater Syria ambitions.
33 Adel Beshara, *Lebanon: The Politics of Frustration: The Failed Coup of 1961* (London: Routledge, 2005), p. 35.
34 Seale, *The Struggle for Syria*, p. 69.
35 Götz Nordbruch, *Nazism in Syria and Lebanon: The Ambivalence of the German Option, 1933–1945* (London: Routledge, 2009), p. 45.
36 Seale, *The Struggle for Arab Independence*, p. 380.
37 At the time, the French consulate in Buenos Aires handled consulate and diplomatic affairs for Syrians and Lebanese living in Latin America.
38 Joseph Walker Leidy, "Antun Saadeh in the mahjar, 1938–1947" (Thesis, Graduate School of The University of Texas at Austin, May 2016), p. 40; see also Steve Hyland, "The Summit of Civilian: Nationalism among the Arabic-Speaking Colonies in Latin America," in *Immigration and National Identities in Latin America*, ed. Nicola Foote (Gainesville: University Press of Florida, 2014), p. 273.
39 Ibid., p. 49.
40 Antoun Saadeh, "The Syrian Social Nationalist Creed and Democracy's Search for a Creed," *Azzawba'a*, June 15, 1942, US Library of Congress.
41 Antoun Saadeh, "The Leader's Speech on the 1st of March," *Azzawba'a*, June 15, 1943, US Library of Congress.
42 This term comes from lughat ad-dhad, the language of dhad, referring to the Arabic letter, since Arabic was thought to be the only language with this particular sound.
43 Antoun Saadeh, "Greater Syria," *Azzawba'a*, July 1, 1943, US Library of Congress.
44 Leidy, "Antun Saadeh in the mahjar, 1938–1947," p. 41.
45 http://antoun-saadeh.com/languages/en/510 (accessed January 4, 2017).
46 The SNP also took part in the 1947 elections and, according to Dr Edmond Melhem, campaigned to make Lebanon's independence "a reality, not a new type of colonization." The party largely failed to gain any seats in parliament. See "The SSNP's Electoral Program during the Lebanese Elections of 1947," June, 16, 2018, http://www.ssnp.com/?p=466 (accessed January 4, 2017).
47 The SSNP Facebook page: "The Red Whirlwind," which in turn cites Dr Jihad Nasri al-Aql, June 1, 2013, https://m.facebook.com/SSNPonline/photos/a.398747906830755/556370501068494/?type=3 (accessed January 5, 2017).

48 Seale, *The Struggle for Arab Independence*, p. 660.
49 Elizabeth Thompson, *Colonial Citizens Republican Rights, Paternal Privilege, and Gender in French Syria and Lebanon* (Columbia University Press, 2000), p. 278.
50 Hisham Sharabi, *Embers and Ashes* (Northampton, MA: Olive Branch Press, 2007), p. 49.
51 Ibid., p. 43.
52 Yusri Hazran, *The Druze Community and the Lebanese State, Between Confrontation and Reconciliation* (London: Routledge, 2014), p. 56.
53 Sulieman, *Political Parties in Lebanon*, p. 96; see also Jumblatt, *Lights on the Truth*, pp. 129–31.
54 Andrew Rathmel, *Secret War in the Middle East, The Covert Struggle for Syria, 1949–1961* (*Lais fi Lubnan al-mustaqqil makan l'il-jawasis wal-khawana*) (Beirut: Lebanese Communist Party, 1947).
55 Seale, *The Struggle for Arab Independence*, p. 531.
56 Moubayed, *Steel & Silk*, p. 322
57 Beshara, *Outright Assassination*, p. 25.
58 Yamak, *The Syrian Social Nationalist Party*, p. 63.
59 Adel Beshara, *Fayez Sayegh, The Party Years 1938–1947* (Black House Publishing, 2019), p. 73.
60 Ibid., pp. 73–86.
61 Yamak, *The Syrian Social Nationalist Party*, p. 63.
62 Ibid., p. 64.
63 Sharabi, *Embers and Ashes*, p. 59.
64 Ibid., p. 53.
65 Ibid., p. 64.
66 Gamliel Cohen, *Under Cover, The Untold Story of the Palmach's Under Cover Arab Unit* (Israeli Ministry of Defense and the Galili Center for Defense Studies, 1951–2002), pp. 296–305; see also Matti Friedman, *Spies of No Country: Secret Lives at the Birth of Israel* (Algonquin Books, 2019), p. 155.
67 Gamliel Cohen's memoir, *Under Cover*, pp. 296–305.
68 For an interesting discussion of the Jummayziah incident, see Dylan Baun, *The Gemmayzeh Incident of 1949: Conflict over Physical and Symbolic Space in Beirut* (Huntsville: University of Alabama).
69 Yamak, *The Syrian Social Nationalist Party*, p. 67.
70 Sharabi, *Embers and Ashes*, pp. 175–6.
71 "SSNP The Martyrdom of the Leader, The Priest Who Knew Him, Part 2," YouTube, posted March 27, 2009, https://www.youtube.com/watch?v=O1XtIc3Xso4 (accessed April 26, 2021).
72 Yamak, *The Syrian Social Nationalist Party*, p. 127.

3 Tahya Suriya! The SSNP's Ideology

1. See the other fundamental principles: Antoun Saadeh, "The Aim and Program of the Syrian Social Nationalist Party," http://antoun-saadeh.com/languages/en/1524 (accessed September 16, 2020).
2. Bashir Mawsli, "The Battle of Maysalun and the Beginning of the Nation's History," July 24, 1920, http://www.ssnp.info/index.php?article=65952 (accessed April, 25, 2021).
3. A Nationalist delegation visits the martyr Yusef al-Azma's tomb on the Anniversary of the Battle of Maysalun, http://www.al-binaa.com/archives/article/171263 (accessed October 10, 2020).
4. Mawsli, "The Battle of Maysalun and the Beginning of the Nation's History," July 24, 1920, http://www.ssnp.info/index.php?article=65952 (accessed April 25, 2021).
5. Dr. Nazeer al-Azma's interview with *Al-Hayat*, November 14, 2014, http://alhayat.com/article/615935 (accessed October 1, 2020).
6. "The Centenary of the Glorious Battle of Maysalun," July 24, 2020, https://www.alqawmi.com/?p=10090&fbclid=IwAR1QQjGGkRlhhvk8ys49uetEm5bOxnyg4L20ly_Pdb5X_CF8qodDsffTBxw (accessed September 15, 2020).
7. SSNP News message to author, January 2019.
8. Joel Veldkamp, "Resurgence of the SSNP in Syria: An Ideological Opponent of the Regime Gets a Boost from the Conflict," December 19, 2014, https://www.joshualandis.com/blog/resurgence-of-the-ssnp-in-syria-an-ideological-opponent-of-the-regime-gets-a-boost-from-the-conflict/ (accessed September 21, 2020).
9. Sharabi, *Embers and Ashes*, p. 59.
10. The dean of foreign affairs meets the ambassador of Cyprus: Lebanon is determined to defend its sovereignty and its right to extract oil, September 20, 2018, http://www.ssnp.com/?p=1819 (accessed September 21, 2020).
11. http://www.ssnp.com/old/library.htm#SSNP%20Anthem (accessed November 4, 2020).
12. Interview with young SSNP sympathizer, online, January 2, 2018.
13. "Group celebrates Saadeh birthday, legacy," *The Arab American News*, March 13, 2009, https://www.arabamericannews.com/2009/03/14/Group-celebrates-Saadeh-birthday-legacy/ (accessed January 5, 2019).
14. Interview with Antoun Issa, who attended the SSNP's youth camps in Australia, but never become a party member, February 5, 2017.
15. Sandra Mackey, *Lebanon, a House Divided* (New York: W. W. Norton), pp. 38–9.
16. Dr. Adel Beshara to author, December 11, 2016.
17. Joshua Landis, "Are There Non-Sectarian Parties in Syria: The Case of the SSNP?," November 23, 2008, https://www.joshualandis.com/blog/are-there-non-sectarian-parties-in-syria-the-case-of-the-ssnp/ (accessed January 8, 2019).

18 Sayegh, *Arab Unity, Hope and Fulfillment*, p. 92.
19 Michael Young, "Remembering the Uprising of Feb. 6, 1984," *The Daily Star*, February 7, 2004.
20 Dr. Garabet K. Moumdjian, translation, 2008, *Remembering Antoine (Antun) Saadeh*, "Part 1. At the Maqasid College, Ahmad Shuman Reminisces," p. 9.
21 Michael W. Suleiman, *Political Parties in Lebanon, The Challenge of a Fragmented Political Culture* (Ithaca: Cornell University Press), p. 105.
22 See, for example, the Saadeh Cultural Foundation Facebook page, September 20, 2020, https://www.facebook.com/saadehculturalfoundation/posts/2760561310865738 (accessed March 10, 2020).
23 http://www.ssnp.com/old/library.htm#Dedicated%20Sections (accessed January 8, 2019).
24 Jesse McDonald, "The SSNP's Military: The Eagles of the Whirlwind & Their Emblem," June 5, 2017, https://www.joshualandis.com/blog/24853-2/ (accessed January 10, 2019).
25 Ibid.
26 Beshara, *Outright Assassination*, p. 22.
27 Hazran, *The Druze Community and the Lebanese State* (London: Routledge, 2019), p. 59.
28 Ibid.
29 Sa'adeh, *Awraq al-Qawmiyya*, fn 3, pp. 206–7.
30 Author's correspondence with Elia Samman, Dr. Ali Haidar's political adviser, January 20, 2017.
31 Interview with young SSNP sympathizer, online, January 2, 2018.
32 Interview with Dr. Milad Sebaaly, February 4, 2017.
33 Beshara, *Outright Assassination*, pp. 13–16.
34 Zeina Maasri, *Off the Wall, Political Posters of the Lebanese Civil War* (London: I.B. Tauris, 2009), pp. 56–7.
35 Hazran, *The Druze Community and the Lebanese State*, pp. 60–1.

4 We Have Avenged Him! The Party and Syria

1 Seale, *Asad: The Struggle for the Middle East*, p. 50.
2 Sami Moubayed, "Farewell Mohammad al-Maghout," April 6, 2006, http://samimoubayed.com/2006/04/06/farewell-mohammad-al-maghout-1934-2006/
3 Salim Mujais, *The Syrian Social Nationalist Party, Its Ideology and History* (Black House, 2019), p. 171.
4 Moubayed, *Steel and Silk*, p. 288.

5 YouTube video interview with Issam al-Mahayri. "History of the SSNP," https://www.youtube.com/watch?v=f5zJi1bBBeU, posted August 1, 2016 (accessed April 25, 2021).
6 Emma Jorum, *Beyond Syria's Borders: A History of Territorial Disputes in the Middle East* (I.B. Tauris, 2014), pp. 92–3.
7 Sarab Al-Jijakli, October 26, 2016, https://sarabiany.wordpress.com/2016/10/26/remembering-adib-shishakli/ (accessed January 18, 2017).
8 Martin Gilbert, *Israel, A History* (New York: William Morrow, 1998), p. 177.
9 Moubayed, *Steel and Silk*, p. 336.
10 Juliette El Mir Saadah, *Muzakarat Al Amina Al 'Ula Juliette El Mir Saadeh* (Beirut: Kutub, 2004), p. 113.
11 Moubayed, *Steel and Silk*, p. 350.
12 Douglas Little, "1949–1958, Syria: Early Experiments in Covert Action," Department of History, Clark University, May 2003, p. 12.
13 Moubayed, *Steel and Silk*, p. 352.
14 Husni al-Zaim, hours before his death, attending a charity dinner by the Red Crescent, August 1949, http://www.syrianhistory.com/en/photos/1853 (accessed April 25, 2021).
15 Seale, *Asad: The Struggle for Syria*, pp. 73–4.
16 Milad Sebaaly to author, February 2017.
17 Mounayed, *Steel and Silk*, pp. 326–7.
18 For an interesting discussion of Shishakli's personality cult, see Kevin W. Martin, "Speaking with the 'Voice of Syria': Producing the Arab World's First Personality Cult," *Middle East Journal*, 72, no. 4 (2018): 361, https://doi.org/10.3751/72.4.15 (accessed April 25, 2021).
19 Joshua Teitelbaum, "The Muslim Brotherhood in Syria, 1945–1958: Founding, Social Origins, Ideology," *Middle East Journal*, 65, no. 2 (2011): 227.
20 Adonis Bouhatab, "Inaam Raad of (Syria Nation Socialist Party): Biography," October 24, 2008, https://adonis49.wordpress.com/2008/10/24/biography-of-inaam-raad/ (accessed April 25, 2021).
21 Moubayed, *Steel and Silk*, p. 288.
22 Seale, *The Struggle for Syria*, p. 126.
23 David Commins and David W. Lesch, *Historical Dictionary of Syria*, 3rd ed. (Lanham: Scarecrow Press, 2014), p. 313.
24 Seale, *The Struggle for Syria*, p. 129.
25 Lesch, *History in Syria*, p. 313.
26 Seale, *The Struggle for Syria*, p. 130.
27 Joshua Landis, "Shishakli and the Druzes: Integration and Intransigence," in *The Syrian Land: Processes of Integration and Fragmentation*, ed. T. Philipp and B. Schäbler (Stuttgart: Franz Steiner Verlag, 1998), pp. 369–96.

28 "One of the Party's Most Prominent Faces in the Jazira Governate ... Comrade Zaki Nizameddine," *al-Binaa*, https://www.al-binaa.com/archives/article/162936 (accessed April 25, 2021).
29 Andrew Rathmell, *Secret War in the Middle East, The Covert Struggle for Syria 1949–1961* (London: I.B. Tauris, 2014), pp. 10–11.
30 An interview with deputy chief-of-staff of the Syrian army, Colonel Adnan al-Malki, in the political daily *al-Jihad* on February 24, 1955, http://syrianhistory.com/en/photos/2641?search=Malki (accessed April 25, 2021).
31 Nabil M. Kaylani, "The Rise of the Syrian Ba'th, 1940–1958: Political Success, Party Failure," *International Journal of Middle East Studies*, *3*, no. 1 (1972): 8.
32 The Nationalists in front of Martyr Ghassan Jadid's tomb: "We will confront normalization, Turkification and Judaization," February 21, 2021, https://ssnparty.org/%d8%a7%d9%84%d9%82%d9%88%d9%85%d9%8a%d9%88%d9%86-%d9%85%d9%86-%d8%a3%d9%85%d8%a7%d9%85-%d8%b6%d8%b1%d9%8a%d8%ad-%d8%a7%d9%84%d8%b4%d9%91%d9%8-7%d9%8a%d8%af-%d8%ba%d8%b3%d9%91%d8%a7%d9%86-%d8%ac%d8%af/ (accessed April 25, 2021).
33 The Martyr Ghassan Jadid, March 3, 2021, https://ssnparty.org/%d8%a7%d9%84%d8%b4%d9%87%d9%8a%d8%af-%d8%ba%d8%b3%d8%a7%d9%86-%d8%ac%d8%af%d9%8a%d8%af/ (accessed April 25, 2021).
34 Moubayed, *Steel and Silk*, p. 58.
35 Online interview with Ali Khalifa (pseudonym), a pro-government Syrian living in Latakia, March 2018.
36 Seale, *Struggle for Syria*, p. 239.
37 Martin, "Syria's Democratic Years, Citizens, Experts, and Media in the 1950s," p. 77.
38 Prior to the Malki assassination, Mahayri was still active with the party's Al-Binaa outlet, publishing a notice on February 15, 1955, for readers to stay informed through the "weapons of knowledge." See Dr Jihad Nasri al-Aql, "Mawsuea Sihafat al-Haraka al-Qawmiyya al-Ijtima'iyya (1933–2008) in 75 Years," *Al Furat*, 2011, p. 89.
39 Moubayed, *Steel and Silk*, p. 86.
40 "Syria: The Roots of Tyranny": The story of Abdul Hamid al-Sarraj who used fear and torture to turn 1950s Syria into a police state. Filmmaker Mohammad Jameel, March 15, 2017, http://www.aljazeera.com/programmes/aljazeeraworld/2017/03/syria-roots-tyranny-170313062353299.html (accessed April 25, 2021).
41 Martin, "Syria's Democratic Years," p. 71.
42 Ibid.
43 Ibid., p. 75.
44 Sami Moubayed, "Farewell Mohammad al-Maghout," April 6, 2006, https://samimoubayed.com/2006/04/06/farewell-mohammad-al-maghout-1934-2006/

(accessed April 25, 2021); another famous Syrian who was imprisoned in the aftermath of the Malki assassination was the world famous poet Adonis.
45 Rathmell, *Secret War in the Middle East*, p. 111.
46 Seale, *Struggle for Syria*, p. 272.
47 Ibid.
48 Memorandum from the Assistant Secretary of State for Near Eastern, South Asian, and African Affairs (Allen) to the Secretary of State, Subject: Adib Shishakli and the Possibility of a Coup in Syria, Washington, June 27, 1956, https://history.state.gov/historicaldocuments/frus1955-57v13/d329 (accessed April 25, 2021).
49 Rathmell, *Secret War in the Middle East*, p. 120.
50 Seale, *Struggle for Syria*, p. 276.
51 Ibid., p. 280.
52 It actually took about two years after the Malki Affair for Sarraj to finally eliminate Jadid. He first attempted to abduct him in Lebanon immediately following the Malki assassination in 1955, but the two Syrian intelligence agents who were dispatched for the mission were betrayed by their informant and the SSNP got the drop on them. The Lebanese government eventually stepped in and negotiated the agents' release back to Syria.
53 Rathmell, *Secret War in the Middle East*, p. 127.
54 Telegram from the Embassy in Syria to the Department of State, Damascus, July 7, 1955, https://history.state.gov/historicaldocuments/frus1955-57v13/d300 (accessed April 25, 2021).
55 Telegram from the Embassy in Syria to the Department of State, Damascus, January 8, 1956, https://history.state.gov/historicaldocuments/frus1955-57v13/d318 (accessed April 25, 2021).
56 Mujais, *The Syrian Social Nationalist Party, Its Ideology and History*, p. 217.
57 "Syria Convicts 15 in Arms Plot," *New York Times*, January 13, 1959.
58 "Leader of the Syrian Revolution Sultan Pasha al-Atrash Remembers Adnan al-Malki," *Al-Jundi Magazine*, July 1955, http://www.syrianhistory.com/en/photos/7022? (accessed April 25, 2021).

5 In the Shadow of Nasser: The SSNP and the Arab Cold War

1 "Military Parade in Cairo, Egypt, United Arab Republic, July 22, 1959," HD Stock Footage, https://www.youtube.com/watch?v=Pz8FBqlGIJA (accessed April 25, 2021).
2 Ibid.
3 SSNP representative from Baalbek, 'Abd al-Satir, wrote in his memoir (pp. 131–3) that the Suez Crisis had actually interrupted Ghassan Jadid and the SSNP's plans to

launch a coup in Syria, causing them to delay the plot because of the external threat to both Syria and Egypt.
4 See Malcolm H. Kerr, *The Arab Cold War. Gamel Abd al-Nasr and His Rivals, 1958–1970*, 3rd ed. (Oxford University Press, 1975).
5 Moubayed, *Steel and Silk*, p. 288.
6 Derek A. Ide, *Socialism Without Socialists: Egyptian Marxists and the Nasserist State, 1952–65* (The University of Toledo Digital Repository, 2015).
7 Kerr, The Arab Cold War, p. 10.
8 Tareq Y. Ismael and Jacqueline S. Ismael, *The Communist Movement in Syria and Lebanon* (Gainesville: University Press of Florida, 1998), p. 59.
9 See "Syria: The Roots of Tyranny."
10 Nabil M. Kaylani, "The Rise of the Syrian Ba'th, 1940–1958: Political Success, Party Failure," *International Journal of Middle East Studies*, 3, no. 1 (1972): 8.
11 Seale, *The Struggle for the Middle East*, p. 39.
12 Elizabeth F. Thompson, *Justice Interrupted: The Struggle for Constitutional Government in the Middle East* (Cambridge, MA: Harvard University Press, 2013), pp. 210–11.
13 Thompson, *Justice Interrupted*, p. 224.
14 Ibid., p. 211.
15 US Embassy Beirut dispatch, No. 272, Memorandum of Conversation between Ambassador Heath and Jawad Bey Boulos, November 7, 1957; US Embassy Beirut dispatch, No. 271, Memorandum of Conversation between Ambassador Heath and Kamal Bey Jumblattt, November 18, 1957.
16 Harold M. Cubert, *The PFLP's Changing Role in the Middle East* (London: Frank Cass, 1997), p. 45.
17 Beshara, *Lebanon, The Politics of Frustration*, p. 45.
18 Kerr, *The Arab Cold War*, p. 17.
19 Adel Beshara, *Lebanon, The Politics of Frustration—The Failed Coup of 1961* (London: Routledge-Curzon, 2005), p. 41.
20 Michael W. Suleiman, "Elections in a Confessional Democracy," *Journal of Politics*, 29, no. 1 (1967): 112.
21 Messih's lieutenant was Iskandar Shawi. According to Michael Sulieman, the other members of Messih's faction included Hassan el-Tawil, Ibrahim Yamut, Yusuf Qa'id Bay, Fadil Kinj, Hanna Kiswani, Mohammed Yusuf Hammoud, George George, Gamil Makhlouf, Mohammed Tabbakh, and Munib el-Husseini.
22 US Embassy Beirut, Confidential Dispatch No. 584, p. 3, 1957.
23 Nada Raad, 'Tueini Talks about His Turbulent Relationship with SSNP', *Daily Star*, May 22, 2004. http://www.dailystar.com.lb/ArticlePrint.aspx?id=1288&mode=print (accessed April 25, 2021).

24 Nada Raad, Electoral System Criticized for Taking Power from the People, *Daily Star*, February 17, 2004.
25 US Embassy Beirut, Confidential Dispatch No. 584, p. 4, 1957.
26 US Embassy Beirut, Confidential Dispatch No. 624, p. 1, Election Results in Mount Lebanon, 1957.
27 Although Issam al-Mahayri was still in prison, some detainees during this period were usually allowed considerable freedom to receive visitors and write; so this is not as strange as it might appear.
28 John Pierre Entelis, *Pluralism and Party Transformation in Lebanon: Al-Kata'ib, 1936–1970* (Brill, 1974), pp. 133–4.
29 Correspondence from Said Taky Deen, president of the Alumni Association of the American University of Beirut, regarding repayment of Sayegh's scholarship loan. J. Willard Marriott Library's Aziz A. Atiya Library, University of Utah, November 12, 1949, https://collections.lib.utah.edu/details?id=841407 (accessed April 25, 2021).
30 Alfred H. Howell, "Sa'id Taky Deen: 1904–1960," *Middle East Quarterly*, 1, no. 3 (Summer 1994): 37.
31 Ibid., p. 25.
32 Howell, "Sa'id Taky Deen: 1904–1960," 37.
33 US Embassy telegram to Secretary of State, No. 1293, October 25, 1957; US Embassy telegram to the Secretary of State, No. 1430, November 4, 1957.
34 Howell, "Sa'id Taky Deen: 1904–1960," p. 37.
35 Rathmell, *The Secret War in the Middle East*, p. 126.
36 Ibid.
37 Beshara, *Lebanon: The Politics of Frustration*, n. 89, p. 183.
38 Samir Khalaf, *Civil and Uncivil Violence in Lebanon, A History of the Internationalization of Communal Conflict* (New York: Columbia University Press, 2002), p. 126.
39 Labib Zuwiyya Yamak, *The Syrian Social Nationalist Party: An Ideological Analysis* (Harvard Middle Eastern Monograph Series, Cambridge: Center for Middle Eastern Studies, 1966), pp. 71–2.
40 Khalaf, *Civil and Uncivil Violence in Lebanon*, p. 125.
41 Ibid., p. 133.
42 US Embassy Damascus, No. 2949, June 9, 1957 by Ambassador to Syria James S. Moose Jr.
43 Khalaf, *Civil and Uncivil Violence in Lebanon*, p. 135.
44 US Embassy telegram to Secretary of State, No. 2841, February 22, 1958.
45 Khalaf, *Civil and Uncivil Violence in Lebanon*, p. 135.
46 Yamak, *The Syrian Social Nationalist Party*, p. 175.

47 William W. Harris, *The New Face of Lebanon, History's Revenge* (Princeton: Markus Wiener, 2009), p. 145.
48 Stephane Malsagne, *Fouad Chehab, 1902–1973, Une figure oubliee de l'historie libanaise* (Alep-Amman-Beyrouth-Damas-Erbil: Presses de l'ifpo, Karthala, Institut francais du Proche-Orient, 2011), p. 216.
49 *Middle East Record, Vol. 1* (Lebanon: Tel Aviv University, The Reuven Shiloah Research Center, 1960), p. 346.
50 Ibid.
51 Khalaf, *Civil and Uncivil Violence in Lebanon*, p. 212.
52 Beshara, *Lebanon: The Politics of Frustration*, p. 51.
53 Ibid., p. 44.
54 Ibid., p. 53.
55 Khalaf, *Civil and Uncivil Violence in Lebanon*, p. 211.
56 Adonis Bouhatab, "Inaam Raad of (Syria Nation Socialist Party): Biography," October 24, 2008, https://adonis49.wordpress.com/2008/10/24/biography-of-inaam-raad/ (accessed April 25, 2021).
57 Ibid.
58 Saʿadeh, ʿAbdullah. *Awrāq Qawmiyya: Mudhakkirāt ʿAbdullah Saʿādah* (The Memoirs of ʿAbdullah Saʿadeh) (Beirut: Nationalist Papers, 1987), p. 71.
59 Beshara, *Lebanon: The Politics of Frustration*, p. 56.
60 Ibid.
61 Awad family members to author, November 2018.
62 Beshara, *Lebanon: The Politics of Frustration*, p. 121.
63 According to Adel Beshara, on the SSNP's Supreme Council, Nadhir al-Azmah, Abdullah Qubarsi, Umar Abu Zlam, Kamil Abu Kamil, and Asad Rihal, and three commissioners, Philippe Musallim, Mustafa Izz ad-Din, and Mustafa Abdul Satir, all expressed skepticism and/or rejected the coup idea. Kamil Abu Kamil, Asad Rihal, and Mustafa Abdl Satir resigned from their leadership positions.
64 Adonis blog; see also Beshara, Lebanon: *The Politics of Frustration*, pp. 126–7, n. 51, p. 202.
65 Ibid., p. 126.
66 Ibid., p. 123.
67 Ibid., p. 127.
68 Ibid., pp. 130–1.
69 *New York Times*, Special Report, "Troops in Lebanon Occupy Rebel Area," January 4, 1962.
70 Beshara, *Lebanon: The Politics of Frustration*, p. 129.
71 Camille K. Chehab, *Le Liban face a l'ouragan by Camille Chehab, ou tout sur le complot du Parti Populaire Syrien "P.P.S."* (Beirut, 1966), introduction.

72 Dana Adams Schmidt, "Lebanon Seeking Tighter Security," *New York Times*, January 11, 1962.
73 Schmidt, "Lebanese Seize Leader of Coup," *New York Times*, January 20, 1962.
74 Ibid., p. 133.
75 "Troops in Lebanon Occupy Rebel Area."
76 British Embassy dispatch, Cairo, January 8, 1962.
77 Chehab, Le Liban face a l'ouragan by Camille Chehab, ou tout sur le complot du Parti Populaire Syrien "P.P.S.", p. 3 (map).
78 Ghassan al-Khalidi, *al-Ḥizb al-Qawmī wa-al-thawrah al-thāniyah, 1961–1962: al-inqilāb wa-al-muḥākamāt* (Bayrū t: Dā r wa-Maktabat al-Turā th al-Adabī , 2003), pp. 255–6.
79 *Middle East Record, Vol. 2, The Attempted NSP Coup* (Lebanon: Tel Aviv University, The Reuven Shiloah Research Center, 1961), p. 398.
80 Nicolas Nassif, *The Republic of Fouad Chehab* (Beirut: Information International, 2008), reposted "The Syrian Social Nationalist Party Military Coup," January 1, 2013, https://monthlymagazine.com/article-desc_681_ (accessed April 26, 2021).
81 Milad Sebaaly to author, February 2017.
82 British Embassy Beirut, confidential dispatch 1011/47/62 No. 8, January 12, 1962, p. 2.
83 Sulieman, *Political Parties in Lebanon*, p. 100.
84 Schmidt, "Lebanon Seeking Tighter Security."

6 Broken Country, Fractured Party: The SSNP and the Lebanese Civil War in the 1970s

1 Ehud Ya'ari, "Behind the Terror," *The Atlantic*, June 1987.
2 See Hisham Melhem, "The Arab World Has Never Recovered from the Loss of 1967," *Foreign Policy*, June 5, 2017, https://foreignpolicy.com/2017/06/05/the-arab-world-has-never-recovered-from-the-loss-of-1967/ (accessed April 26, 2021).
3 Samir Khalaf, *Civil and Uncivil Violence in Lebanon, A History of the Internationalization of Communal Conflict* (New York: Columbia University Press, 2002), p. 211.
4 See Itamar Rabinovich, *The Civil War for Lebanon, 1970–1985* (Cornell University Press, 1985), pp. 28–39, for how the PLO established a strong militant presence in Lebanon under President Charles Hilu.
5 Richard L. Homan, "Jumblatt: Enigmatic Mystic with Clout," *Washington Post*, March 17, 1977, https://www.washingtonpost.com/archive/politics/1977/03/17/jumblatt-enigmatic-mystic-with-clout/66e75049-8dd8-4a35-a84b-2940a1b5c12d/?utm_term=.bf2caedfca2e (accessed April 26, 2021).

6 Nazih Richani, *Dilemmas of Democracy and Political Parties in Sectarian Societies: The Case of the Progressive Socialist Party of Lebanon 1949–1996* (New York: St. Martin's Press, 1998), pp. 80–1.
7 Suleiman, *Political Parties in Lebanon*, p. 92.
8 Khalaf, *Civil and Uncivil Violence in Lebanon*, p. 218.
9 Dr. Milad Sebaaly, "Inaam Raad Biography," YouTube video, May 19, 2012, https://www.youtube.com/watch?v=Djwr1OGxv8A (accessed April 26, 2021).
10 Richani, Dilemmas of Democracy and Political Parties in Sectarian Societies, p. 117.
11 Ibid.
12 Raad, *Al-Kamila al-Akhira Mudhakarat wa Watha'iq* (Beirut: Mu'assasat In'ām Ra'ad al-Fikriyya, 2002), pp. 106–8 and 211–13.
13 Ibid., pp. 211–13.
14 Ibid.
15 'Abdullah Sa'adeh, *Awrāq Qawmiyya: Mudhakkirāt 'Abdullah Sa'ādah* (The Memoirs of 'Abdullah Sa'adeh) (Beirut: Nationalist Papers, 1987), pp. 206–7.
16 Farid el Khazen, *The Breakdown of the State in Lebanon* (Cambridge, MA: Harvard University Press, 2000), p. 74.
17 Ibid.
18 Interview conducted by Ruwan Al-Rejoleh with Firas Tlass, the son of former Syrian Defense Minister Mustafa Tlass, September 2018.
19 Raad, "The Last Words."
20 Raad, *Al-Kamila al-Akhira Mudhakarat wa Watha'iq*, p. 220.
21 Taha Ghaddar, "The Social Institutions in Saadeh's Party: The National and Consultative Councils Are in Conflict with Saadeh's Constitutional Ideology," December 15, 2011, SSNP.Info/?article=69692 (accessed April 25, 2021).
22 Raad, *Al-Kamila al-Akhira Mudhakarat wa Watha'iq*, p. 198.
23 Ibid., p. 197; Inaam Raad wrote in his memoir:

> I should've been more diplomatic and adopted the language of courtship. I had read at some point that (Gaddafi and the Libyan Revolutionary Command Council) had nationalized (or dispossessed) the churches, so when I arrived in Libya, I asked if there were any Christian sects here? I was told no, so I visited the churches and found them to be in the Italian style, I said you have not persecuted the Libyans but have closed down what the Italians left behind. I added, "We understand that the Islamic factor is important and foundational in the National Movement's struggle against colonialism, particularly French and Italian, namely against Italy's actions in Libya and France's in Algeria. Colonialism, sadly, used religion and religious missionaries as one of its weapons, going all the way back to the Crusades, but please understand that we in the East are comprised of a number of different religious groups, and that Eastern Christians are fellow

citizens who have lived in their countries and fought on their behalf, thus what brings us together is nationalism built on the unity of life."

24 Interview conducted by Ruwan Al-Rejoleh with Firas Tlass, the son of former Syrian Defense Minister Mustafa Tlass, September 2018.
25 This petty behavior of letting the air out of car tires was something that the Syrian government officials had experienced themselves from their Baath Party rivals in Iraq.
26 Interview conducted by Ruwan Al-Rejoleh with Firas Tlass, the son of former Syrian Defense Minister Mustafa Tlass, September 2018.
27 Interview with an anonymous former Kataeb fighter, April 4, 2017.
28 Reuven Avi-Ran, *The Syrian Involvement in Lebanon since 1975* (Boulder: Westview Press, 1991), p. 58.
29 Author interview with Adel Beshara, December 2016.
30 Elias Gergi Qanayzeh was born in Tartus on March 18, 1913, and joined the SSNP's branch in Tartus in 1935. He went on to become the pro-Syrian factions' president in 1975 and was president of the SSNP's Supreme Court during the 1990s. He died in 1997.
31 Avi-Ran, The Syrian Involvement in Lebanon since 1975, pp. 27, 44.
32 Other Khawarij were Mufeed al-Qintar, Adnan Tayara, Haitham Abdulqadir, Wadee' El Hellu, and Nasir Rammah. Most Khawarij were from the Munnazamat El Zawaba'a, the whirlwind's organization (militia).
33 Firas Shoufi, "'The Nationalists' in Lebanon and Syria: Larger Than a Crisis and Smaller Than a Split," *Al Akhbar*, May 29, 2012, https://al-akhbar.com/Politics/70386 (accessed April 26, 2021).
34 Danny Haddad, "The Phalange and the Nationalists: Two Parties with Many Objections," *Al Akhbar*, December 1, 2018, https://al-akhbar.com/Politics/148258 (accessed April 26, 2021).
35 Interview with SSNP News, December 2018.
36 Interview conducted by Ruwan Al-Rejoleh with Firas Tlass, September 2018.
37 Adonis Bouhatab, "Inaam Raad of (Syria Nation Socialist Party): Biography," October 24, 2008, https://adonis49.wordpress.com/2008/10/24/biography-of-inaam-raad/ (accessed April 25, 2021).
38 Interview with an anonymous former Kataeb fighter, 2017.
39 Zuraiq believed that a collective mobilization was required for the Arabs to confront their predicament and that "ideologically and historically, challenges had always stimulated the development of civilizations and that it should be assumed that the defeat [of the Arabs in 1948 by Israel] would play this role for the Arabs." Furthermore, "the strengthening of the sense of the Zionist danger in every Arab country, international contacts, involvement of the popular forces in the battle, and dissatisfaction with the role of the [Arab] regimes' forces," were needed to confront the state of Israel and deliver salvation for the Palestinians. This notion of

a complete restructuring of Arab society and thinking became the basis of Habash's and the PFLP's ideology. Husri, in turn, emphasized that secularism was needed in order to foster a healthy environment for nationalism. See Harold M. Cubert, *The PFLP's Changing Role in the Middle East* (London: Frank Cass, 1997), pp. 29–30.
40 Eyal Zisser, "The Syrian Phoenix: The Revival of the Syrian Social National Party in Syria," *Die Welt des Islams*, 47, no. 2 (2007): 188–206.
41 Dr. Adel Beshara to author, October 4, 2018.
42 The Arabic term "Izz" is not exactly glory (*Majd*) or honor (*Sharaf*), but this is the closest translation to it. The term in Arabic, *Waqfat Izz* ("Stand of Glory/Honor"), is one of the most common exclusive SSNP phrases and goes back to the Antoun Saadeh era.
43 Kuwkab Malouf, "Four Decades of the Aintoura Massacre," *Al-Binaa*, http://www.al-binaa.com/archives/article/977?fbclid=IwAR34IvN5VFj_AckufiXIY2wEMc7tNz3VGII3TUNaD5SZjlkEyiRSxwwljEI (accessed April 26, 2021).
44 Firas al-Shoufi, "Aintoura Has Not Forgotten the Time the Kharijites Were Eradicated," *Al-Binaa*, April 9, 2013, https://al-akhbar.com/Politics/49085?fbclid=IwAR1Vi_2RFNbeDaBpJwW0jk8-nsDGcyWE4PApfRtOFgPVJ5kzdy_NVulT37M (accessed April 26, 2021).
45 Bouhatab, "Inaam Raad of (Syria Nation Socialist Party): Biography."
46 For some background, see Lorena De Vita, "How the GDR Capitalized on the Arab-Israeli Conflict," June 5, 2017, https://www.wilsoncenter.org/blog-post/how-the-gdr-capitalized-the-arab-israli-conflict (accessed April 26, 2021).
47 Imad Salamey, *The Government and Politics of Lebanon* (London: Routledge, 2017), p. 45.
48 P. Augustus Richard Norton, *Amal and the Shi'a, Struggle for the Soul of Lebanon* (Austin: University of Texas Press, 1987), pp. 26–7.

7 Guerrilla War to Politics: The SSNP's Role in Lebanon's Politics

1 See Sune Haugbolle, *War and Memory in Lebanon*, 1st ed. (Cambridge: Cambridge University Press).
2 Zeina Maasri, *Off the Wall, Political Posters of the Lebanese Civil War* (London: I.B. Tauris, 2009), p. 73.
3 *PFLP Bulletin*, no. 39 (June 1980): 22.
4 Beshara, *Outright Assassination*, p. 275.
5 Slaying is denounced by Reagan; "U.S. Fears New Burst in Fighting," *New York Times*, September 15, 1982.

6 Colin Campbell, "Gemayel of Lebanon Is Killed in Bomb Blast at Party Offices," *New York Times*, September 15, 1982, https://www.nytimes.com/1982/09/15/world/gemayel-of-lebanon-is-killed-in-bomb-blast-at-party-offices.html

7 Georgi Azar, "Bashir Gemayel's Assassins Sentenced to Death," *An-Nahar*, October 20, 2017, https://en.annahar.com/article/688404-bachir-gemayels-assassin-sentenced-to-death

8 Afif Diab, "Habib al-Shartouni Striking the Head of Collaboration," *al-Akhbar*, July 23, 2012, https://web.archive.org/web/20180413125127/https://english.al-akhbar.com/content/habib-al-shartouni-striking-head-collaboration (accessed April 20, 2021).

9 Scott Preston, "Lebanon's Civil War Scars Re-emerge with Assassination Case Verdict," *al-Monitor*, October 27, 2017, https://www.al-monitor.com/pulse/originals/2017/10/lebanon-bashir-gemayel-killer-sentence-timing.html

10 "Lebanese Court Issues Death Sentence over 1982 Gemayel Assassination," Reuters, October 20, 2017, https://www.reuters.com/article/us-lebanon-politics-trial/lebanese-court-issues-death-sentence-over-1982-gemayel-assassination-idUSKBN1CP22E (accessed September 16, 2020).

11 Salah Jadid himself was a member of the SSNP for a period of time before joining the Baath Party. His two brothers, Ghassan and Fuad, stayed on with the SSNP.

12 "Alliance between Ideology and Politics 2: 'National Interest,'" *al-Nahda Magazine*, February 17, 2014.

13 Saadeh, *Awraq Qawmiyyah*, p. 306.

14 "Crisis in Lebanon," *New York Times*, February 8, 1984, https://www.nytimes.com/1984/02/08/nyregion/wednesday-february-8-1984-crisis-in-lebanon.html

15 Ranwa Yehia, "Alwan's One-Man War Remembered," *Daily Star*, September 30, 2000, http://www.dailystar.com.lb/News/Lebanon-News/2000/Sep-30/12717-alwans-one-man-war-remembered.ashx

16 For the allegations about this assassination attempt, see Daniel Pipes, "Radical Politics and the Syrian Social Nationalist Party," *International Journal of Middle East Studies* (August 1988): 303–24.

17 Habib Shartouni writes about his friend, Khaled Alwan, the hero of the Wimpy operation, May 21, 2015, Friend of Shartouni blog, http://www.friendsofshartouni.com/2015/05/blog-post_21.html (accessed April 26, 2021); information published for the first time about Marytr Khaled Alwan, who carried out the Wimpy operation, September 25, 2016, *al-Khabar*, https://alkhabar-sy.com/%D9%85%D8%B9%D9%84%D9%88%D9%85%D8%A7%D8%AA-%D8%AA%D9%86%D8%B4%D8%B1-%D9%84%D8%A3%D9%88%D9%84-%D9%85%D8%B1%D8%A9-%D8%B9%D9%86-%D8%A7%D9%84%D8%B4%D9%87%D9%8A%D8%AF-%D8%AE%D8%A7%D9%84%D8%AF-%D8%B9%D9%84/ (accessed April 26, 2021).

18 Milt Freudenheim, Henry Giniger, and Richard Levine, "The World; Bombing in the Bekaa," *New York Times*, August 4, 1985.
19 "Israelis Stage New Air Raid on Militia Base in Lebanon," *New York Times*, October 25, 1988.
20 "Around the World; 9 Killed in Bekaa Clashes between Lebanese Units," *New York Times*, June 13, 1986.
21 Edgar O'Ballance, *Civil War in Lebanon, 1975–92* (New York: St. Martin's Press, 1998), p. 166.
22 Ibid., p. 171; see also Robin Wright, "Feared 'Pink Panthers' Prowl the Battle-Scarred Streets of Beirut," *Christian Science Monitor*, February 9, 1982, https://www.csmonitor.com/1982/0209/020930.html
23 Interview conducted by Ruwan Al-Rejoleh with Firas Tlass, September 2018.
24 "Around the World; 9 Killed in Bekaa Clashes between Lebanese Units."
25 "Lebanon Reports 8 Killed in Shiite Village and Blames Israelis," *New York Times*, April 14, 1985.
26 Ibid, p. 173.
27 Nawwaf Hardan, "We Remember You," March 6, 2008, Ssnp.info/?article=38587 (accessed April 26, 2021).
28 There are several chiefs in the party: the chief of the interior, the chief of the state, the chief of the media, the chief of finance, and the most important one is the defense at that time.
29 Interview conducted by Ruwan Al-Rejoleh with Firas Tlass, September 2018.
30 SSNP News email correspondence to author, December 2018.
31 United Press International, "Foreign News Briefs," October 22, 1987, https://www.upi.com/Archives/1987/10/22/Foreign-News-Briefs/9082561873600/ (accessed April 26, 2021).
32 Interview with an anonymous source close to the SSNP, November 2018.
33 Adel Beshara to author, December 11, 2016.
34 Hezbollah, *The Changing Face of Terrorism*, p. 40.
35 "The Heroes of the Naharia Operation. Glory to the Martyrs and Victory to the Revolution," http://www.signsofconflict.com/Archive/poster_details/2099 (accessed September 18, 2020).
36 Nazih Richani, *Dilemmas of Democracy and Political Parties in Sectarian Societies: The Case of the Progressive Socialist Party of Lebanon 1949–1996* (New York: St. Martin's Press 1998), p. 118.
37 Interview with Antoun Issa, who attended the SSNP's youth camps in Australia, but never become a party member, February 5, 2017.
38 *al-Nahar*, 21 September 1987, p. 4. For an interesting discussion of the PLO's relations with Gaddafi and the participation of other leftist factions in the Libya-Chad conflict, see Ajmad Arafat, "A Story from the History of the Palestinian's

Military Activities … When the PLO Fought with Gaddafi against Chad," Raseef 22, December 4, 2018, https://raseef22.net/article/173109-%D9%82%D8%B5%D8%A9-%D9%85%D9%86-%D8%AA%D8%A7%D8%B1%D9%8A%D8%AE-%D8%A7%D9%84%D9%86%D8%B4%D8%A7%D8%B7-%D8%A7%D9%84%D8%B9%D8%B3%D9%83%D8%B1%D9%8A-%D8%A7%D9%84%D9%81%D9%84%D8%B3%D8%B7%D9%8A%D9%86%D9%8A (accessed September 17, 2020).

39 Interview conducted by Ruwan Al-Rejoleh with Firas Tlass, September 2018.
40 Patrick Seale, *Abu Nidal: A Gun for Hire* (New York: Random House, 1992), p. 226.
41 "Abu Nidal Is Reportedly Placed under House Arrest by Libyans," *New York Times*, November 28, 1989.
42 Neil A. Lewis, "U.S. Links Men in Bomb Case to Lebanon Terrorist Group," *New York Times*, May 1988, https://www.nytimes.com/1988/05/18/world/us-links-men-in-bomb-case-to-lebanon-terrorist-group.html (accessed April 26, 2021).
43 Dr. Milad Sebaaly, "Inaam Raad Bbiography," YouTube, posted May 19, 2012, https://www.youtube.com/watch?v=Djwr1OGxv8A (accessed April 26, 2021).
44 Salamey, *The Government and Politics of Lebanon*, p. 121.
45 Ihsan A. Hijazi, "Syria-Lebanon Cooperation Pact Signed," *New York Times*, May 23, 1991, https://www.nytimes.com/1991/05/23/world/syria-lebanon-cooperation-pact-signed.html (accessed April 26, 2021).
46 Eyal Zisser, "The Syrian Phoenix: The Revival of the Syrian Social National Party in Syria," *Die Welt des Islams*, 47, no. 2 (2007): 201.
47 Richani, *Dilemmas of Democracy and Political Parties in Sectarian Societies*, p. 116.
48 Ibid., p. 118.
49 Ibid.
50 "Ad-Diyar," November 5, 1998, https://www.addiyar.com/article/725390- (accessed September 10, 2020).
51 Interview with an SSNP Intifada faction member, January 20, 2017.
52 Andrew Tabler, *In the Lion's Den* (Chicago: Lawrence Hill Books, 2011).
53 Sabine Darrous, "SSNP Chooses 'reformer' Araiji to Lead Party toward Legality in Syria," *Daily Star*, January 6, 2001.
54 Ibid.
55 Ibid.
56 Author's interview with a party member, 2018.
57 Nada Raad, "Tens of Thousands to March in Support of Lebanon's Links with Syria," Daily Star, November 30, 2004, http://www.dailystar.com.lb/ArticlePrint.aspx?id=4718&mode=print (accessed September 19, 2020).
58 Rola el-Husseini, *Pax Syriana, Elite Politics in Postwar Lebanon* (Syracus University Press, 2012), pp. 95–6.
59 "Last Contingent of Syrian Troops Returns from Lebanon," The Associated Press, April 26, 2005, YouTube, https://www.youtube.com/watch?v=wVQ5ZgUPSu4 (accessed December 10, 2020).

60 Are Knudsen and Michael Kerr (eds), *Lebanon, After the Cedar Revolution* (Oxford University Press); Picard, *Lebanon in Search of Sovereignty*, p. 100.
61 See Aron Lund, *Russia in the Middle East* (The Swedish Institute of International Affairs, 2019), p. 15.
62 Nicholas Blanford, *Killing Mr Lebanon, The Assassination of Rafik Hariri and Its Impact on the Middle East* (New York: I.B. Tauris), p. 176.
63 "Lebanese Release Hariri Suspect," BBC News, August 31, 2005, http://news.bbc.co.uk/2/hi/middle_east/4199984.stm (accessed September 19, 2020).
64 "Seemline, Father of Hassan Nasrallah, Ghadi Francis," YouTube, October 27, 2014, https://www.youtube.com/watch?v=qxrr9zqWpOM&feature=youtu.be&ab_channel=freebratfrancis (accessed September 17, 2020).
65 Carsten Wieland, *Syria: A Decade of Lost Chances, Repression and Revolution from Damascus Spring to Arab Spring* (Cune Press, 2012), p. 240.
66 "Lebanese Security Officials Display Weapons Confiscated from Pro-Syrian Party," *Daily Star*, December 23, 2006, http://www.dailystar.com.lb/News/Lebanon-News/2006/Dec-23/43570-lebanese-security-officials-display-weapons-confiscated-from-pro-syrian-party.ashx (accessed September 16, 2020).
67 *Al-Binaa*, reproduced in Dr. Jihad Nasri al-Aql, *Mawsuea Sihafat al-Haraka al-Qawmiyya al-Ijtima'iyya (1933–2008) in 75 years* (Beirut: Al Furat, 2011), p. 806. The names of the martyrs are as follows: Ahmad Na'was, Khalil Suleiman, Mohammad Ghanim, Fadi al-Sheikh, Mohammad Darwish, Ahmad Khalid, Nasr Hamoudha, Mahmoud al-Turk, Khalid al-Ahmad, Khalid Ibrahim, and Zafer Abujaj Hamoudha.
68 el-Husseini, Pax Syriana, Elite Politics in Postwar Lebanon, pp. 95–6. Knudsen and Kerr, Lebanon, After the Cedar Revolution; Picard, *Lebanon in Search of Sovereignty*, Post-2005 Security Dilemmas, p. 101.
69 Robert F. Worth and Nada Bakri, "Deal for Lebanese Factions Leaves Hezbollah Stronger," *New York Times*, May 22, 2008, https://www.nytimes.com/2008/05/22/world/middleeast/22lebanon.html
70 Wieland, Syria: A Decade of Lost Chances, p. 194.
71 "Asaad Harden Assumes SSNP's Reins," *Daily Star*, June 4, 2008.
72 The Nationalist Party's Supreme Council confirmed the party court's decision to strip Charles Ayyoub of the rank of trustee and expel him from the party, September 7, 2019, http://www.ssnp.com/?p=7710 (accessed September 18, 2020).
73 Charles Ayyoub, September 8, 2019, https://twitter.com/charlesayoub6/status/1170799702327078914 (accessed September 17, 2020).
74 Saeed Maalawi, "Paving and Rehabilitating Roads in the Villages of Hasbaya and Marjayoun … and the Kfir People and Their Activists Thank MP Hardan," October 25, 2018, https://ssnp.online/%D8%AA%D8%B9%D8%A8%D9%8A%D8%AF-%D9%88%D8%AA%D8%A3%D9%87%D9%8A%D9%84-%D8%A7%D9%84%D8%B7%D8%B1%D9%82%D8%A7%D8

%AA-%D9%81%D9%8A-%D9%82%D8%B1%D9%89-%D8%AD%D8%A7%D8%B5%D8%A8%D9%8A%D8%A7-%D9%88%D9%85%D8%B1/ (accessed April 26, 2021).

75 "Hassan Diab Garners 69 Votes in Binding Parliamentary Consultations," December 12, 2019, http://www.naharnet.com/stories/en/267390-hassan-diab-garners-69-votes-in-binding-parliamentary-consultations (accessed April 26, 2021).

76 Salim Saadeh, social media post, January 2, 2020. Abdullah Saadeh's son, Salim, was first elected to parliament in 1992, representing Koura, lost his seat in 1996, but regained it in the 2018 elections. https://twitter.com/SalimSaadeh/status/1212642695509938176 (accessed April 26, 2021).

77 "MP Saadeh Addresses Parliament after Being Injured in Protesters Attack," February 11, 2020, http://www.naharnet.com/stories/en/269055-lawmaker-injured-in-protesters-attack-in-beirut?fbclid=IwAR0ztMLJ7e0jOZbsz0S6aD-2OEiibJf6jbdyC_pQyPbB358l91B4CzFSLsY (accessed April 26, 2021); see also Salim Saadeh, social media post, February 11, 2020, https://twitter.com/SalimSaadeh/status/1227180253958868992 (accessed April 26, 2021).

78 SSNP Online, August 12, 2020, https://ssnp.online/%D8%A7%D9%84%D9%82%D9%88%D9%85%D9%8A-%D8%B4%D9%83%D9%91%D9%84-%D9%87%D9%8A%D8%A6%D8%A9-%D8%B7%D9%88%D8%A7%D8%B1%D9%89%D8%A1-%D8%A7%D8%AC%D-8%AA%D9%85%D8%A7%D8%B9%D9%8A%D8%A9-%D8%B6%D9%85%D9%91/ (accessed September 21, 2020).

79 "Emmanuel Macron Visits Beirut to Reshape Lebanon," *The Economist*, September 1, 2020, https://www.economist.com/middle-east-and-africa/2020/09/01/emmanuel-macron-visits-beirut-to-reshape-lebanon (accessed September 18, 2020).

80 "Foreign Dealings with Lebanon after the Beirut Explosion," Al Alam TV, August 7, 2020, https://www.alalamtv.net/news/5088536/%D8%A7%D9%84%D8%AA%D8%B9%D8%A7%D8%B7%D9%8A-%D8%A7%D9%84%D8%AE%D8%A7%D8%B1%D8%AC%D9%8A-%D9%85%D8%B9-%D9%84%D8%A8%D9%86%D8%A7%D9%86-%D-8%A8%D8%B9%D8%AF-%D8%A7%D9%86%D9%81%D8%AC%D8%A7%D8%B1-%D8%A8%D9%8A%D8%B1%D9%88%D8%AA (accessed April 26, 2021).

81 Nationalist Intifada: We are alert to the plans of the foreign countries that are now declaring their support while yesterday they economically besieged the country: National News Agency, August 9, 2020, http://nna-leb.gov.lb/ar/show-news/495772/ (accessed September 18, 2020).

82 https://www.facebook.com/watch/live/?v=2683030205318688&ref=search (accessed September 18, 2020).

83 *al-Binaa*, https://www.al-binaa.com/archives/263064?fbclid=IwAR3cBdk-z9ywEO_GJA45zzIaloJTyp3E781p6_8-pJrAKWxORcgmtlqnsJ8 (accessed September 18, 2020).

8 Battles and Ballots: The SSNP and the Syrian Civil War

1 SSNP Field Media tweet images covering Anas Mohammed Saeed Kerkutli's funeral. He was an SSNP militia fighter killed in action during clashes in Al-Hajar al-Aswad, outside of the Palestinian Yarmouk refugee camp, May 10, 2018.
2 Carl Yonker, "Wither the Syrian Ba'th? Down, But Not Out," Moshe Dayan Center for Middle Eastern and African Studies, March 28, 2018, https://dayan.org/content/wither-syrian-bath-down-not-out (accessed April 26, 2021).
3 Interview with an anonymous Intifada faction member, 2017.
4 "Pro-Assad Enforcers Attack Protesters in Beirut," *Los Angeles Times*, August 3, 2011, https://latimesblogs.latimes.com/babylonbeyond/2011/08/syria-human-rights-lebanon-violence-protests.html (accessed April 26, 2021).
5 Josh Wood, "Refugees from Syria on Edge in Lebanon," *New York Times*, February 22, 2012, https://www.nytimes.com/2012/02/23/world/middleeast/refugees-from-syria-on-edge-in-lebanon.html (accessed April 26, 2021).
6 Lizzy Davies, "Bashar al-Assad Sends Private Message to Pope Francis," *The Guardian*, December 29, 2013.
7 Joseph Nasr, "Syrian Refugees, German Govt. Condemn Far-Right Trip to 'Normal' Syria," March 7, 2018, https://www.reuters.com/article/us-mideast-crisis-syria-germany/syrian-refugees-german-govt-condemn-far-right-trip-to-normal-syria-idUSKCN1GJ21T (accessed April 26, 2021); see also Nick Grinstead, Jesse McDonald, and Christopher Solomon, "Eagles Riding the Storm of War: The Role of the Syrian Social Nationalist Party," January 15, 2019, https://www.clingendael.org/publication/role-syrian-social-nationalist-party-civil-war (accessed April 26, 2021).
8 Jean Aziz, "Syrian Government Insists: No Conditions on Dialogue," *Al-Monitor*, February 22, 2013, https://www.al-monitor.com/pulse/originals/2013/02/obstacles-remain-syria-negotiations.html (accessed April 26, 2021).
9 Joseph Sweid takes the constitutional oath as the Syrian Social Nationalist Party head in Syria, *Golan Times*, February 27, 2016, http://golantimes.com/news/3250 (accessed April 26, 2021). The assertation that Issam al-Mahayri retired to the United States was denied by SSNP Amana faction member Abdullah Mnine in an e-mail to the author, January 30, 2020.
10 For examples, see "Assad Forms Committee to Change Syria's Constitution," *Reuters*, October 15, 2011, https://www.reuters.com/article/us-syria-assad-constitution-idUSTRE79E1TF20111015 (accessed April 26, 2021); Hugh Naylor and Zakaria

Zakaria, "Syria's Assad Holds Elections Despite Peace Talks in Geneva," *Washington Post*, April 13, 2016, https://www.washingtonpost.com/world/syrias-assad-holds-elections-despite-peace-talks-in-geneva/2016/04/13/2883ceec-00e2-11e6-8bb1-f124a43f84dc_story.html?utm_term=.a0a294bc5570 (accessed April 26, 2021).

11 The full name of the Intifada faction's leader, Dr. Ali Haidar.

12 Agnes Favier and Marie Kostrz, "Local Elections: Is Syria Moving to Reassert Central Control?," European University Institute, Robert Schuman Center for Advanced Studies, February 3, 2019, https://cadmus.eui.eu/handle/1814/61004?fbclid=IwAR2v0-DIi1NjMXCAdArYgnSqYqmI2mRoKVaVNTmla6vcHj61vBp6IxNvkTY (accessed September 19, 2020); Syrian Social Nationalist Party, "Umm Ruwaq Directorate," Facebook post, September 11, 2018, https://www.facebook.com/amrwaq.ssnp/posts/1101489646668838 (accessed September 19, 2020).

13 Dr. John Eibner, "Comments from Nouhad Samaan, Head of SSNP in Homs," *Syria Comment*, January 2, 2015, https://www.joshualandis.com/blog/footnotes-on-the-ssnp-comments-from-nouhad-samaan-head-of-ssnp-in-homs/ (accessed April 26, 2021).

14 Chris Tomson, "Syrian Army Goes All in on Aleppo as More Reinforcements Pour into the City—Map Update," *Al Masdar News*, November 25, 2016, https://www.almasdarnews.com/article/syrian-army-goes-all-in-on-aleppo-as-more-reinforcements-pour-into-the-city/.

15 "Al Mayadeen Culture Documentary," YouTube, January, 28 2018, https://www.youtube.com/watch?v=vyQhjz-yPP4.

16 Joel Veldkamp, "Resurgence of the SSNP in Syria: An Ideological Opponent of the Regime Gets a Boost from the Conflict," *Syria Comment*, December 19, 2014, https://www.joshualandis.com/blog/resurgence-of-the-ssnp-in-syria-an-ideological-opponent-of-the-regime-gets-a-boost-from-the-conflict/ (accessed April 26, 2021).

17 Video analysis of the combat footage featured in the *Al Mayadeen* documentary conducted on March 2, 2018, by Roland Bartetzko, a former German paratrooper who fought with the Croatian Defense Council in Bosnia and the Kosovo Liberation Army.

18 Interview conducted by Ruwan Al-Rejoleh with Firas Tlass, September 2018.

19 In May 2012, Dr. Ali Haidar's son, Ismael, was shot and killed along with other Intifada faction members near Homs allegedly by antigovernment militants.

20 "Eagles of the Whirlwind, a Militia in Nationalist Clothing, Are Killing Syrians in the name of 'Christians,'" January 7, 2017, http://www.shaam.org/news/syria-news/%E2%80%9C%D9%86%D8%B3%D9%88%D8%B1-%D8%A7%D9%84%D8%B2%D9%88%D8%A8%D8%B9%D8%A9%E2%80%9D-%D9%85%D9%84%D9%8A%D8%B4%D9%8A%D8%A7-%D8%A8%D9%84%D8%A8%D9%88%D8%B3-

%D9%82%D9%88%D9%85%D9%8A-%D8%AA%D9%82%D8%AA%D9%84-%D8%A7%D9%84%D8%B3%D9%88%D8%B1%D9%8A%D9%8A%D9%86-%D8%A8%D8%A7%D8%B3%D9%85-%E2%80%9C%D8%A7%D9%84%D9%85%D8%B3%D9%8A%D8%AD%D9%8A%D9%8A%D9%86%E2%80%9D.html (accessed September 20, 2020).

21 "The Eagles of the Whirlwind Are Recruiting Children to Fight for Iran in Syria," SY24, July 17, 2019, https://www.sy-24.com/news/%D9%85%D9%8A%D9%84%D9%8A%D8%B4%D9%8A%D8%A7-%D9%86%D8%B3%D9%88%D8%B1-%D8%A7%D9%84%D8%B2%D9%88%D8%A8%D8%B9%D8%A9-%D8%AA%D8%AC%D9%86%D8%AF-%D8%A7%D9%84%D8%A3%D8%B7%D9%81%D8%A7%D9%84-%D9%84%D9%84/ (accessed September 20, 2020).

22 Leith Aboufadel, "Syrian Forces in Sweida Hang ISIS Fighter after Terrorist Attack," *Al Masdar News*, https://www.almasdarnews.com/article/graphic-18-syrian-forces-in-sweida-hang-isis-fighter-after-terrorist-attack/ (accessed March 16, 2019).

23 Eagles of the Whirlwind militia member, Malek Khoury, e-mail to author, August 7, 2018.

24 Author's correspondence with SSNP News nonofficial outlet, anonymous, September 2018.

25 https://www.wsj.com/articles/russia-offers-a-carrot-to-embattled-syrian-rebels-1535799600?mod=cx_picks&cx_navSource=cx_picks&cx_tag=contextual&cx_artPos=6#cxrecs_s (accessed April 26, 2021).

26 Alexey Naumov, "Swastika over Damascus," March 20, 2017, https://lenta.ru/articles/2017/03/20/syrian_ns/ (accessed April 26, 2021).

27 Yuri Lyamin, "The SSNP Party's Militia in Syria," June 24, 2017, https://imp-navigator.livejournal.com/628708.html (accessed April 26, 2021).

28 "Syrian Social Nationalist Party Urges Adding Damascus to Syria Talks Platforms," *Sputnik*, April 4, 2017, https://sputniknews.com/middleeast/201704041052293385-syria-damascus-gene/ (accessed September 15, 2020).

29 "Qatar Diplomatic Row Could Affect Astana Talks—Syrian Opposition Member," *Sputnik*, June 5, 2017, https://sputniknews.com/politics/201706051054329094-qatar-astana-syria-opposition/ (accessed September 15, 2020).

30 "Potential Kurdish State Allegedly Backed by Israel May Upset Region—Politician," *Sputnik*, August 15, 2017, https://sputniknews.com/middleeast/201708151056489271-israel-kurdistan-netanyahu/ (accessed September 15, 2020).

31 "Minister Haidar: We Work with Russian Coordination Center in Hmeimem as One Team to Boost Local Reconciliations," December 18, 2017, http://sana.sy/en/?p=121734 (accessed September 20, 2020).

32 For a discussion on the party's activities and screenshots of the images of the Russian military awards, see Jesse McDonald, "The Syrian Social Nationalist

Party's (SSNP) Expansion in Syria," *Syria Comment*, April 22, 2018, https://www.joshualandis.com/blog/the-syrian-social-nationalist-partys-ssnp-expansion-in-syria-by-jesse-mcdonald-jjmcdonald10/ (accessed September 21, 2020).
33 "Syria Interior Minister Out in Government Reshuffle," Agence France-Presse, November 26, 2018, https://www.france24.com/en/20181126-syria-interior-minister-out-government-reshuffle (accessed April 26, 2021).
34 Jonathan Steele, "The Price of Peace? How Damascus Strikes Deals with Beaten Rebels," *Middle East Eye*, October 5, 2017, https://www.middleeasteye.net/big-story/price-peace-how-damascus-strikes-deals-beaten-rebels (accessed April 26, 2021).
35 Sam Heller, "Four Perspectives on Syria, Round II," The Century Foundation, March 30, 2017, https://tcf.org/content/report/four-perspectives-syria-round-ii/
36 Author interview with Intifada faction political adviser to Ali Haidar, Ilya Samman, January 20, 2017.
37 Jonathan Steele, "The Price of Peace? How Damascus Strikes Deals with Beaten Rebels," *Middle East Eye*, October 5, 2017, https://www.middleeasteye.net/big-story/price-peace-how-damascus-strikes-deals-beaten-rebels (accessed April 26, 2021).

9 Fires on the Mountain Tops: Women, Youth, and Social Media

1 https://ouacs.wordpress.com/2006/10/27/fawaz-trabulsi/ (accessed April 26, 2021).
2 Rahbani Brothers, *The Night and the Candles: A Song of Two Seasons* (Dynamic Graphic for Printing and Publishing, 2003).
3 Laura Lavinia and Alberto Rodríguez, "Freedom, Duty, Discipline and Power: The SSNP in 28 Questions," 14Milimetros, July 8, 2020, https://14milimetros.com/freedom-duty-discipline-and-power-the-ssnp-in-28-questions/? (accessed September 15, 2020).
4 Lina Mounzer, "The Girl in the Red Beret," *Bidoun*, 17 (Spring 2009), https://www.bidoun.org/articles/the-girl-in-the-red-beret (accessed April 26, 2021).
5 RimaSalameh, "Suicide Car Bombing in Christian Town," *Associated Press*, July 17, 1986, https://www.apnews.com/f447c7b0126f9762b14bf9ddb23fb51f (accessed April 26, 2021).
6 Interview by Robert Baer with Munir al-Jamali, *The Cult of the Suicide Bomber*, documentary, directed by David Batty and Kevin Toolis, June 2, 2006.

7. "SSNP Rally in Beirut," July 2007, YouTube, February 14, 2009, https://www.youtube.com/watch?v=pJordOBYVi8& (accessed April 26, 2021).
8. Randa Baa'qalini's father, Mansour Hanna Baa'qalini, took a lot of the party's most sensitive missions and escaped assassination numerous times; he later headed an SSNP field hospital during the Lebanese Civil War; he died in September 2014. See "The Party Mourns Comrade Mansour Baa'qalini," September 8, 2014, https://ssnp.info/index.php?article=96948 (accessed April 26, 2021).
9. Al-Qubaysiat is a mysterious Islamic women's movement with over 70,000 members, *Al Arabiya*, May 3, 2006, https://www.alarabiya.net/articles/2006/05/03/23408.html (accessed April 26, 2021); KatherineZoepf, "Islamic Revival in Syria Is Led by Women," *New York Times*, https://archive.nytimes.com/www.nytimes.com/ref/world/middleeast/29syria.html (accessed April 26, 2021).
10. For background on the Qubaysiat movement in Syria, see Lama Rajeh, "My Journey with Al-Qubaysiat Sisterhood," *Al Jumhuriya*, June 22, 2017, https://www.aljumhuriya.net/en/content/my-journey-al-qubaysiat-sisterhood (accessed April 26, 2021); Ibrahim Hamidi, "The Qubaysi Women's Islamic Movement," *Syria Comment*, May 16, 2006, http://joshualandis.oucreate.com//syriablog/2006/05/qubaysi-womens-islamic-movement-by.htm (accessed April 26, 2021); Zoepf, "Islamic Revival in Syria Is Led by Women."
11. SSNP News Twitter post with translations provided, October 1, 2018.
12. Mohammed Manar Hmijou, "On Women's Day, President Assad Refers the Draft Law Abolishing Honor Crimes to the People's Assembly," *Al Watan*, March 9, 2020, http://alwatan.sy/archives/235538 (accessed April 26, 2021).
13. Ahmad Merhi tweet, March 8, 2020, https://twitter.com/AhmadAMerhi/status/1236636449379926016 (accessed April 26, 2021).
14. Interview with a young SSNP supporter, online, October 2016.
15. Ibid.
16. Syrian Social Nationalist Party, youth camp Facebook post, September 13, 2018, https://www.facebook.com/permalink.php?story_fbid=1990161721033881&id=1941841432532577 (accessed September 21, 2020).
17. Syrian Social Nationalist Party, youth camp Facebook post, September 3, 2018, https://www.facebook.com/permalink.php?story_fbid=1977756762274377&id=1941841432532577 (accessed September 21, 2020).
18. SSNP Online, Facebook post, August 24, 2018, https://www.facebook.com/SSNPonline/posts/1960832527288944 (accessed September 21, 2020).
19. SSNP Directorate in Sahnaya, Facebook post, August 1, 2019, https://www.facebook.com/sehnayassnp/posts/2109835262461753 (accessed September 21, 2020).
20. Aziz Ibrahim to author, February 28, 2020.
21. Interview with a young SSNP supporter, online, October 2016.

22 Ibid.
23 Yamen Moghrabi, August 31, 2020, https://english.enabbaladi.net/archives/2020/08/why-do-syrian-youth-refrain-from-joining-political-parties/ (accessed September 21, 2020).
24 Author email correspondence with an anonymous attendee of an SSNP youth camp in Australia, March 30, 2020. They also noted the party was a "product of its own environment" and the attitudes regarding social issues in the youth camps in the diasporic community were a markedly different setting compared to Lebanon and Syria, and that there was also a factor of competing influences between the diaspora and homeland.
25 Samy Akil, a Syrian political researcher from Aleppo who focuses on the SSNP, email to author, December 2020.
26 Interview with Dr Milad Sebaaly, February 4, 2017.
27 Joel Veldkamp, "Resurgence of the SSNP in Syria: An Ideological Opponent of the Regime Gets a Boost from the Conflict," *Syria Comment*, December 19, 2014, https://www.joshualandis.com/blog/resurgence-of-the-ssnp-in-syria-an-ideological-opponent-of-the-regime-gets-a-boost-from-the-conflict/ (accessed April 26, 2021).
28 Jesse McDonald, "[The] Syrian Social Nationalist Party (SSNP) and the War in Syria," *Syria Comment*, May 11, 2016, https://www.joshualandis.com/blog/syrian-social-nationalist-party-ssnp-war-syria/ (accessed April 26, 2021).
29 8th of July Movement, Facebook page, https://www.facebook.com/8Tamouz/ (accessed August 2020).
30 8th of July Movement, Facebook page, May 5, 2020, https://www.facebook.com/8Tamouz/photos/a.1725476937707564/2554375614817688/?type=3&theater (accessed April 26, 2021).
31 The General Authority for the Social Nationalist Renaissance Movement: Our goal is to return the party to the path of achieving its vision and goal: November 24, 2018, https://alkalimaonline.com/Newsdet.aspx?id=344162 (accessed September 17, 2020).
32 A source close to the Intifada faction, e-mail to author, August 16, 2020.

10 Invisible Leaders: The Future of the SSNP

1 The Amana's Youth Camp took place in Saydnaya and lasted from September 1 to September 7 of 2015, culminating in the graduation ceremony featured in the video. Syrian Social Nationalist Party YouTube page, July 28, 2016, https://www.youtube.com/watch?v=U3XGUvxD23I&feature=youtu.be (accessed September 14, 2020).

2   The martyrs the named were Assad al-Omar, Mohammad Issa Fneir, Zulfaqqar Hassan, Arab al-Johanni, Ali Qayruz, and Louay al-Saadi.
3   The lyrics to the song played during the mock rescue demonstration:

> O' Zionist, if I go mad, I shall come at you in the darkness of the night.
> And with the sparks of anger from my eyes, I shall demolish the mountains of the world upon you.
> With blood we have written for freedom and shook the occupier's throne.
> And with my people's revolutionary unity, the dawn of victory rises upon us.
> With the eye we challenged the awl and the undying souls.
> And we shall tirelessly resist until we erase David's star.

4   "All's Not Well in Top Echelons of Syria Ruling Structure," *Gulf News*, May 9, 2020, https://gulfnews.com/world/mena/alls-not-well-in-top-echelons-of-syria-ruling-structure-1.71412035 (accessed October 15, 2020).
5   Susan Muhanna, "Rami Makhlouf and His Relationship to the Syrian Social Nationalist Party," *al-Arabiya*, May 28, 2020, https://www.alarabiya.net/ar/politics/2020/05/28/%D8%B1%D8%A7%D9%85%D9%8A-%D9%85%D8%AE%D9%84%D9%88%D9%81-%D9%88%D8%B9%D9%84%D8%A7%D9%82%D8%AA%D9%87-%D8%A8%D8%A7%D9%86%D8%B4-D-9%82%D8%A7%D9%82-%D8%A7%D9%84%D8%AD%D8%B2%D8%A8-%D8%A7%D9%84%D8%B3%D9%88%D8%B1%D9%8A-%D8%A7%D9%84%D9%82%D9%88%D9%85%D9%8A?fbclid=IwAR1fP7wXz6-mxcwVU4aVXNUO9jI8X_OxkNxJBD6hQOgI1nj8VQgT5mB0b0A# (accessed September 15, 2020).
6   Suleiman Al-Khalidi, Maha El Dahan, Tom Perry, and Michael Georgy, "Special Report: A Collapsing Economy and a Family Feud Pile Pressure on Syria's Assad," *Reuters*, August 13, 2020, https://www.reuters.com/article/us-mideast-syria-tycoon-special-report-idUSKCN2591C3 (accessed September 10, 2020).
7   "The Intractable Roots of Assad-Makhlouf Drama in Syria," The Newlines Institute for Strategy and Policy, May 15, 2020, https://newlinesinstitute.org/about/ (accessed October 9, 2020).
8   "Trouble in Bashar al-Assad's Own Ranks," *The Economist*, May 16, 2020, https://www.economist.com/middle-east-and-africa/2020/05/16/trouble-in-bashar-al-assads-own-ranks (accessed September 12, 2020).
9   "Assad Disbands Makhlouf Militias, Renames 'Tiger Forces,'" *Asharq Al-Awsat*, August 30, 2019, https://english.aawsat.com//home/article/1878961/assad-disbands-makhlouf-militias-renames-tiger-forces (September 12, 2020).
10 Nick Grinstead, "Assad Tends to His Base by Making Amends with the Makhloufs," Middle East Institute, August 26, 2020, https://www.mei.edu/blog/assad-tends-his-base-making-amends-makhloufs (accessed August 31, 2020).
11 Anonymous Syrian from Latakia to author, 2018.

12 Lea Al-Qazi, "Is He Resigning as President of the Nationalists Today?" *al-Akhbar*, June 20, 2019, https://www.al-akhbar.com/Politics/272201/%D8%A7%D9%84%D9%86%D8%A7%D8%B4%D9%81-%D9%8A%D8%B3%D8%AA%D9%82%D9%8A%D9%84-%D9%85%D9%86-%D8%B1%D8%A6%D8%A7%D8%B3%D8%A9-%D8%A7%D9%84%D9%82%D9%88%D9%85%D9%8A-%D8%A7%D9%84%D9%8A%D9%88%D9%85?fbclid=IwAR2hk4seMvJSBSR6v-zi6reX_lqRLrPpMgqC6pvXKYi3bxyFo_Ju_1xE77s

13 Leah Al-Qazi, "The Syrian Social Nationalist Party Head Resigns," *al-Akhbar*, February 26, 2020, https://al-akhbar.com/Politics/284723?fbclid=IwAR2_G3OW-yOdDsnjfXQe8QZW0Eh-bYbgEsLelvAbGUwRwb7P7HB3usKdbtI (accessed February 28, 2020). Faris Saad had a long history in the SSNP and has been a party member since 1960. He was one of Inaam Raad's Supreme Council faction's main leadership members. He was born in Ain Zhalta (Inaam Raad's village), Chouf District, Mount Lebanon Governorate in 1941 to an Evangelical Protestant family. Saad held many positions, most notably as the party's dean of economy. He became a trustee in 1977. He is also the editor-in-chief of a number of economic newspapers. He became president in July 2019; his resignation tendered on January 25, 2020 was accepted by the Supreme Council on May 19, 2020.

14 "The Baath and the Syrian Nationalists in Lebanon: It Is Necessary to Coordinate with Syria," July 25, 2020, http://www.sana.sy/?p=1191192&fbclid=IwAR0eEgWIpb_PqVaQYpE_bIL7uz-w7xhKSviS5syvv2TSApPJUCe8BvMoLRE. Coincidently, the Lebanese Baath Party is also in the midst of a leadership dispute. Assem Qanso and Numan Shalq have been at odds since the 2018 Lebanese parliamentary elections.

15 July 8 Movement Facebook post, July 29, 2020, https://www.facebook.com/8Tamouz/posts/2625547067700542 (accessed September 21, 2020).

16 In addition, in the video, Nashef outlined the July 8 Movement's grievances with the bureaucratic violations that have become commonplace within the Markaz faction. Nashef indicates that he has sent a note to the president with issues that needed to be discussed at the General Assembly, but it has not been distributed or taken seriously. He also points out that invites to the sub-meetings were sent from an internal unit outside of its mandate as opposed to be coming from the General Assembly's bureau and its president himself. This is a practice that runs against the party's constitution and norms. He was not notified that these invites to the side meetings were being sent, questioning legitimacy and transparency. Nashef explains that he had sent a note on this issue to the president protesting this structure and called for a delay of the General Assembly and the party elections by one year so the assembly's bureau can follow procedure and arrange the sub-meetings, take members' suggestions, and commission studies in order to allow the assembly to be effective.

17 Leah al-Qazi, *al-Akhbar*, September 14, 2020, https://www.al-akhbar.com/Politics/293837/ (accessed September 21, 2020).

18 "Hardan Challenges the Nationalist Elections: Towards a New Crisis?" *al-Akhbar*, September 21, 2020, https://www.al-akhbar.com/Politics/294124/%D8%AD%D8%B1%D8%AF%D8%A7%D9%86-%D9%8A%D8%B7%D8%B9%D9%86-%D9%81%D9%8A-%D8%A7%D9%86%D8%AA%D8%AE%D8%A7%D8%A8%D8%A7%D8%AA-%D8%A7%D9%84%D9%82%D9%88%D9%85%D9%8A-%D9%86%D8%AD%D9%88-%D8%A3%D8%B2%D9%85%D8%A9-%D8%AC%D8%AF%D9%8A%D8%AF%D8%A9 (accessed September 21, 2020).

19 Sakr, described by party sympathizers as a successful diplomat, has fostered relations with regional and international parties, particularly in Europe and the West, as well as being an active social media figure.

20 Hassan Sakr, Twitter post, September 20, 2020, https://twitter.com/HassanTSakr/status/1307640508727078913 (accessed September 21, 2020).

21 See "War Profiteers in Syria Enter Politics," Center for Global Policy, July 13, 2020, https://cgpolicy.org/articles/war-profiteers-in-syria-enter-politics/ (accessed September 11, 2020).

22 "Parliamentary Election in Syria to Become Vital Step Toward Constitution Change—Lawmaker," *UrduPoint*, July 16, 2020, https://www.urdupoint.com/en/world/parliamentary-election-in-syria-to-become-vit-975395.html (accessed September 16, 2020).

23 "Syrian Social Nationalist Party's Bloc in Parliament," Facebook page, July 21, 2020, https://www.facebook.com/permalink.php?story_fbid=1388402004883838&id=742626412794737 (accessed September 12, 2020).

24 "President Assad Issues a Decree That Includes the Names of the People's Assembly Winners from the Third Legislative Round," July 30, 2020, http://www.sana.sy/?p=1194167 (accessed September 9, 2020).

25 Manuel Hanna Facebook livestreaming broadcast, July 20, 2020, https://www.facebook.com/manuelloooo/videos/2626386157679771/ (accessed July 25, 2020).

26 "Representatives in Parliament, The Medication File Is Sick … And the Citizens Have Lost Confidence in the Deputies and the Government," June 2020, https://shamra.sy/news/article/1a5a3153ae60da1f564186652ff7e482 (accessed September 10, 2020).

27 Mazen Azouz, Facebook post, July 20, 2020, https://www.facebook.com/mazen.azouz.3/posts/2617618415179075.

28 Kamal Thebian, "Is the Syrian Embassy Dinner the Beginning of the Unification of the Nationalists?," March 28, 2017, http://lampress.net/News.php?ID=6639 (accessed September 10, 2020).

29 Author's correspondence with Eagles of the Whirlwind member, Ali Ibrahim, November 2017.

30 Eagles of the Whirlwind militia official spokesperson to Jesse McDonald, via WhatsApp, July 10, 2018.
31 Ibid.
32 Nour Samaha, "Eagles of the Whirlwind," *Foreign Policy*, March 28, 2016, https://foreignpolicy.com/2016/03/28/the-eagles-of-the-whirlwind/ (accessed October 5, 2020).
33 Nour Samaha, "Eagles of the Whirlwind," *Foreign Policy*, March 28, 2016, https://foreignpolicy.com/2016/03/28/the-eagles-of-the-whirlwind/ (accessed October 5, 2020).
34 Syriana TV Facebook post, June 16, 2014, https://www.facebook.com/syrianatv/posts/702049619830662 (accessed October 20, 2020).
35 Interview via Twitter with SSNP-M supporter using the pseudonym in March 2018.
36 Carnegie Middle East Center, "Syria in Crisis," January 1, 2012, https://carnegie-mec.org/diwan/48565?lang=en (accessed September 14, 2020).
37 "Syrian-Based Opposition Group Call for Election Reform," March 31, 2012, YouTube, https://www.youtube.com/watch?v=__AAtRiNMIM&ab_channel=APArchive (accessed September 29, 2020).
38 Author's correspondence with Elia Samman, Dr. Ali Haidar's political adviser, January 20, 2017.
39 It should be noted that the YPG has also been guilty of its own repression of political opposition in its territories, but not to the extent of the Baath Party.
40 Consider, for example, the March 2004 Qamishly riots and antigovernment clashes, along with the issue of the Kurdish language being taught in Syrian schools.
41 Ayad Moussalli, "From Saladin, Yousef al-Azma, and Ibrahim Hananu, to the Kurds: No Federalism and No Dissonant Factions But Rather National Unity," *al-Binaa*, https://www.al-binaa.com/archives/article/163802 (accessed September 19, 2020).
42 "UAE Reopens Syria Embassy in Boost for Assad," Reuters, December 27, 2018, https://www.reuters.com/article/us-mideast-crisis-syria-emirates/uae-reopens-syria-embassy-a-boost-for-assad-idUSKCN1OQ0QV (accessed October 15, 2020).
43 Mark Landler and David M. Halbfinger, "Trump, with Netanyahu, Formally Recognizes Israel's Authority over Golan Heights," *New York Times*, March 25, 2019, https://www.nytimes.com/2019/03/25/us/politics/benjamin-netanyahu-donald-trump-meeting.html (accessed October 15, 2020).

Bibliography

Avi-Ran, R. *The Syrian Involvement in Lebanon since 1975*. Westview Press, 1991.

Baun, Dylan. "The Gemmayzeh Incident of 1949: Conflict over Physical and Symbolic Space in Beirut Dylan Baun." *Arab Studies Journal*, 25, no. 1 (2017): 92–122.

Beshara, Adel. *Fayez Sayegh—The Party Years 1938-1947*. Black House, 2019.

Beshara, Adel. *Lebanon: The Politics of Frustration—The Failed Coup of 1961 (History and Society in the Islamic World)*. 1st ed. Routledge, 2005.

Beshara, Adel. *Outright Assassination: The Trial and Execution of Antun Sa'adeh, 1949*. 1st ed. Ithaca Press, 2010.

Binder, Leonard. *Ideological Revolution in the Middle East*. Hoboken, NJ: John Wiley, 1964.

Blanford, Nicholas. *Killing Mr. Lebanon: The Assassination of Rafik Hariri and Its Impact on the Middle East*. 1st ed. I.B. Tauris, 2008.

Cohen, Gamliel. *Under Cover, The Untold Story of the Palmach's Under Cover Arab Unit*. Israel: Israeli Ministry of Defense and the Galili Center for Defense Studies, 2002.

Collelo, Thomas. *Syria: A Country Study*. Washington, DC: Federal Research Division, 1987.

Commins, David, and David Lesch. *Historical Dictionary of Syria (Historical Dictionaries of Asia, Oceania, and the Middle East)*. 3rd ed. Scarecrow Press, 2013.

Cubert, Harold. *The PFLP's Changing Role in the Middle East*. 1st ed. Routledge, 1997.

El-Husseini, Rola. *Pax Syriana: Elite Politics in Postwar Lebanon*. Syracuse University Press, 2012.

El-Khazen, Farid. *The Breakdown of the State in Lebanon 1967–1976*. Harvard University Press, 2000.

Entelis, John. *Pluralism and Party Transformation in Lebanon: Al-Kata Ib (Social, Economic and Political Studies of the Middle East and Asia, No 10)*. Brill Academic, 1997.

Favier, Agnes, and Marie Kostrz. *Local Elections: Is Syria Moving to Reassert Central Control?*. San Domenico di Fiesole: Middle East Directions, 2019, doi:10.2870/18582.

Fisk, Robert. *Pity the Nation: The Abduction of Lebanon (Nation Books)*. 4th new American ed. Bold Type Books, 2002.

Friedman, Matti. *Spies of No Country: Secret Lives at the Birth of Israel*. Illustrated ed. Algonquin Books, 2019.

Gani, J. *The Role of Ideology in Syrian–US Relations: Conflict and Cooperation (Middle East Today)*. 1st ed. Palgrave Macmillan, 2014.

Gelvin, James. *The Arab Uprisings: What Everyone Needs to Know®*. Oxford University Press, 2012.

Gilbert, Martin. *Israel: A History*. 1st ed. William Morrow, 1998.

Ginat, Rami. *Syria and the Doctrine of Arab Neutralism: From Independence to Dependence*. Sussex Academic Press, 2010.

Harik, Judith Palmer. *Hezbollah: The Changing Face of Terrorism*. 1st ed. I.B. Tauris, 2004.

Harris, William. *The New Face of Lebanon: History's Revenge (Princeton Series on the Middle East)*. Revised ed. Markus Wiener, 2009.

Haugbolle, Sune. *War and Memory in Lebanon (Cambridge Middle East Studies)*. Reissue. Cambridge University Press, 2012.

Hazran, Yusri. *The Druze Community and the Lebanese State: Between Confrontation and Reconciliation*. Routledge, 2014.

Herf, Jeffrey. *Undeclared Wars with Israel: East Germany and the West German Far Left, 1967–1989*. Cambridge University Press, 2016.

Howell, Alfred. "Sa'id Taky Deen: 1904–1960." *Middle East Quarterly* (1994).

Hyland, Steven. *The Summit of Civilian: Nationalism among the Arabic-Speaking Colonies in Latin America, in Immigration and National Identities in Latin America*. University Press of Florida, 2014.

Ide, Derek. Socialism without Socialists: Egyptian Marxists and the Nasserist State, 1952–65. Toledo, OH: University of Toledo, 2015.

Ismael, Tareq, and Jacqueline Ismael. *The Communist Movement in Syria and Lebanon*. 1st ed. University Press of Florida, 1998.

Jörum, Emma Lundgren. *Beyond Syria's Borders: A History of Territorial Disputes in the Middle East*. I.B. Tauris, 2015.

Kaufman, Asher, and Asher Kaufman. *Reviving Phoenicia*. I.B. Tauris, 2004.

Kaylani, Nabil M. "The Rise of the Syrian Ba'th, 1940–1958: Political Success, Party Failure." *International Journal of Middle East Studies*, 3, no. 1 (1972): 3–23, doi:10.1017/s0020743800030014.

Kerr, Malcolm. *The Arab Cold War: Gamal 'Abd al-Nasir and His Rivals, 1958–1970*. Oxford University Press, 1975.

Khalaf, Samir. *Civil and Uncivil Violence in Lebanon: A History of the Internationalization of Communal Conflict (History and Society of the Modern Middle East)*. Columbia University Press, 2004.

Knudsen, Are, and Michael Kerr. *Lebanon: After the Cedar Revolution*. 1st ed. Oxford University Press, 2014.

Landis, Joshua. "Shishakli and the Druzes: Integration and Intransigence." In *The Syrian Land: Processes of Integration and Fragmentation. Bilad al-Sham from the 18th to the 20th Century*, edited by Birgit Schäbler and Thomas Philipp, 369–96. Stuttgart: Franz Steiner Verlag, 1998.

Leidy, Joseph. *Antun Saadeh in the Mahjar, 1938–1947*. Austin: University of Texas, 2016.

Little, Douglas. "Cold War and Covert Action: The United States and Syria, 1945–1958." *Middle East Journal*, 44, no. 1 (1990): 51–75, www.jstor.org/stable/4328056.

Lund, Aron. "Russia in the Middle East." UI Paper (2019), www.ui.se/globalassets/ui.se-eng/publications/ui-publications/2019/ui-paper-no.-2-2019.pdf.

Maasri, Zeina. *Off the Wall: Political Posters of the Lebanese Civil War*. Illustrated ed. I.B. Tauris, 2008.

Mackey, Sandra. *Lebanon: A House Divided*. Illustrated ed. Norton, 2013.

Majāʿiṣ, Salīm. *Antoun Saadeh: Years of the French Mandate*. Kutub, 2004.

Malsagne, Stéphane. *Fouad Chéhab, 1902–1973: Une Figure Oubliée de l'histoire Libanaise*. Karthala, 2011.

Martin, Kevin. *Syria's Democratic Years: Citizens, Experts, and Media in the 1950s (Public Cultures of the Middle East and North Africa)*. Indiana University Press, 2015.

Martin, Kevin W. "Speaking with the 'Voice of Syria': Producing the Arab World's First Personality Cult." *Middle East Journal*, 72, no. 4 (2018): 631–53. doi:10.3751/72.4.15.

Melhem, Edmond. *Syrian Women: Their Struggle in Society and Their Empowerment through the Syrian Social Nationalist Party*. 1st ed. CreateSpace, 2018.

Moubayed, Sami. *Steel & Silk: Men & Women Who Shaped Syria 1900–2000*. Cune, 2005.

Mujais, Salim. *The Syrian Social Nationalist Party: Its Ideology and History*. Black House, 2019.

Nassif, Nicolas. *Fouad Chehab's Republic*. Beirut: Dar Al Nahar and The Fouad Chehab Foundation, 2008.

Nordbruch, Götz. *Nazism in Syria and Lebanon: The Ambivalence of the German Option, 1933–1945*. 1st ed., Routledge, 2012.

Norton, Augustus Richard. *Amal and the Shi'A: Struggle for the Soul of Lebanon (Modern Middle East Series)*. 1st ed. University of Texas Press, 1987.

O'Ballance, Edgar. *Civil War in Lebanon, 1975–92*. Palgrave Macmillan, 1998.

Perthes, Volker. "A Look at Syria's Upper Class: The Bourgeoisie and the Ba'th." *Middle East Report*, 170 (1991): 31. doi:10.2307/3013248.

Phillips, Christopher. *Everyday Arab Identity: The Daily Reproduction of the Arab World (Routledge Studies in Middle Eastern Politics)*. 1st ed. Routledge, 2012.

Picard, Elizabeth. "Lebanon in Search of Sovereignty: Post 2005 Security Dilemmas." In *Lebanon: After the Cedar Revolution*, edited by Are Knudsen and Michael Kerr, 156–83. Hurst, 2012.

Pipes, Daniel. *Greater Syria: The History of an Ambition*. Oxford University Press, 1992.

Rabinovich, Itamar. *Syria under the Ba'th, 1963–66: The Army-Party Symbiosis*. 1st ed. Israel Universities Press, 1972.

Rabinovich, Itamar. *The War for Lebanon, 1970–1985*. Revised ed. Cornell University Press, 1985.

Rahbani Brothers. *The Night and the Candles: A Song of Two Seasons*. Dynamic Graphic, 2003.

Rathmell, Andrew. *Secret War in the Middle East: The Covert Struggle for Syria, 1949–1961 (Library of Modern Middle East Studies)*. I.B. Tauris, 2013.

Richani, Nazih. *Dilemmas of Democracy and Political Parties in Sectarian Societies: The Case of the Progressive Socialist Party of Lebanon 1949–1996*. 1st ed. Palgrave Macmillan, 1998.

Saʻādah, Khalīl. *Caeser and Cleopatra: An Historical Romance*. London: Edwin Vaughan, 1898.

Salamey, Imad. *The Government and Politics of Lebanon*. 2nd ed. Peter Lang, 2021.

Salibi, Kamal. *A House of Many Mansions: The History of Lebanon Reconsidered*. 1st ed. University of California Press, 1990.

Saunders, Bonnie. *The United States and Arab Nationalism: The Syrian Case, 1953–1960*. Praeger, 1996.

Sayegh, Fayez. *Arab Unity: Hope and Fulfillment*. 1st ed. Devin-Adair, 1958.

Seale, Patrick. *Abu Nidal: A Gun for Hire: The Secret Life of the World's Most Notorious Arab Terrorist*. 1st ed. Random House, 1992.

Seale, Patrick. *Asad: The Struggle for the Middle East*. University of California Press, 1989.

Seale, Patrick. *The Struggle for Arab Independence: Riad El-Solh and the Makers of the Modern Middle East*. Cambridge University Press, 2010.

Seale, Patrick. *The Struggle for Syria: A Study in Post-War Arab Politics, 1945–1958*. New ed. Yale University Press, 1987.

Sharabi, Hisham. *Embers and Ashes: Memoirs of an Arab Intellectual*. Interlink Books, 2007.

Suleiman, Michael. *Political Parties in Lebanon: The Challenge of a Fragmented Political Culture*. 1st ed. Cornell University Press, 1967.

Suleiman, Michael W. "Elections in a Confessional Democracy." *Journal of Politics*, 29, no. 1 (1967): 109–28. doi:10.2307/2127814.

Tabler, Andrew. *In the Lion's Den*. New York: McGraw-Hill, 2011.

Taqī al-Dīn, Saʻīd. *Bridge under the Water: This Is How We Chased Eisenhower Out of La République Libanaise (Arab World Series)*, vol. 2, Lebanon, n.p., 1957.

Teitelbaum, Joshua. "The Muslim Brotherhood in Syria, 1945–1958: Founding, Social Origins, Ideology." *Middle East Journal*, 65, no. 2 (2011): 227, www.jstor.org/stable/23012146.

Thompson, Elizabeth. *Colonial Citizens: Republican Rights, Paternal Privilege, and Gender in French Syria and Lebanon (History & Society of the Modern Middle East)*. Columbia University Press, 2000.

Thompson, Elizabeth. *Justice Interrupted: The Struggle for Constitutional Government in the Middle East*. Illustrated ed. Harvard University Press, 2013.

Tucker, Ernest. *The Middle East in Modern World History*. 1st ed. Pearson, 2012.

Wieland, Carsten. *Syria: A Decade of Lost Chances: Repression and Revolution from Damascus Spring to Arab Spring*. First ed. Cune, 2012.

Yamak, Labib Zuwiyya. *The Syrian Social Nationalist Party: An Ideological Analysis.* Harvard Center for Population and Development Studies, 1966.

Zisser, Eyal. "The Syrian Phoenix: The Revival of the Syrian Social National Party in Syria." *Die Welt Des Islams*, 47, no. 2 (2007): 188–206. doi:10.1163/157006007781569918.

Works in Arabic

Abd al-Satir, Mustafa. *Ayyam Wa Qadiyya: Min Mu'anayat Muthaqaf 'Arabi.* Beirut: Mu'assasat Fikr li-l-Abhath wa-l-Nashr, 1982.

Al-Mīr Saʻādah, Jūlyīt. *Muzakarat Al Amina Al 'Ula Juliette El Mir Saadeh.* Beirut: Kutub, 2004.

Khalidi, Ghassan al. *Al-Ḥizb al-Qawmī Wa-al-Thawrah al-Thāniyah, 1961–1962: Al-Inqilāb Wa-al-Muḥākamāt.* Beirut: Dār wa-Maktabat al-Turāth al-Adabī, 2003.

Nasri al-Aql, Jihad. *Mawsūʻat Ṣiḥāfat Al-Ḥaraka al-Qawmiyya al-'Ijtimāʻiyya Fī 75 ʻĀman, 1933–2008,* vol. 5, Beirut: al-Furāt, 2011.

Raʻad, Inʻam. *al-Kalimāt al-Akhīra: Mudhakkirā wa Wathāʼiq.* Beirut: Muʼassasat Inʻām Raʻad al-Fikriyya, 2002.

Saadeh, Abdallah. *Awrāq Qawmiyya: Mudhakkirāt ʻAbdallah Saʻādah.* Beirut: Nationalist Papers, 1987.

Saadeh, Antoun. "Greater Syria," *Azzawbaʻa,* July 1, 1943, US Library of Congress.

Saadeh, Antoun. "The Leader's Speech on the 1st of March," *Azzawbaʻa,* June 15, 1943, US Library of Congress.

Saadeh, Antoun. "The Syrian Social Nationalist Creed and Democracy's Search for a Creed," *Azzawbaʻa,* June 15, 1942, US Library of Congress.

Index

Abd al-Malik 23
Abd Messih, George 15, 28, 31, 53, 57, 59, 61, 64, 74, 76–77, 85, 101, 104, 163
Abu Nidal Organization 104, 105, 119
Aflaq, Michel 5–6, 7
al-Akhbar 112
al-Alam, Nabil 111
Al-Baath 5
Aleppo's People Party 53
Al-Hayat, 2006 60, 61
al-Majallah 13
Amana faction 131–134, 142, 153, 155–157, 160, 167
American University in Beirut (AUB) 14
American University of Technology 150
anti-Arabist movement 38
anti-corruption 18, 27, 50, 72, 127, 128, 134, 154, 156, 157, 161, 164, 166
anti-Hardan tendency 123, 126, 154, 158, 159, 167
anti-imperialism 34, 158
anti-Phoenicianism 38
anti-sectarianism 39, 151, 157
anti-Semitism 37–40, 60
anti-UAR secessionist government 7
anti-Zionism 25, 40, 60, 102, 107, 110, 131
Arab Socialist Baath Party 5, 56, 57
  Baathist–Communist 60
  Baathist Iraq 105
  Baathists 6, 7
  Baathist Syria 3
  Baath-led National Progressive Front 160, 164
  Baath movement 56
  Baath Party 5–9, 34, 39, 43, 86, 102, 113, 160, 162, 165
Arab Christians 49, 101–102, 106–107, 110
Arab Cold War 68, 87, 94
Arab Deterrent Force (ADF) 102

1948 Arab-Israeli War 25, 28–29, 50–51
Arabization 39
Arab Liberation Army 50
Arab Liberation Movement (ALM) 54, 57
Arab nationalism 49, 56, 57, 59, 64, 67, 68, 71, 77, 86, 94, 100, 164, 165
Arab Nationalist Movement 95
Arab societies 6
Arab Spring 4
Arab Sunnis 4
Arab unification 6
Arafat, Yasser 7, 98, 106
Araiji, Gebran 105, 122–3, 153,
al-Arsuzi, Zaki 5, 49, 113
al-Ashqar, Assad 28, 64, 73–75, 82, 83, 98, 102
al-Assad, Bashar 1, 8, 129, 136
al-Assad, Hafez 4, 7, 8, 34, 58, 61, 93, 100, 102, 106, 109, 112, 114, 121–123, 156, 157, 162
al-Atassi, Hashim 49
authoritarianism 5, 7, 58, 162
Axis of Resistance 8, 129, 168
al-Aysami, Shibli 7
al-Azma, Yousef 35

Bab al-Tabbaneh–Jabal Mohsen conflict 131
Bakdash, Khalid 14, 15, 70
Banat, Rabi Noureddine 158, 167
Begin, Menachem 109
Beirut International Airport 26, 62–63, 125
Bekaa Valley 115
Beshara el-Khoury 23, 27, 30–31, 74,
Black September 98
Blue Declaration, Beirut 17
British military garrison 47
Burj el-Barajneh Palestinian refugee camps 118
Bustan Organization 156, 157

Caliphate, Ottoman 128
capitalism 44
Cedar Revolution 4
Central Treaty Organization (CENTO) 72
1987 Chad War 119
Chamoun, Camille 23, 26, 68, 73, 74,
Chehab, Fuad 30, 79, 80–84, 86, 94, 172
Christian movement 3
Cohen, Gamliel 29–30,
Coalition for Peaceful Change Forces 163
Cold War 7, 42, 51, 54, 120, 122
colonialism 12, 16, 17, 19, 24, 26, 27, 31,
  33, 35, 37, 40, 41, 47–51, 54, 55,
  61, 65, 68, 79, 80, 95, 101, 110, 113,
  114, 128
Comite Central Syrien 38
communism 26, 34, 42, 51, 68, 70–73,
  76, 86, 97
Communist Party 14, 116, 135, 163
Communist University of the Toilers 56
Communist Workers Party 105
conservatism 61, 96, 105, 130, 152
corporatism 43
Corrective Movement 93
Council of Commissioners 32
Counter-revolution 34, 143
Covid-19 pandemic 127, 160

Damascus Spring 4, 7, 8
Dashnak party 64, 89, 95
Deauville Congress 99
Democratic Union Party (PYD) 9
Deuxieme Bureau 60, 128
Diario Siriolibanes 21
Druze 45, 75, 78, 95, 101–103, 121,
  126, 142

Eagles of the Whirlwind 40–42, 130,
  134–143, 151, 153
  National Defense Forces (NDF) 134
  Pro-government militias 134
Economy 5, 48, 53, 79, 157, 166
Egyptian intelligence 59
Egyptian–Saudi alliance 55
Egypt's British-backed monarchy 67
Elections
  general elections 23
  internal party elections 159
  Lebanese elections 121

parliamentary elections 19, 75, 112, 126,
  133, 160
Emergency Council 119, 121
European colonialism 5
European imperialism 3
excommunication 45

Facebook 153, 158
fascism 20, 25, 41–2, 148
Fatah Party 98
feminism 150
Fertile Crescent 1, 97–8, 98, 113
First Popular Social Uprising 30, 47, 117
First World War 13, 14, 38, 47, 48, 165
Foreign Affairs Committee 128, 132
foreign influence 131
France 12, 27, 54, 55, 72, 117, 128
Franco–Syrian Treaty of Independence,
  1936 49
Free Nationalists 28
French language 148
French Mandate 2
French–Soviet alliance 18
Future Movement, Beirut 125

Gaddafi, Moammar 100, 101, 105, 119
Gemayel, Amin 106
Gemayel, Bashir 106, 107, 110, 111, 112
Gemayel, Nadhim 112
Gemayel, Pierre 18, 19, 75
gender equality 150
General Executioners Movement 103
Genesis of Nations 16
geopolitics 49, 146
Ghoqa, Abdulqadir 115
Greater Syria 3, 33, 113, 122, 151,
  154, 166
Great Syrian Revolt, 1925 14

al-Hafiz, Amin 7
Haidar, Ali 121, 133, 139, 141–142, 148,
  161, 163, 167, 173,
Hardan, Assaad 117–118, 123, 126–127,
  158–159, 161, 167, 173
Hariri, Rafik 4, 123, 125
Hariri, Saad 125, 127
Hashemite 38, 52, 55, 72, 85
Hassanieh, Wael 156, 158

Hatay 3, 8, 26, 33, 36, 47–49, 165
Hezbollah 4, 107, 111–119, 121, 124–125, 128–131, 135, 186
High Council 32, 97, 126, 159
Hitler, Adolf 2, 20
Hmeimim Air Base 141
honor killings 149
Battle of the Hotels 102
Hrawi, Elias 120
Hundred-Days War 106
Hussein, Saddam 3, 119

Ibrahim, Sa'ad Eddin 7
Ideology
    Alexandretta 35, 47, 49
    Antioch 47, 49
    Cilicia 33, 165
    Cyprus 2, 26, 33, 36, 47
    Hatay 8, 26, 36, 47, 49, 165
    irredentist geopolitical aspirations of 2
    Ottoman Empire 14, 47, 48, 69
Idlib Province, 2018 139
imprisonment 11–12, 19, 22, 24, 30, 32, 43, 51–52, 60–61, 62, 64, 69, 74, 86, 89, 93, 95, 97, 99, 100, 112, 115, 120, 145
infiltration 29, 30, 64, 119
informational warfare 110
inter-Lebanese confrontation 69
internal purge 27
Intifada faction 35, 43, 64, 74, 85, 99, 101, 121, 122, 127, 128, 130, 132, 133, 139, 142, 148, 152, 154, 157, 161–164, 167, 168
intimidation 11
Iran–Syria partnership 119
Iraqi government 52
The Iraqi Plot 64, 77
Iraq–Jordan Arab Federation 72, 73
Islamic State 4, 39
Islamic Tahrir Party 86
Islamist government 130
Islamist insurgency 5
Islamist movements 8
Islamization 39
Israeli Air Force 115
Israeli Defense Forces (IDF) 107, 111

Israeli–Hezbollah conflict 4, 107, 111–119, 125
Israeli military 155
Israeli–Palestinian conflict 165

Jadid, Ghassan 57–59, 61, 62
Jadid, Salah 7
Jaish al-Fateh militant group 135
Jammoul 107, 111
July 8 Movement 154, 158–161
Jumahuriya 7
Jumalikaya 7
Jumblatt, Kamal 23, 101, 106
Jumblatt, Walid 115, 120, 125
Jummayziah incident 30

Kairallah, Shawki 85
Kanafani, Ghassan 119
Karim, Ali Abdul 161
Kataeb Party 18, 30, 69, 79, 96, 111, 118
Kayrouz, Habib 118
Khaddam, Abdul Halim 8
Khalaf, Samir 78
Khalil, Antoine 126
Khawarij faction 102–103, 106
Khouri, Nasri 121
Kurds 141, 164–165, 184
Kurdish secessionism 130

laïcité 38
Lebanese American University 31
Lebanese Armed Forces 125
Lebanese Baath Party 111
Lebanese Civil War
    Christian militias 7
    geopolitics 146
    Guerrilla Operations 110
    intelligence-gathering 1
    Kataeb party 101
    Saadeh, Abdullah 96
Lebanese Communist Party (LCP) 17, 26, 86, 95, 96, 115, 118, 135
Lebanese Democratic Party 135
Lebanese government 11
Lebanese National Movement (LNM) 94–6, 100–7, 111
Lebanese National Salvation Front 107
Lebanese People's Party. *See* Lebanese Communist Party (LCP)

Lebanese–Syrian unity 122
Lebanon Crisis, 1958 73–80, 101
  anti-Nasser political coalition 74
  Assad al-Ashqar 75
  Khoury, Beshara 74
  Lebanese Chamber of Deputies, 1957 74
  Progressive Socialist Party 75
  Syrian Social Nationalist Party 75
Lebanon School 23–27, 32, 42, 73, 96, 167
Lebanon's National Struggle 27
Levantine-Iraqi unity 23
LGBT issues 152
Luftwaffe 138

Macron, Emmanuel 128
al-Mahayri, Issam 12, 48, 53, 60, 62, 64, 69, 75, 88, 89, 102–3, 118, 119, 121, 132, 133
mahjar 20
Majlis al-Tawari 119
Makhlouf, Anisa 61, 157
Makhlouf, Badi 60, 61
Makhlouf, Hussein 156
Makhlouf, Rami 132, 156, 158
al-Malki, Adnan 56–60, 63, 64, 65, 70, 83, 89
al-Mallouhi, Inas Mohammed Khair 147, 161
Maoism 105
marriage 148, 167
Marka International Airport 53
Markaz (Center) faction 154, 158
martyrdom 12, 40, 45, 111, 116, 119, 129, 158
Marxism 71
  cultural sympathizers 105
  organization 99
Marxist cultural sympathizers 105
massacres 7, 105–6, 112, 125
Maysalun, Battle of 35
Melkart Conference 98
mercenaryism 119
Merei, Ahmad 160
Mountain War 114
Mossad 115, 119
Mehaidili, Sanaa 92
Mukhaiber, Albert 86

munafi dhiyyat 16, 99
Muslim Brotherhood (MB) 53

al-Nashef, Hanna 126, 158, 159
Nasrallah, Abdulkarim 124
Nasrallah, Hassan 125, 129
Nasser, Adonis 135
Nasser, Gamal Abdul 6, 53
Nasserists 6, 111
National Alliance for the Liberation of Syria 7
National Defense Forces (NDF) 147
nationalism 5
  Lebanese Front 102
  Nationalist Council 99
  Nationalist marriages 148
  National Pact 45
  National Progressive Front 134
  natural nationalism 37
  pan-Arab nationalism 8
  self-determination 43
  Syrian nationalism 8, 36, 79
Nazi Germany 2, 11, 18, 20, 21, 23, 36, 41, 49
New Year's Eve coup 43, 80–84, 94, 96, 99, 127
Non-Aligned Movement 7
non-political Lebanese community 151
non-violence 101, 139

Oslo Accords 7
Operation Grapes of Wrath 121
Operation Straggle 61
Orthodox 15, 16, 29, 38, 51, 75, 81, 116, 121, 128, 140, 141, 163, 164
Ottoman Empire 13, 14, 22, 47, 48, 69, 128

Palestinian Liberation Organization (PLO) 93, 98, 104
  anti-Arafat Palestinian forces 118
  leftist coalition 7
pan-Arabism 4, 5, 6, 17, 22, 23, 25, 28, 29, 33, 38, 39, 45, 54, 65, 69, 79, 94, 98, 102, 103, 110, 114, 126, 162
pan-Syrianism 2, 4, 8, 54, 102, 122, 161
Parti Populaire Syrien (PPS) 16
People's Council 133
Phoenicianism 4, 22

political crime 86
political pragmatism 34
political violence 1
Popular Front for Change and Liberation (PFCL) 133, 163. *See also* Coalition for Peaceful Change Forces
Popular Front for the Liberation of Palestine (PFLP) 104, 107
post-independence period 17
Port of Beirut explosion 127
prison letters 43, 97
Progressive Socialist Party (PSP) 26, 69, 77, 94, 115
Pro-Khomeini elements 118
propaganda 40, 41, 53, 62, 106, 110, 129, 131, 143, 153, 154
pro-Syrian forces 123, 125
Putin, Vladimir 124

Qanayzeh, Elias Gergi 53, 102
Qanayzeh, Tammuz 154
Qanso, Ali 121–123, 126, 153, 161, 172
Qanso, Assem 102, 204n14
Qatar 165
Qasim, Abd al-Karim 73, 83
Qonsol, Zaki 23
Qubaysiat 148, 149
Qustantin Zuraiq 104
Quwatli, Shukri 50

Raad, Inaam 81, 83, 93–106, 110, 118–123, 138–140, 172
Rammah, Nassir 103
reformers 105
Reconciliation efforts 5, 78, 139, 141–143, 162, 172
Regenerative Congress, Damascus 133
Rejectionist Front 104
religion 8, 37–39, 43, 58, 71, 78, 124, 149, 150, 153, 154, 162, 189
religious-oriented violence 154
revolutionary movements 2
Revolution Day 67
Romantic Nationalism 40
Rosewater Revolution 74, 80
Russia 5, 8, 14, 34, 124, 134, 141, 143, 147, 157, 164, 165
Russian Coordination Center 141

Saadeh, Abdullah 93, 97–100, 105, 127
Saadeh, Antoun 1–3, 11, 12, 13–24, 26–45, 47–49, 51, 53–54, 60, 69–70, 73–75, 81–82, 84, 87, 93, 95, 96, 98–9, 101, 103, 105, 106, 109, 110, 111, 114, 117, 119, 124, 27, 126, 128, 145, 150, 160, 162, 166, 168
 al-Ayyam newspaper 14
 Argentina 22
 Baath Party 57
 cultural activities 37
 early life 13
 Genesis of Nations 16
 Jews 39, 40
 Kataeb Party 30
 marytrdom, example of 106, 111
 National Pact 45
 political beliefs 13
 social beliefs 13
 Syrian-Lebanese Communist Party 14
 Syrian nationalism 13
 Syrian National Party (SNP) 15–20, 23–27
Saadeh, Juliette El-Mir 20, 51, 52, 60
Saadeh, Salim 127
Sabra and Shatila Palestinian refugee camps 112, 118
Sakr, Hassan 159
Salafist Islam 8
Salim, Mohammed 117
Samman, Nouhad 137, 160
Sanjak of Alexandretta 47
Al-Sarraj, Abdul Hamid 60, 62, 70, 77, 128, 163
Sati al-Husri 104
Sayegh, Fayez 6, 13, 27, 38, 75
Second World War 1, 18, 19, 21, 23, 25, 26, 51, 75, 138
secularism 11, 37–40, 152, 158
self-determination 43
Shaheen, Ilyas Mtanious 133
Shartouni, Habib 111–112, 120
Sharabi, Hisham 13, 25, 28, 29, 44, 62, 63
Shishakli, Adib 49–57, 61, 63, 65
Shishakli, Salah 61, 62, 76
Siniora, Fouad 125
Six-Day War, 1967 110
socialism 42, 44, 99, 103

social media 127, 129, 134, 139, 140, 150, 153–4
  Whirlwind's military 153
  Twitter 153
Social Nationalist Renaissance Movement 154
Social Nationalists 29
al-Solh, Riad 53
South Lebanon Army (SLA) 107, 111
Soviet Central Committee 116
Soviet Union 26, 34, 56, 58, 59, 67, 72, 81, 95, 96, 98
SSNP. *See* Syrian Social Nationalist Party (SSNP)
Suez Crisis 67
suicide attacks 1, 116, 117, 129, 146, 147
Sunni community 8
Sunni conservatism 8
Sunni Muslims 4, 149
Supreme Council 99–100, 121, 159
Sweid, Joseph 132
Sykes–Picot Agreement 12, 35, 98, 128
Syrian Arab Republic 35, 155
Syrian Civil War 3, 5, 8, 9, 129, 151, 154, 157
Syrian Communist Party 56, 69, 163
Syrian Democratic Forces (SDF) 9, 164, 165
Syrian Intelligence 60, 62, 68, 70, 77, 118, 119, 121, 123, 163
1976 Syrian intervention in Lebanese Civil War 107
Syrian–Lebanese Commission 121
Syrian-Lebanese Community Party 56
Syrian-Lebanese politics 12
Syrian regime 1, 3, 7, 61, 39, 76, 101, 102, 104, 117, 139, 157
Syrian Social Nationalism 101
Syrian Social-Nationalist Ideology 21
Syrian Social Nationalist Party (SSNP) 1, 2, 4, 5, 9, 28
  Alexandretta 35, 47, 49
  Antioch 47, 49
  Baghdad Pact 72
  British support 30, 47, 62, 67, 85
  Cilicia 33, 165
  Cyprus 2, 26, 33, 36, 47
  Deuxieme Bureau 60, 70, 84
  France 12, 27, 54, 72, 117, 128
  Hatay 8, 26, 36, 47, 49, 165
  Iraq-Jordan Arab Federation 72–3
  Libyan support 34, 100, 105–6, 115, 119, 189
  Ottoman Empire 14, 47, 48, 69
  Russia 5, 14, 32, 36, 134, 141
  Soviet Union 25, 34, 58, 67, 96
  Turkey 3, 33, 47–9, 72, 164–5
  United States 61–2, 67, 96, 97, 133
Syrian Social Nationalists 161

Tahya Suriya 33
Taqiyaddin, Said 28, 31, 61, 75, 76, 80, 82
Tawari 119
Tay, Hasan 127
Ten Point Program 104
Tishreen University, Latakia 151
traditional democratic system 18
training 30, 62, 78, 117, 119, 125, 139, 150
tripartite aggression 68
Trustee 34
Tueini, Ghassan 28, 74–75

United Arab Republic (UAR) 6, 58, 67, 68
  Aflaq, Michel 7, 17, 49, 70, 78
  Arab Socialist Movement 71
  Bakdash, Khalid 70
  Bitar, Salah al-Din 70
  Popular Front for the Liberation of Palestine (PFLP) 72
  Syrian Baath 69
University of Damascus 48

Vatican 132
violence 11, 79, 82, 93, 102, 109, 117, 128
Voice of Reform 78

Wadi Private International University 151
al-Wazzan, Shafik 111
Western imperialism 6, 68
Western intelligence 61, 62, 64, 73
Western-linked conspiracy theories 40, 61, 62, 131, 136
Al-Wimbi Operation 114

Yamak, Labib Zuwiyya 12, 18, 28, 32, 77, 79
youth 150–3

YPG. *See* Syrian Democratic Forces (SDF)

Za'im, Husni 19, 30, 31, 45, 51–52
Zahreddine, Issam 142
Zawbaa 21, 23, 24, 29, 41, 110, 118, 120, 129, 130, 142, 147, 166

Zeineddine, Rabi 154
Zhalta, Ain 81, 95, 120, 204
Zidan, Yousef 154
Zineddine, Waseem 90, 103
Zionism 25, 40, 60, 100, 110, 131, 202

www.ingramcontent.com/pod-product-compliance
Lightning Source LLC
Chambersburg PA
CBHW062215300426
44115CB00012BA/2077